Makayla —

We love you and an
praying for your
success and blessings

May God's purpose for your life
be fulfilled and great joy

Yours — Grandma,
Gramps

THE
COURAGE TO STAND

—A NEW AMERICA—

DR. SHON NEYLAND

authorHOUSE®

AuthorHouse™
1663 Liberty Drive
Bloomington, IN 47403
www.authorhouse.com
Phone: 1 (800) 839-8640

Scriptures taken from the Holy Bible, New International Version®, niv®. Copyright © 1973, 1978, 1984 by Biblica, Inc.™ Used by permission of Zondervan. All rights reserved worldwide. www.zondervan.com

Cover photo by James Little

Published by AuthorHouse 10/25/2017

ISBN: 978-1-5462-0789-4 (sc)
ISBN: 978-1-5462-0790-0 (hc)
ISBN: 978-1-5462-0788-7 (e)

Library of Congress Control Number: 2017913927

Print information available on the last page.

Any people depicted in stock imagery provided by Thinkstock are models, and such images are being used for illustrative purposes only. Certain stock imagery © Thinkstock.

The views, illustrations, or photos in this book do not necessarily represent those of the Department of Defense, or the United States Air Force, or the Air Force Chaplain Corps. All photos are used with permission or from public domain. The illustrations in this book do not represent any particular person unless otherwise noted. All interviews, pictures, and personal examples are included with the permission of the persons involved.

This book is printed on acid-free paper.

CONTENTS

To my lovely wife, Madeline, to whom I am eternally grateful for being with me on this journey called life. I also dedicate this book to my loving children: Ashley, Shontae, and Shon II. I am proud of each of their successes in life, and they motivate me to continue serving our nation.

PREFACE

America is at a crossroads in its history, and I believe there is an opportunity to go forward and shape the future. I am convinced this is a message that is needed for America, perhaps now more than ever. We have an opportunity to turn a pivotal corner in our society. In my estimation, the United States is the greatest nation on earth, but there are times when the nation seems irretrievably broken. Our leaders seem to make decisions that erode the fabric of society. All too often, the country seems to respond to issues across racial, religious, or political lines rather than basing decisions on what is right, moral, legal, and ethical. A divided nation cannot stand, and one individual or group of people is not enough to repair its cracks. It will take a nation coming together to stand. As a military veteran of more than thirty-three years at the publishing of this book, I understand what it means to sacrifice in service to others. I know about giving oneself to great causes, such as participating in the defense of our nation, serving in wars away from family, and putting the needs of the nation before personal gain. My view of America as the greatest nation on earth may sound like American exceptionalism, but in this instance, I believe America, along with other nations that espouse democracy, honor, moral courage, and justice, is a special nation. I know that other people believe their country is the greatest nation on earth, but when you think of the opportunities available in America and its contributions to the world, one simply has to acknowledge that America is indeed among the greatest nations in the history of the civilized world, if not the greatest. I know this comment will cause some controversy, but I believe in America, and I hope you do as well. This is without a doubt the land of opportunity, the home of the brave, and the land of the free. As we say in the military, America is the land of the free because of the brave—those who fight for freedom. But we are also the land of the free because of great political and religious leaders who have sacrificed much to ensure America would be great. Further, we are the land of the free because of all Americans who make the nation great. Each person in America makes an invaluable contribution to society and to the well-being of this nation, with each person doing his or her part, big and small. The world looks to America because the nation is special and unique and plays a major role in the future of our world. The United States leads the world in humanitarian outreach, democracy, and financial aid and supports the world's largest economy and most powerful military. We make no excuses, and America is not perfect, but it is a nation that strives to grow and develop, and its citizens are grateful for that. We are a nation of destiny born out of purpose in that the United States is unique for its opportunities and social mobility.

However, I and many would argue that our nation is not where it needs to be in terms of equality, fairness, and prosperity for all. Many point to the ethnic divide, the hatred, and the heinous crimes we sometimes commit against one another. There is still much evidence that covert discrimination and unfair treatment exist, and these realities hinder the growth of America. These grievances happen in all walks of life; they happen to the rich and the poor alike, to people of all colors and ethnicities, and to all genders. The impact affects all economic, educational, physical, and emotional facets of life and well-being. A case can be made that our nation can improve in many areas. As the leader of the free world, America must now move even further up the moral plane toward harmony and respect for all. Many might say this is an arrogant statement, but I do not believe it to be so. America has done much to overcome discrimination, prejudice, and racism. I am convinced that America has grown tremendously in many areas of equality, fairness, and prosperity for all, yet there is more work to be done.

Even though America is a great nation, there is incredible violence in America, and the path our nation is on appears to be antireligious. Why would we attack religion, when it was the quest for freedom of the right to practice religion that birthed our great nation? This is akin to saying we believe Americans should have the right to trample or burn the American flag or not honor it even though it is the flag that represents the very freedom for which so many died. Recently, some professional athletes have not honored the American flag or the national anthem before the start of a game. I believe it is wrong and disrespectful to our nation and all it stands for not to honor the American flag. I support peaceful protests for what may be considered injustices, but do not dishonor the flag or national anthem. Believe it or not, it has been reported in the news that some are offended because the American flag is being flown in their neighborhoods. Homeowner associations across America have begun to institute strict guidelines for flag flying. Recently, I saw an article that stated the US Supreme Court upheld a ban on wearing US American flag shirts at a high school during Cinco de Mayo in order to create a more positive environment.[1] Evidently, there had been disciplinary issues between whites and Mexicans, with approximately thirty fights between the ethnicities. Due to the discipline issues, we ban the wearing of the American flag, or because of a homeowner association's newly established rules, we can't show American pride and fly the flag, because it doesn't fit within the rules. Does this make sense? Is this what we have become—a place where the very rights of freedom can be erased by an outcry or judgment of a few?

Further, I believe it is incredible when we examine how many youth are killed daily in America with little to no media coverage. Rape, domestic violence, road rage, and mass killings have almost become routine. I know this statement is somewhat harsh, but we tolerate and accept the unthinkable. Think about it for a minute. How often do you wake up to national news of heinous crimes in the inner cities and suburbs of America? Not often. Indeed, you will find the news highlighted in the local papers and media of the city in which the crime took place, but where is the national outcry to stop the violence? Where is the economic aid to counter the attacks on humanity? Much of the violence is found in the inner cities of America, where many of the poor and unemployed dwell. It is normally the poor of all ethnicities who have the highest murder rates, abortion rates, crime, imprisonment, etc. We live in a time when the birth of a celebrity's child gets more coverage in the media than the loss of life of a military member fighting on the front lines in war. I am simply submitting that we choose to value sports and entertainment news rather than address what is troubling our nation and unfolding before our eyes. We have to take a stand, speak out, and change our paradigms. How do we change this phenomenon? More Americans die daily on the battlefields of our streets than on the battlefields in Iraq or Afghanistan. I am convinced that we can and should challenge each other to combat this American tragedy. This book is a cry for change, self-awareness, responsibility, and accountability. This book is not about pitting one ethnicity against another or finding blame; it is about giving hope to America and bringing Americans together. Many of my closest friends are of Caucasoid (or European) ethnicity. Of course, I have friends of Asian, African, and Hispanic descent, as well as Pacific Islanders, Middle Easterners, and Native Americans. I am not attempting to be the moral police, but it is my hope to galvanize a movement to change America for the better. Many of the statistics in this book will be alarming for the reader, but by no means do I mean to say this is the plight of all; on the contrary, these statistics are meant to bring attention to the situation and hopefully spur a change Americans can truly believe in.

As a military veteran still on active duty, I believe the air force gives me a distinct viewpoint on ethnic relations. I try to see all people as one human race, regardless of ethnicity, because for most of my adult life, that approach was all I knew. I have friends in every major people group. I have been militarized, which many say is good, though some say it is bad. I love America! Yes, I am a patriot, and I love this land. I have known respect for all people from my first day in the military in 1984. I was afforded equal opportunity to excel in every aspect. I realize I stand on the shoulders of those who suffered great persecution in early America. Speaking of veterans, I want to reach out to the many veterans of all ethnicities who serve our great land. Many of them live in atrocious situations and feel their lives are not worthy, with as many as twenty-two veterans ending their lives daily, more than double the rate of the general population.[2] This should not be, and America has to do more for our veterans who sacrificed so much for our freedom—this is part of a new America.

Let me be clear. Despite my relatively smooth journey in the military as compared to those who went before me, I do not imply that the military is perfect or free from racism today, but it does lead American society as a whole with regard to equality for all. For instance, any member of the military can actually be punished for discriminatory practices and for using racial epithets. This is not the standard in American society, unless you are in the media, politics, or entertainment. The average American has no concept of this. The military has led society in ethnic relations and equality. A woman in the military makes the exact same pay as a man with the same rank. This is not the case, however, in America at large, with women generally making seventy-eight cents for every dollar a man makes. The gap is greater for women of different ethnicities, with Hispanic women at the bottom of the pay scale, earning only fifty-four cents for every dollar a man earns.[3] The military has led the way in opening the door of equality for all people regardless of ethnicity. The famed Tuskegee Airmen were a prime example of what a chance at equality can provide, as they became the nation's first black pilots. The military, under President Harry Truman, led the way in the United States in breaking racial discrimination and segregation in the armed forces. President Truman's Executive Order 9981 in 1948 directed the integration of the military, and it is almost certain that the performance of the Tuskegee Airmen influenced his decision.[4] By the early 1950s, segregation was no longer an official or legal part of the military, especially in light of the Korean War. Conversely, segregation dominated America at large well into the mid-1960s and only started to truly erode in the late 1970s, despite the Civil Rights Act of 1964. The battle for equality was being fought on many levels at the same time, including within the fields of entertainment, professional sports, medicine, engineering, and academics. It was not only a battle for those of African descent to gain their footing but also a time for people of all ethnicities and creeds to begin to make gains.

I know some might be thinking this is just another book about equality for those of African descent or other disenfranchised ethnicities, but it is not. I assure you, it is about America gaining greater strength when we all succeed. In some sense, it is about national security in that it seeks to prevent self-destructive behavior in America. Only Americans can truly destroy America. It is about responsibility, accountability, and growth for America and all Americans. I am not pushing for reparations, only for a fair opportunity for all Americans. I am pushing for reconciliation in America between all ethnicities. Yes, what we now call the "race problem" will be addressed, and solutions will be offered, but it is more than that, for this is a book that will deal with the moral fabric of a people—Americans. I lay out a road map for how we as Americans can change. Please understand that I am dealing with the rights of all people, the human race, and not one ethnicity. For instance, I do not believe in the term *reverse discrimination* (generally meaning discrimination against whites), for discrimination against any ethnicity of people is wrong. A great example would be when Irish Americans had to struggle in the early 1920s to be accepted in American society. They were considered outcasts because they did not fit in. They were slandered, not because of the color of their skin but because they were different. What about the Italians who struggled as well to migrate into American society? Some of the most vicious acts of racial profiling took place against Italians. Early Italian Americans worked in the fields of the Deep South to earn a modest living. What did they all have in common? They were Europeans (white) who were discriminated against because they were different. Thus, this book is a call for a higher ground where all people are accepted for who they are and have the right to pursue happiness, peace, and the American way.

I always have held that discrimination, prejudice, and hatred of one people group has never truly been limited to the color of one's skin but are about the capacity for evil. This is not to say that the color of one's skin does not often serve as a part of the larger picture of discrimination. The color of one's skin indeed often serves as a catalyst or a reason to discriminate. I have observed that it is more about prejudice against another group because they are different rather than because of the color of the others' skin. If you examine the wars around the world between nations, tribes, and villages, you quickly learn that prejudice is not about skin color primarily; rather, it's about a disdain for someone who happens to be different from you. Here are some clear examples. In Africa, the war and genocide of the Hutus and the Tutsis in Rwanda was not about skin color essentially (although one group was slightly taller than the other) but about one people group feeling superior over the other. The conflict between the groups was exacerbated first by Belgian colonialism and then by economics—one group was wealthier than another and held more economic power. This conflict resulted in approximately eight hundred thousand to one million Tutsis being killed. What about the annihilation and ethnic cleansing of the Serbs in Bosnia and Herzegovina; the eight-year Iran and Iraq War, in which more than four hundred thousand died on both sides; the Irish and the British wars; the French and the Spaniards; the Armenians and the Turks; or the Germans practically against the world? Whether these conflicts rose from religious, economic, or colonial-era issues, hatred was held for one group against the other even though their color of skin and ethnicity were similar. Note that the Germans did believe their particular breed of European descent or DNA was superior to all other ethnicities, but it was not limited to skin color. In almost every case, it was one ethnicity believing it was greater or superior than the other, and the battles were often laced with religious, cultural, political, and economic motives. Again, in most of the cases I named above, the color of the skin of those who fought and were viciously killed was the same as the color of skin of those they were fighting against.

It is within this backdrop that I craft this book. As I have stated several times, I believe America is exceptional and filled with opportunities to succeed far greater than the average nation. As a young man who grew up in the inner city of New Orleans, Louisiana, I could not help but notice that I had every opportunity afforded me to succeed. It was up to me to decide and thrive. I don't consider myself to be wealthy at all and don't intend to brag, but I realized a few years ago that my annual income is well over the average income in America. That is amazing for a kid who once dreamed with one of my best friends, Kevin George, that if we could "only make $50,000 per year," we would be set for life. We meant it at the age of sixteen, because we could only see so far. In fact, we weren't too far off, as the median income for American households today is approximately $50,000 to $55,000. Today I stand on the shoulders of giants and pioneers who led the way for freedom and democracy. I was able to go forward with little prejudice and discrimination because of those who suffered for my freedom. I am referring to those of African descent, European descent, Hispanic or Latino descent, Native American descent, and Asian descent who marched and fought for freedom in America throughout its history. Thus, not only do I honor my military heritage and those who fought to keep America free, but I stand on the shoulders of those who had to overcome horrific acts of inhumane treatment to simply survive and make a change.

I believe you will be inspired as you read this book, for I believe America is still strong, the leader of the free world, and capable of even greater accomplishments through a paradigm shift and through embracing one another in love. The words of Dr. Martin Luther King Jr. ring in my ears. His dream was that his four kids would one day live in a nation that judges its people based on their character rather than the color of their skin. I am also reminded of President Thomas Jefferson, who etched the words in our Declaration of Independence that guaranteed liberty, life, and the pursuit of happiness for all men. Now is the time for America to take a stand and make a change, a change that will galvanize the nation and move us forward to ensure the legacy of America continues for generations to come. This book is a call for all Americans to live out the true meaning of our creed.

ACKNOWLEDGMENTS

I must acknowledge the host of relatives, friends, and mentors who have inspired me over the years to keep going and never quit. I am truly standing because of their support and love over the years. This book deals with a new way forward with regard to human relations, advocating for the nation to come together with love for all persons regardless of ethnicity, religion, or national origin, and I can attest that those who have influenced my life over the years are from diverse ethnicities and have certainly led the way in America in making a difference with the courage to stand.

I also acknowledge the great love and support of my immediate family, who were pivotal in my life and directly shaped my earlier years: my uncle Edgar Sr. and aunt Marguerite Williams, my nonbiological grandparents, the late Dave and Bertha Williams; my parents, the late Millard and Phyllis Neyland; and my sisters, Shannon and Kecie Neyland.

COUNTERING THE DEGRADATION OF A NATION

Proclaim liberty throughout all the land unto all the inhabitants thereof.

—Liberty Bell inscription, 1751

Liberty Bell

The famed Liberty Bell was commissioned out of Whitechapel Foundry in London, and it is believed to have cracked upon its first attempt to ring in 1751.[5] However, the bell would ring for a solid ninety years until the 1840s, when it could no longer ring due to the growing crack that made it unusable. Mystery still surrounds how the bell first got its crack, but we do know the repair attempt in the 1840s did not work. By the way, the large crack is actually a part of the repair attempt. The crack in the bell could be seen as indicative of our struggle in America—it's broken, yet the bell keeps ringing for freedom, at least symbolically. Abolitionists used the symbol and the inscription on the Liberty Bell (which was not called by that name until the 1800s) as a rallying cry against the hypocrisy and double standards in America for women, blacks, and disenfranchised people of all ethnicities and colors, including poor white people. This included many female abolitionists who were also part of the women's suffrage movement (the fight for voting rights). It is also fascinating that the Liberty Bell was located in Independence Hall, which was founded in 1732, the same year President George Washington was born. I find it ironic that it would be General George Washington who led our country during the American Revolution and then served as our first president. Independence Hall, Philadelphia, is where the great documents that framed our nation were birthed and signed by the great leaders of our nation. I have walked those hallowed grounds, viewing the Liberty Bell and other historical artifacts and documents. It is an amazing story of resilience and persistence for something new and something great. This is what America was founded on. The Liberty Bell would ring to gather the people to Independence Hall to hear vital news concerning the nation. On special occasions, the Liberty Bell would be struck as a symbol of freedom and hope, such as on D-day, June 6, 1944, when the Allied Forces invaded Normandy, France, to bring down the tyrannical reign of Adolf Hitler and his forces across Europe.[6] Today I call for the Liberty Bell to ring in our hearts as we gather to read the vital news that will shape our future.

There is a growing division in our nation that must be addressed. We can see through a variety of recent cases that have captivated the nation that ethnic relations appear to be challenged across America. Additionally, while the crime rate has remained steady for the most part, or even decreased in some cases, the egregious manner in which crimes are carried out has caught America's attention. In fact, each day, we hear or read about heinous crimes taking place within the borders of our great nation. Hardly a two-week period goes by when I don't get a social-media blast with racist rants about an altercation between police and citizens. Not only that, but as a member of the armed forces, I see an erosion of the appreciation for the freedoms we enjoy in America. In fact, some can make a case that our citizens have taken our freedom for granted. I can assure you that our freedom is not free, and it has come at a great cost. Most people realize that our freedom is not free, but it appears that fact can be sometimes forgotten. In recent years, some of the types of incidents we have seen in the news include a mother killing her babies; drug use increasing dramatically; murder in hospitals; women being attacked and having their babies literally cut out of their wombs; bullying; young students brutally shot in elementary schools; false imprisonment of women, children, and boys; young college students kidnapped and murdered; shootings in airports; shootings on military installations; home terrorist attacks; children killed in our schools; children shooting children; shootings in movie theaters; mass college campus murders; snipers on bridges; random punching of the elderly in the streets; police brutality; elderly couples being killed while trying to sell a car; serial killers in major cities; snipers shooting random people; road rage that leaves young children dead; teachers having sex with students; a man shooting his children and himself; a mother driving off the road and killing herself and her young children; sixteen youth being killed over a weekend in one city; shootings on the Fourth of July in one city; random murders of police officers; rape; widespread murder; murder of entire families; and a man going into an armory to kill others. I could list enough of these types of incidents to fill several pages of this book. I am making the point that a certain degradation has taken place in America in recent years. The respect for human life has been greatly degraded. This is not to argue that crime has not been in the world since the beginning of time or that human degradation was not shown through slavery and discrimination in America from the very beginning. Wherever there has been humans, there have been crime and wrongdoing. Crime is not limited to America, of course; it is rampant around the world in every nation, whether prosperous or not. However, I am speaking out on taking time to stand because America is still one of the greatest nations on the earth. We must turn the tide. We have to gain the courage to stand and make a difference wherever we can. America is not perfect, but we have a great message to tell the world. America is strong because of our democratic state.

This is a democracy that was founded by the people for the people. America was founded on the principles of freedom and the right to pursue happiness for each of its citizens. It took some time, but today we are closer to living out the meaning of the words of our Constitution and Declaration of Independence. America was founded with ideals that respected the rights and security of all citizens. Not only that, but America has set the way ahead for democracies around the world. The preamble of the Constitution starts off by saying,

> We the people, in order to form a more perfect union, establish justice, insure domestic tranquility, provide for the common defense, promote the general welfare, and secure the blessings of liberty to ourselves and our posterity, do ordain and establish this Constitution for the United States of America.

America is a nation that was built on the ideals of equality for all men and women, although we are well aware that the true quest for equality was not manifested in the beginning and is an ongoing battle. The quest to ensure the equality of all men and women began with the foundation of our nation. Again, while it is true that America has never been perfect, we have always sought and fought for equality for all men and women on one level or the other. Equality has not yet been realized, and perhaps it will never be, but it's certainly the goal we strive for.

If America is to gain its footing and reach its full potential, it must deal with the key areas that continue to impair our nation. In this book, I will deal with those issues that are currently dividing and causing derision in our nation. We are amazed when we see horrific crimes of mass violence in our nation or when the innocent lives of children are taken through senseless murders (such as in Columbine, Colorado, or Newtown, Connecticut), but the reality is that we have slowly moved away from what has made America great. We have lowered our care and respect for one another through our desire to be powerful and successful. I will make a case that common courtesy and general caring for one another have declined over the years. Some would say our love is waxing cold, to use an old biblical reference. I submit to you that we have moved away from basic right and wrong and dignity for human life and rights. We don't build relationships with our neighbors like we used to. In the pursuit to ensure that all people feel accepted in America, we have slowly drifted from the values and morals that have made us strong in the past. In our arduous search for religious plurality, we have sometimes trampled on the rights of the spiritual. In various arenas, there seems to be an outcry against those who are spiritual. Some who are spiritual are told they cannot express themselves freely without feeling persecution. The news is littered with stories of individuals being told not to pray in public or even in private—in my estimation, this is a denial of our basic rights found in the First Amendment, which guarantees the right to the free exercise of religion. These kinds of changes have caused America to slip away from the principles that our nation was founded upon.

Moreover, I will address key issues that I believe are affecting America and each of its citizens. Of course, this is not an all-inclusive list, but it illustrates seven key areas I believe will make America stronger when addressed. First, America remains a nation that struggles with division with regard to ethnic relations. There has been a resurgence of "black versus white," and that should not be. Although we are no longer dominated by the racism, discrimination, and prejudice that were once commonplace in America, there are still obstacles that hinder our great nation. There is a residue of discrimination, prejudice, and inequality that haunts us—mostly covertly but sometimes overtly. One only has to look with intention, and he or she will find covert and even overt racism still being perpetrated. I believe we are a nation that is sincerely attempting to make a change toward acceptance of all, but there are obstacles in our way. Second, along the lines of prejudice and ethnic tension, there is the issue of derogatory words against all ethnicities, which only exacerbate tensions and cause further divisions. No ethnicity should be put down with stereotypical names that demean and belittle. What I am proposing deals with ethnic relations in a unique way, and I believe that if it is embraced, this approach will profoundly change the world we live in. Third, America must deal with the pursuit of equality. Equality is only going to come through a belief in oneself that one can become what one sets out to be. Low self-esteem, self-hatred, and the cycle of stagnation have to be addressed. This means our education system must be examined for its disparities between those who are limited economically and those who are not. We must acknowledge the economic gap between ethnicities and find creative ways to close it.

Educational inequality is not limited to ethnicity but is also based on economics. This also requires a close examination of illicit drug use, crime, gang warfare, and poverty. Our justice system must also be examined and revamped to ensure fairness and equality for all. America must close the education gap for those who are poor, and education must improve for all Americans (not based on ethnicity or skin color) as we strive to lead the world in innovation and technology. The defense of our nation rests with innovation, science, engineering, craftsmanship, and a strong working middle class. Fourth, America must not let its pursuit of religious plurality stop freedom of religion for all Americans. It appears that the real goal for some is not plurality of religion for America but an America without any religious rights or references to God, or what some would call a "secular society." Some advocate for a theocracy of sorts, while others seek a godless nation. The issue of religion and spirituality in America is a key component to our greatness and peace and prosperity for all. A fifth area that I address is the makeup or the breakup of the American family. A strong family is critical to a strong America. I will analyze the state of the family and the ramifications of a clearly shifting paradigm of singleness and children growing up in single-parent households. The data is overwhelmingly clear, with empirical evidence that two-parent households impact America in a positive way. The challenge is how to get the next generation to embrace the concept of family rather than move toward a mind-set that promotes the opposite. A sixth component that will be key to improving America is establishing and increasing mentorship programs for both boys and girls of all ethnicities. Investment in the lives of our youth and next generations will have a true impact on our future. Seventh, we need to examine a new way forward with regard to relationships, focusing on respect and unconditional love for one another. It is the genuine love for one another that will keep America strong and ever growing. Intentional kindness sounds esoteric, but it is unleashing soft power in America for the better. Finally, I will wrap up the book with a call for a new America. This chapter will use case studies to show how success is in our grasp and how everyday Americans and citizens from different walks of life have made it to the next level and found happiness and peace.

America can live up to its potential, truths, and values so that all Americans are Americans. Today is perhaps the worst political division of America since the Civil War. Republicans and Democrats can be seen year after year fighting one another and stalling progress in America. Let's put America first. Put self-gain and political ambitions on the sidelines in order to have a stronger nation where all can prosper. Unfortunately, we see politics divided by ethnic lines. Today I am in the minority as a Republican with brown skin. How could this be, when the Republican platform represents conservative values, which many brown-skinned people espouse? Somewhere along the way, we have convinced ourselves that Hispanics and African Americans belong to the Democratic Party, and the Republican Party consists of mostly Europeans or white Americans. This shifted between the 1950s and 1960s. However, many would be surprised to know that it was the Southern Democratic platform that espoused slavery and disenfranchised different ethnicities, while the Republican Party pushed for equality for all. Note, not all in the Republican Party agreed for full rights of slaves. Some were divided in the Civil War, with some wanting abolition and some wanting slaves deported, and others didn't care about abolition at all. Even while the Republicans fought to end slavery, there were many who certainly did not want equality for women, Native Americans, or other ethnicities, such as the Chinese or Japanese. Remember, most people of brown color voted Republican until the early to mid-1950s. However, the Democratic Party fought for desegregation and full civil rights by the late 1920s. The reason southerners left the Democratic party beginning in the 1930s and in droves in the 1960s was first because of the New Deal and President Franklin Roosevelt's efforts to expand civil rights to African Americans and then, most importantly, because of President John Kennedy's and President Lyndon Johnson's pursuit of full civil rights and integration for African Americans in all areas of life. After 1960, the Republican Party was heavily composed of former Southern Dixiecrats who had fled the Democratic Party, and the issue of segregation is what drove the solid South from the Republican to the Democratic Party. The heart of conservatism is the care and success of all people but without dependence on the government. The government is a means for security and safety, but it is not designed to dominate every aspect of our lives. We need to change the dynamics of our country and become progressive to where America is first, and then we can side with our political allegiances. Today, even when America is attacked by terrorists and militant groups, the first thing the politicians and some in the media generally do is blame the Republicans or the Democrats instead of uniting to fight and defeat the attackers of our nation. This is a far cry from America only a decade and a half ago, when America was attacked on 9/11. The growing division in America has to be analyzed closely to understand its root causes. I don't want to be pessimistic and state that we cannot change, for I see positive change taking place in politics in some locations, but change needs to become the norm in America.

A short review of American history reveals interesting paradigms in the formation of our nation and what was to ensue in America. In 1607, early settlers from England arrived at Jamestown, Virginia, after fleeing England to the Netherlands and seeking religious freedom.[7] Some argue that the settlers from England came to Jamestown to make money through plantations because the 102 Pilgrims who sailed from Plymouth, England, were authorized to travel and expand the British Empire. They did not come to Massachusetts in 1620 to form a new nation.[8] The government of England was spiritually oppressive, especially when King Henry VIII reigned (1509–47). Yet a major task of the Pilgrims was to represent the king of England in a newly discovered land. Among the 102 Pilgrims on the *Mayflower* were at least thirty-five Pilgrims who were traveling to America to escape the Church of England, which they thought was corrupt, to gain religious freedom.[9] They were known as Separatists and Puritans because they were trying to find religious freedom from the oppression of the church. You may recall that it was illegal to form different congregations outside of the Church of England; thus, those who wanted to escape the religious oppression were called Separatists. This is most interesting as we fast forward to today with those who would suppress religion of all forms. Some in America would strike down religion in America if given the chance, yet it was religion that led the colonists to Jamestown in 1607, and many on the 1620 voyage were also seeking religious freedom. The irony is that some in America want to limit religious freedom in America. It was not until the early settlers began to realize that they were experiencing taxation on their produce without representation that thoughts of a revolt were birthed. It would be approximately 150 years after landing on the American continent that the descendants of the early settlers and newly arrived settlers would begin to believe that independence was the expedient move for America.

By the mid-1700s, there were several key reasons for the quest for independence. Remember that not all of the colonists were in agreement

THE COURAGE TO STAND: A NEW AMERICA

on independence from Britain. Essentially, most of the colonists were ready to break their ties with the British Empire because of unfair and continually rising taxation on the produce from the American colonists. This growing taxation on the produce did not bring greater security or gain for those who would labor but paid for major economic needs in the British Empire. The British Empire was experiencing deep debt due to the French and Indian War of 1754–63 and needed additional revenue.[10] To gain that revenue, Britain began placing heavy taxes on the American colonies with the 1764 Sugar and Currency Act; the 1765 Stamp Act to gain money on any printed documents; and the 1767 Townshend Act, which raised taxes on high-demand products coming from Britain to America.[11] Again, please understand the irony when one thinks that America was formed to break away from the oppression and tyranny of the British Empire that treated them like indentured slaves. Unfortunately, America would continue oppression of a people even as she gained her freedom. Tensions continued to mount between Britain and America when Britain sent military soldiers to stem the tide of the growing rebellion with the rise of the Sons of Liberty, who would begin to take the rebellion into their own hands by fighting independently against oppression. In 1770, the famed Boston Massacre was a confrontation between British soldiers and colonists, with shots being fired by the former into the crowd, killing several Americans. The 1773 Tea Act, which was designed to ensure a failing British East India Company had the monopoly on trading tea with the colonists, led to the infamous Boston Tea Party, in which colonists, dressed as North American Native Indians, snuck onto a British ship to to stop the tea from being imported into America. They dumped the tea into Boston Harbor and feathered and tarred the ship's captain.[12] This was followed by the 1774 Intolerable Acts by the British, who sent more troops to America, closed Boston Harbor, demanded that the colonists feed and house the troops as needed, and forbade all town hall meetings to quash any uprisings. However, this action only unified the American spirit and led to the first Continental Congress in 1774, with twelve of the thirteen colonies (Georgia withheld) meeting and calling for a boycott of all British goods.[13] By 1775, the first open conflict between British soldiers and the colonists took place in both Lexington and Concord, killing eight Americans and seventy-four British troops. This incident led to the formation of the Continental Army led by General George Washington.[14]

9

The American Revolution began in 1775 as the Second Continental Congress was formed, with all thirteen colonies taking part. King George III declared the colonies in open rebellion following the Battle of Bunker Hill; even though the Declaration of Independence was signed in 1776, the war would not be officially over until the Treaty of Paris in 1783.[15] America was formed out of a struggle for freedom and independence. Although the nation gained its independence, and despite the language in the Declaration of Independence, America would continue the practice of indentured servitude, disenfranchisement of certain groups, and, like Britain, the debilitating practice of slavery. However, I must point out that at least some of the Founding Fathers in fact wanted to end slavery. They were in conflict with society and the values they knew were right. Though they displayed tremendous courage to break away from the motherland, they could not muster up the courage to end slavery in their lifetimes. Many of our prominent leaders owned slaves, including Thomas Jefferson, Benjamin Franklin, George Washington, Patrick Henry, and James Madison. Many of them left wills directing the freedom of their slaves at their deaths. George Washington is reported to have written to a friend, "I can only say that there is not a man living who wishes more sincerely than I do to see a plan adopted for the abolition of slavery."[16] In particular, Alexander Hamilton, Benjamin Franklin, and John Jay became tremendous advocates for the abolition of slavery and were critical to pushing forward the Act for the Gradual Abolition of Slavery, which was the first successful plan to eliminate slavery over a thirty-year period.[17] The Act for the Gradual Abolition of Slavery was started in Pennsylvania and did not work as intended, but it was the first plan that actually countered slavery and was eventually adopted by other states.

We have indeed come a long way since the early 1600s and 1700s, when our nation was an extension of the British Empire and independence was only a dream held by a few. As I have stated above, when America was not yet America, there was an opportunity to live out the true meaning of the Founding Fathers' dreams, but politics, obstinate views, and economics would not let it happen. The ethnic divide was only in its early stages, for there were free "blacks" and free Irishmen in the early 1700s who owned land and businesses, yet at the same time, there was the beginning of slavery. Slavery was not limited to Africans; those of Irish descent were also sold into slavery. There are some who would still hold America back into a time of ethnic divide and oppression. There are those who would love for America to be stuck in the times of Jim Crow laws, when the ethnic divide and prejudice were deep and crippling to the progress of all people. Sometimes I hear people say, "This is not the America we are used to, and I am not happy with the way we are going." This has meaning both ways. Personally, I am glad America is not the segregated America of the 1700s, 1800s, and early to mid-1900s, nor do I believe we should go back to a time when, if you were of Irish, Asian, Latino, Jewish, or Italian descent, you would be enslaved in some cases or ostracized in society. Remember, Irish Americans were not considered white among others; they often served as indentured servants, which meant they provided labor in exchange for food, clothing, and shelter. Unlike slaves, they were able to earn their freedom within a set number of years. The indentured servitude was in exchange for payment for the passage over. If you were not Protestant and immigrated to the United States, you were most likely going to face prejudice, because some feared the genetic outcome of the new blood mixing with the current nation's residents.[18] Further, in 1882, Congress passed the Chinese Exclusion Act, excluding anyone of Chinese descent from entering the United States, and in 1907, twenty-five years later, an executive agreement was reached to also exclude all Japanese attempting entry into the United States.[19] Imagine if that were happening today where one group or ethnicity was excluded from America simply because of their ethnicity. Indeed, it is happening, at least in rhetoric, as some of the 2016 presidential candidates had openly stated they would, on the basis of religion and ethnicity, not be eligible for certain types of visas and actually ban all Muslim immigrants. That is not the America we want; unfortunately, it was the America of the past. Interestingly, the America of the past was dominated by the idea of the superiority of one ethnicity over another. In fact, in 1917, Congress voted to only allow entry in America to those who could pass a literacy test, and in 1924, Congress put a cap on all immigrants entering the United States based on ethnicity from the 1890 census population size.[20] In the backdrop of all the immigration laws, restrictions, and limitations, the Statue of Liberty, given as a gift from France to mark the hundredth anniversary of America, stood in the New York Harbor and became a symbol of freedom, embracing immigration from around the world. America welcomes immigrants, and that is why we are the land of the free and the home of the brave. While I address the illegal immigration issues we face in America later in the book, we cannot get to a place where we discriminate against any ethnicity because they are different. Illegal immigration must be mitigated in America. *The Courage to Stand* calls for us to come together as Americans despite the differences in ethnicities.

I am saddened that our respect for one another and for life has seemed to decline in many more areas as well. Further, one can rightly argue that even in those early years, how could there be respect and decency in America when we literally deemed some ethnicities or nationalities inferior to others, and heinous crimes against humanity could be carried out without any penalty or punishment? Perhaps the answer is that America has always wrestled with equality and dignity for all, and we continue to grow to self-actualize as a nation. With technology and change, violence has increased in some cases; crime has become more sophisticated. Statistically speaking, violent and property crime in America has decreased in some areas and increased in others. For instance, violent and property crime actually declined in 2013 and 2014, but rose in 2011 and 2012.[21] In that same period, the United States recorded the lowest murder rate since 1960.[22] In 2015, there was a rash of violence across America that began to rise to numbers that had not been seen in years. In other words, although America has been slowly moving to a more civil nation, there are still periods where violence can erupt across our major cities and capture the attention of all concerned. In late 2013, the United States was looking at the highest rise of violent crime since 2011, with rates spiking 17 percent since 2012.[23] Keep in mind this was after one of the largest declines of violent crime (murder, rape, aggravated assault, etc.) in America since 1993. CNN reported in June 2015 that there was a slight resurgence of violent crime, especially murder, in urban areas and in major cities, and that the type of crimes appear to be more callous and reckless.[24] I will show an empirical link later in the book with regard to violence and poverty. The major cities of the United States are plagued by low income per capita and thus higher-than-average violent crime rates. Therefore, even though crime has declined from a peak in 1991 and 1993, there has been a slight increase beginning in 2013, as noted above.

In some ways, we as Americans, like all people globally, are drawn to the sensationalism of these negative events. I recently read about some Americans criticizing the media for not showing enough of the positive things that go on in America every day. There are people of all ethnicities helping people in America. I am not amazed when I see a black male helping an elderly white female in the airport or a white female coming to the aid of a disabled Hispanic male. I actually see it across America frequently, especially in the military. Recently, the media reported that a young kid lost control in the snow and ice and crashed into a pole in Washington, DC. Several Americans pulled over to help the young man and basically pulled him from the wreckage before the vehicle was engulfed in flames. During the interview, I was not surprised to learn that the two gentlemen interviewed were of different ethnicities—one was black and one was white—the victim was white. Why was there not a big deal about the ethnicity of the rescuers? Because it does not matter! These are strangers helping strangers and showing love and intentional kindness. They were humans helping humans. I am not amazed, because it is what makes America great—it is the very principles that we are founded upon. However, these acts of kindness and types of behaviors are often not covered in the media. In the case above, the media covered it briefly, but the headlines did not read "Black and White Man Rescue White Teen." The point is that if this were a scandalous incident regarding ethnicity, then the ethnicity would be emphasized to drive up ratings. Again, this is not to imply that kind acts are never covered, but ethnicity is what drives the media to focus on the horrific acts of violence or the scandalous implications of acts against society, especially regarding one ethnicity against the other.

I know I sound idealistic in advocating for a new America where all people respect and honor one another and treat each other with dignity despite their ethnicity or tone of their skin. In 2015, I was out with my wife and some friends and was trying to figure out the parking rules in downtown Washington, DC. If anyone has lived or tried to park in downtown Washington, DC, you know it can be one of the most confusing places, with sometimes up to four signs with seemingly incongruent instructions on one pole. In fact, the local news even did a feature recently on the confusing nature of signs in downtown DC. It is an amazing experience, but you want to avoid violating the rules because violators attract the meter personnel in minutes. I was trying to ensure I wasn't violating the rules (not paying when I needed to) as I was reading the two signs, so I thought I would ask for assistance. From a safe distance, I approached a European descent couple who was getting in their car, and I simply asked if it were legal to park my car in the location without paying. The couple looked at me, ensured their doors were locked, and simply drove off. I must admit, I was shocked because that is not the norm for me. Not to be undone, following dinner, I was coming back to my vehicle with my male friend as our wives went into another store, when out of nowhere, a woman of European descent rolled down her window to ask for instructions to a particular building. Neither of us knew the location, but she was very grateful that we stopped, listened, and tried to assist. You may be wondering what the point of this story is. I submit to you that what I just shared is an everyday occurrence in America where you have polar opposite reactions. If I built my perception of Americans of European descent on my interaction with the first couple, I could have concluded that all those of European descent in America are racist and prejudiced and that I was ignored because of the color of my skin. Conversely, if I built my experience around the second interaction with the woman of European descent who stopped, pulled next to me, and rolled down her window to ask for instructions, I could conclude that Americans of European descent are no longer racists and prejudice is going by the wayside, for she treated me like a human being and my skin color did not matter. The truth probably lies somewhere in between. There are some in America who want to see us divided, and there are others who are intent on judging individuals by their character and not by the color of their skin. We cannot lump everyone into the same pool based on their color or ethnicity. By the way, this entire process could have been reversed, where a person of European descent was looking for assistance and ignored by those of African descent—that too happens every day. This short anecdote from my life is filled with many nuggets that can shed light on the state of America's ethnic relations. I was most likely stereotyped by the couple based on what they have experienced in the past or seen in the media regarding people of a brown hue despite my articulation and clean-cut look (military). Yet the European woman in the second car displayed no such indifference to me and may have a background of experiences filled with people of all nationalities in her life; hence, I was simply another human who might be able to help her reach her destination. Perhaps the first couple did not realize what I was asking, but I doubt that, because before the door was completely closed they clearly heard me say, "Excuse me!" Yet they looked at me, closed and locked the doors, and glanced at me briefly a second time with no response. In their defense, I would argue that I would want my daughters or son to do the same, depending on the circumstance, and to be cautious no matter what the skin color of the person. However, in this case, I was standing in front of the restaurant with people dining on the sidewalk and servers working in broad daylight. They were leaving the restaurant to get into their vehicle that was parked on the curb of the restaurant; I stayed back at least ten feet or so when asking my question. While I would like to give them the benefit of the doubt or an alibi, I submit that it appeared they represented that part of America that perpetuates the ethnic divide in America, while the second young lady represents the unity of what America can be. It is up to each of us to decide what we want our nation to look like in the end. I can tell you from one who strives to have friends of all colors and ethnicities, the second encounter made my day. As a side note, I often see Americans coming together during crises helping one another where the skin tone of the person does not matter, but the quest is to build an America where this is the standard every day.

The next day as I was flying out of Reagan International Airport, a young man of European descent was flying by himself with his toddler. He had a lot of baby supplies, including the stroller (all parents have been there). His wife was a pilot and had to catch her flight; it was moving to watch the family say goodbye as she dashed off to fulfill her work requirements. We were sitting next to each other in the food-court area, and the gentleman had to go check his flight information at one of the gates, so he asked without hesitation if I could watch the stroller, baby bags, and luggage while he checked his flight arrangements. Of course I obliged and was happy to lend a hand as he checked on his flight status. It made me feel good in that I was not judged as dangerous or aggressive because I am of a light brown hue, and I could help my fellow American with a different hue (less melanin) as a human being and do a good deed. That is respect and the standard we should all strive for!

I could give anecdotes like this continually throughout this book. The challenge has been set. How does America move to the next chapter of its historic place in the world? Throughout this book, I push for change in America where all people are accepted and free. Of course, I don't have all of the answers, but I believe that what I am sharing can make a positive impact to America. It will take the American people to push together for the change that I am advocating. Perhaps the words I write will inspire legislation and other tangible changes that will make our nation greater. I am a calling for a new America, an improved America, where we build on the legacies of so many who have died and sacrificed all to build up our great nation. This is a journey of equality that can only happen when we the people come together and embrace the change. I challenge the reader to review the following chapters with an open mind and get ready to be challenged, for it will take every one of us to make this a reality. America can continue to grow and expand as the world's leader for humanitarian and equal rights.

In the preface, I spoke about America's exceptionalism, and I am reminded by others that I should be careful when espousing such a position. However, let me give you some world rankings of America at the time of publishing of this book that demonstrates why I think America is indeed a great nation—not the perfect nation or the best, but one of the best the world has ever seen in regard to leading the world to a new place of democracy and freedom. Yes, despite the times when America embraced practices of slavery and mistreatment of others that were wrong and saturated with corruption, the nation is still great. There are many statistics that speak to America's greatness, and I will not try to list them all here. A closer examination reveals that America was ranked number three in human development by the United Nations' 2011 Human Development Index with a score of 0.910, which ranked nations for health, education, and income.[25] In May 2009, the United States ranked third in innovation, according to the Economists Intelligence Unit, with a score of 9.50.[26] These areas are simply samples of what America does for the world—and please note, the nations ranked above the United States are very small countries. Let's look deeper at why I believe America leads the world. According to the 2015 World Gross Domestic Product (GDP) ranking, America has the world's largest economy, leading China by $7 trillion with an $18 trillion economy.[27] The GDP is the monetary value of all of the nation's finished goods and the services produced within the nation over a period of time.[28] A popular formula of the GDP equals C+G+I+NX—where C equals consumer spending, G equals government spending, I equals the nation's investment and business capital expenditures, and NX equals the nation's total net exports (exports minus imports).[29] A closer examination reveals that in 2013, the United States ranked tenth in the world with a GDP per capita at $52,939.[30] Note that most of the nations that rank above the United States are small countries that are not considered major players in the world economy nor would they be called on for military intervention or even to offer major economic aid. No other potential superpower comes close, with nations such as France ranking at number twenty-one with a GDP per capita at $44,000, the United Kingdom ranking at number twenty-two with a GDP per capita at $41,000, Japan ranking at number twenty-five with a GDP per capita at $38,000, Russia ranking at number fifty-three with a GDP per capita at $14,000, and China ranking at number eighty-four with a GDP per capita at almost $7,000.[31] This clearly shows that America leads the way when compared to large countries that are considered major economic and military superpowers.

Another major area in which I would challenge America is in balancing the budget and reducing the national debt. Currently the deficit, which is the difference between how much the government receives in income (taxes) and how much it spends, has been reducing over the last five years, while the national debt continues to grow. The deficit finally dropped below $1 trillion in 2013 to $973 billion, and the Obama Administration predicted the deficit to decrease to $475 billion by 2018.[32] When the deficit is reduced to zero, we would have our first budget surplus since the Clinton Administration of the 1990s. However, the only way to change the national debt is to reduce government spending with a balanced approach to taxes. There may even be a requirement for some temporary tax increases as President Ronald Reagan had to do during his presidency. I am a huge proponent for small businesses, smaller government, and fewer taxes, but because of the recession, we had to take action that included a balanced approach of raising taxes on the American people while cutting spending. Further, sequestration (extreme cuts to government spending) was implemented by an agreement between Democrats and Republicans that no one thought would ever be instituted. In other words, the proposed governmental cuts of sequestration were so nonsensical, that everyone, including former President, Barack Obama, predicted it would never go into effect before another sensible budget agreement was reached. Unfortunately, that did not happen and sequestration was implemented. The strain sequestration placed on the Department of Defense has been well documented because of the mandatory, nonsensical cuts. The interesting thing is that it was sequestration that caused much pain in the federal government operations, but it was the catalyst for deficit reduction. Austerity was forced on the American people because those in the highest offices in our land could not agree on the national budget and the way forward.

The national debt is the total of all the money owed by the federal government (accumulated deficits), and it is growing each day. Whenever there is the deficit for a given year, the government has to borrow money to counter the deficit, which continues to build the debt. At the publishing of this book, the national debt was at an astounding $18 trillion and growing.[33] The federal debt grew from $6 trillion in 2000 to $10 trillion in 2008.[34] Once the recession hit America, that, coupled with major spending in the form of a government bailout ($700 billion) and increased military spending, made the federal debt grow from $10 trillion in 2008 to $16 trillion in 2012.[35] Think of the federal debt as what it takes to run the nation and provide programs. I am advocating that a strong America is one that has limited but effective government with the opportunity for entrepreneurship based on personal responsibility, fiscal restraints, accountability, and stewardship. Our federal government continues to grow at a pace that will basically bankrupt America if not changed with a balanced budget—our economy cannot withstand increased spending limits with no change in sight. Quantitative easing, which is a monetary policy that calls for the central banks to stimulate the economy by buying assets from other commercial banks to increase money supply when standard monetary policy has become ineffective, cannot last forever.[36] In 1913, it was estimated that federal government expenditures accounted for 2.5 percent of the GDP as compared to over 35.6 percent of total government expenditures as the percentage of the GDP in 2012.[37] The year 1913 was significant because the Sixteenth Amendment was ratified. It allowed the federal government to levy, for the first time, a federal income tax upon the American people.[38] The government was much smaller and collected a variety of taxes on other things, such sales and consumption.[39] Many Constitutional historians believe that the federal government was created in 1776 to protect its citizens' rights, but after 1913, the federal government slowly moved to ensuring economic success of the citizens with welfare programs and government assistance, especially after World War II and many Great Society programs.[40] Obviously, ensuring economic success for citizens has grown out of control. Spending for the government can be broken down into mandatory spending and discretionary spending. Discretionary spending is what is negotiated annually between the president and Congress, and it can be changed annually. The discretionary budget is $1.168 trillion for fiscal year 2016.[41] Mandatory spending (already authorized by Congress through law) accounts for 60 percent of the budget and includes items such as Social Security ($938 billion), Medicare (aid for seniors, $583 billion), Medicaid (aid for the poor, $351 billion), immigration reform ($8 billion), and welfare (entitlement programs, $662 billion), while discretionary spending accounts for 33.5 percent of total spending, two-thirds of which is military spending at more than $534 billion for fiscal year 2016.[42] The remainder of the budget (6.5 percent) is interest on the national debt. At our current debt rate, Social Security benefits will be questionable after the next thirty years because the workforce is shrinking, and not enough funds are being given to Social Security. Today America spends roughly $79.9 billion on Health and Human Services; $70.7 billion on Education; $70.2 billion on Veterans Administration; $41.2 billion on Homeland Security; $29.9 billion on the Energy Department; $41 billion on Housing and Urban Development; $14.9 billion on the Justice Department; $46.3 billion on the State Department and Foreign Aid; and $18.5 billion on NASA.[43] It is not my intent to deal with our financial concerns in great detail, but to highlight the fact that a strong America is a fiscally responsible America. It is my position that fiscal irresponsibility, more than any other issue, is the gravest threat to America.

Let's look further before concluding this section on American strength despite our fiscal spending challenges. How does the United States rank in the world with foreign aid? The North-South Institute 2013 report lists the United States as the number-one nation in the world in providing foreign aid, giving more than $30 billion annually, which is by far the leading sum for a single nation. The next closest nation, the United Kingdom, gives $13 billion annually.[44] In fact, America gives more foreign aid annually than the entire European Union combined. I could show more world facts that will corroborate my claim that America is indeed exceptional in its economy, world outreach, humanitarian aid, and military power. No nation our size does what we do for the free world in terms of democracy, economic power, and human rights. Of more than 196 nations, America is a world leader in democracy and freedom. The president of America is often introduced (and rightly so) as the "leader of the free world." Our freedom index is ranked very high with other industrial nations. According to the 2015 Freedom House Index, America's status is "free," with a freedom rating of one out of seven, including a rating of one out of seven in civil liberties and one out of seven in political rights.[45] A ranking of one means a strong emphasis on the ideal and compliant, whereas a seven represents noncompliance. Of course, it can almost go without saying that we are the world's most sophisticated and most dominant military. No one can project airpower, sea power, or land power like America, with such agility, speed, reach, and precision. Our global reach is second to none. I am not saying this as a National War College graduate with prejudice, but these are simply the facts. In 2015 America was the number-one-ranked military in the world with more than 1.4 million active troops, spending $577 billion on military infrastructure, with a navy that had 3.4 million tons of hardware, almost fourteen thousand aircraft, and almost nine thousand tanks.[46] We spend more on our military than the next top nine nations combined, including Russia, China, India, the United Kingdom, France, South Korea, Germany, Japan, and Turkey.[47] Only China has more military troops on active duty with 2.3 million, while Russia and China have more tanks with fifteen thousand and nine thousand, respectively.[48]

We are world changers, no matter how you slice it. It is from this backdrop that I believe we can translate this freedom and greatness to a new level in America. There is no doubt that America is probably the most diverse nation on the planet. Of course, this is what makes America great, and it is my intent to show how this diversity can be leveraged so that economic and social equality can be reached by all. I am trying to present a balanced approach in which I acknowledge the greatness of America. At the same time, I realize we have much to improve upon, but I will not accept that America is a terrible nation, and I will not sit by idly and listen to those who trash America for being broken or for not doing enough for the world. I truly believe that the American dream is still alive, and one can work his or her way up the levels of life. People fight to get into this nation. With an estimated 11.1 million illegal immigrants in our nation as of 2012, there are no serious political discussions that do not address immigration problems in America.[49] Illegal immigration does bring with it a host of problems, such as higher crime rates in some southern border areas and government aid for education and emergency medical costs, as illustrated in a Research and Development (RAND) corporation study showing medical costs for illegal immigration at $1.1 billion in 2000.[50] Further, there are costs associated with providing education resources, legal expenses, and uncompensated care for those who illegally entered and gave birth to children in America. One example in 2006 shows that Oklahoma spent $9.7 million on emergency Medicaid services for delivery of babies.[51] Imagine these costs amplified throughout the states. But the reason this is a problem is because America is so great, and many are trying to get into this nation legally and illegally. There is not an equal number trying to exit our great land. There is no doubt that America is still the place to be. America should welcome all who would come into our nation legally. There is a process for entry, and perhaps that process should be reviewed for improvement as far as timing, requirements, and bureaucratic practices. I also believe our borders must be protected with a fence line that actually keeps the illegal immigrants from entering at the southern part of America, yet there must be a fair way to help them enter our nation if they so choose. Those who are in America illegally must not be deported but given a chance to earn their citizenship like everyone else through a comprehensive plan. However, illegal immigrants must acknowledge they are here illegally and self-identify. Further, those who are criminals and illegal in the United States must be deported. Don't let the naysayers who say America is on a decline deceive you. In the political seasons, this especially becomes the rhetoric—that we are weak worldwide—but it is not true. We are still the world's only superpower. No one can mobilize a military as we can and, at the same time, provide needed support in a major catastrophe or natural disaster. America is not on a decline, but her best days are ahead, and this turmoil with regard to ethnicity shall be overcome—of that I am confident. I am proud to be called American. I simply want us to continue to grow and expand our freedom and liberties to all.

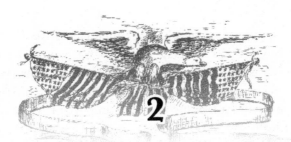

2
A NEW TERMINOLOGY: CLOSING
THE RACIAL DIVIDE

Four score and seven years ago our fathers brought forth on this continent, a new nation, conceived in Liberty, and dedicated to the proposition that all men are created equal.
—President Abraham Lincoln,
Gettysburg Address

President Abraham Lincoln

In 1989, I was the president of what was then called the Black History Committee at Dyess AFB, Abilene, Texas. I learned a lot about black history and why it was so important to celebrate and remember. America had indeed come a long way—this was clear to me. However, I also determined that somehow we were missing something important to the growth of America. Specifically, the air force base had several other heritage groups: Native American, Hispanic, Asian Pacific, and Women's Heritage. It was clear to me that while it was important to recognize each of the ethnicities or classes and what they contributed to America, we were neglecting what made us strong as a nation—we were all Americans. I called for a special meeting of all committee heads to discuss the possibility of creating a new group: the American Heritage group. My vision was simple. All of the groups would merge and work on the recognition of each special ethnicity or minority group during the year at the designated time and then culminate with a grand presentation of American Heritage Month in June and July, with July Fourth celebrations ending the heritage year, if you will. The idea was well received by the other heritage groups, but before we could implement the concept and make a formal proposal to the air force base leadership, I was selected to attend officer training school in San Antonio, Texas. Thus, the American Heritage Committee idea faded with my transition to a new location. Although we never implemented the idea, I believe the concept is the right one and something we should consider in the military community and across America, where there are American Heritage committees that recognize contributions of all groups.

In 2013, America recognized the contributions of Dr. Martin Luther King, African American civil rights leader, to our society and reflected on his famous "I Have a Dream" speech. Perhaps this speech, more than any other, has become a beacon for change and racial reconciliation. The Pew Research Center conducted a poll and asked Americans about the progress we have made with regard to equality for those of all ethnicities since 1963. The Pew Center found that 81 percent of Americans across all groups believe that some or a lot of progress has been made, with only 4 percent saying no progress at all has been made.[52] The data also showed exactly 80 percent of Americans acknowledge that much more needs to be done with regard to racial equality.[53] America agrees that we have come a long way, and I certainly see it, but there is indeed more to be done to bring us together as a nation. This is why I love America; it is a nation of resilient individuals who are ready for change, and at least in one poll, 80 percent agree that more change is needed with regard to racial reconciliation. Again, I believe that a diverse America is a strong America.

Racial reconciliation has been a major subject in recent times. I remember attending a Promise Keepers conference in the mid-1990s for pastors. There must have been more than fifty thousand men converging in Atlanta for this dynamic conference. In fact, the men almost filled the Georgia Dome. The crowd was diverse but mostly white, as the Promise Keepers organization was a men's movement born out of the Evangelical community, which is of mostly European ancestry. However, that was not our focus, and it made no difference to the interracial group I was traveling with. We had traveled from Montgomery, Alabama, and our goal was simply to experience God and grow as men—racial concerns were not an issue. However, as the meeting went on, one of the most significant moments came when the leaders of the conference unexpectedly openly repented for the discrimination that has been perpetrated since the birth of our nation. It was a moving moment in history, with more than fifty thousand men crying and weeping for our nation and asking God for forgiveness for participating and for the church for indolently sitting on the sidelines while these egregious acts were committed year after year. This event was amazing to witness firsthand, and I am probably not painting the emotional picture well. At the end of the prayer and confession of sins for racial injustice, the leaders of the conference asked the white men in the audience (remember, they were all pastors in some capacity) to find someone of the Native American, black, Hispanic, or Asian descent so they could apologize and pray for them. I was prayed for and felt grateful, although I had not experienced a lot of overt racism in my life, but I saw those around me literally sob as this experience unfolded. I am still not sure of the ramifications of that moment on my life or in our American history, but perhaps that is why I am writing this book right now. The moment did demonstrate that we can come together as a nation, and I saw men take responsibility and ownership for wrong and ask for forgiveness. While this is certainly a great start, what is often lacking in moments like these is follow-up. For instance, it would be interesting to note how many of those congregations became racially integrated as a result of the change in the pastors across all ethnicities. I would also be curious to know how many went out and made legitimate friendships with people who did not look like them and welcomed them into their families. I understand this can be difficult to implement at every level, but it's this kind of change I am advocating—a change that allows people of like interests, regardless of the color of their skin, to live in harmony, bond, and build healthy relationships.

As I have intimated, despite the attempts for racial reconciliation over the years in various forums, one of the most divisive issues America deals with remains racial injustice and the perceptions thereof. In 2013, the Pew Center found that in the preceding year 10 percent of whites say they were discriminated against, while 35 percent of blacks say they experienced discrimination, and 20 percent of Hispanics say they experienced discrimination.[54] This is a significant, for it means that approximately 22 percent of all Americans say they were discriminated against regardless of ethnicity from 2012 to 2013. In my assessment, any discrimination is wrong. I don't suppose we will ever be discrimination free, but we can work toward that end. Remember, our nation has come from a time when there was great inequality for many ethnicities. In June 2015, a white police officer was put on administrative leave for treating a young black girl in swimming gear with over-the-top force during a pool party altercation. The images swept across the social-media circuit and made headline news. Evidently, a neighbor heard the noise from the neighborhood pool party as a fight broke out in McKinney, Texas, and called the police.[55] The video evidence, in what has become the norm today, captures the insensitivity of the police officer and the aggressive behavior. In fact, at one point, as police officers were trying to round up the teens who were running frantically, one police officer, David Eric Casebolt, drew his weapon. Two other officers quickly confronted those who were swarming Officer Casebolt, and it appeared then and only then did the officer holster his weapon. The other police officers were in control and did not do anything out of the ordinary, but this was apparently not case for Officer Casebolt. It was amazing to see the behavior, as it was clear there was no need to pull out the weapon. The police chief, Greg Conley, acknowledged that the behavior of Officer Casebolt was incongruent with police training and practices. Instead of simply speaking with the youth, who obviously had no weapons as they were in swimming attire, the officer in question tried to use roughhouse tactics with knees to the backs, heads, and other body parts. It was actually sad for me to watch. The girl was not booked, but detained and released to her parents. A few days later, Officer Casebolt would officially resign and apologize for his behavior.[56] He cited stress and the fact that he had recently responded to a suicide completion and suicide attempt. Officer Casebolt stated that he did not intend to mistreat anyone and was only reacting. I believe Officer Casebolt was sincere in his apology, but he overreacted. I only place this story here in response to what the 2013 Pew Center reported. This is why the numbers are so unbalanced. Listen, make no mistake about it, police officers must protect themselves at all times, and they risk their lives for our safety every day. I have great admiration for police officers, and I thank them for their service to our nation. However, I call for sensitivity training. A review of the circumstances will clearly show that while the officer was being provoked, his behavior was not congruent with the situation. The police chief describes the officer's action as "indefensible."[57] Thank goodness there was not another case of a young teen needlessly killed. That happens enough already, with hundreds of all ethnicities losing their lives across America monthly. I will speak to this subject in more detail later in the book.

Another bizarre incident ended in a tragedy in 2015. A University of Cincinnati police officer, Raymond Tensing, shot and killed Samuel DuBose, who refused to get out of his car during a routine traffic stop because he was missing a front license plate.[58] Officer Tensing, a white male, was fired by the university and indicted by a grand jury for murder and voluntary manslaughter of Dubose, a black man. The body camera has shown that Tensing wanted DuBose to get out of the vehicle, but DuBose refused to get out. A brief tussle with the door ensued and Officer Tensing fatally shot DuBose. In the video, Officer Tensing noticed a gin bottle on the floor and DuBose gave the bottle to Officer Tensing, telling him that it was not gin, but an air freshener. The county coroner has not stated whether DuBose was intoxicated, but the bottle that was found in the car, also shown to Officer Tensing, was in fact a fragrance of some sort and not gin as it was marked.[59] Again, sensitivity training is needed in America's law enforcement. These types of acts only exacerbate the age-old debate that if you are black in America, you are not treated with the same dignity by law enforcement, and you are somehow less than. This type of thinking and these actions have dogged America throughout its history, and now is the time to change the paradigms and make the promises of democracy a reality.

A quick review of world history reveals that that the terms *black* and *white* were devised in history, essentially in the mid to late 1600s, to cause the divide we still experience today. In truth, all humans have the same skin colors in their genes, from dark to light. The genetic material is called melanin, and it is why we have brown colored skin and hair, but in varying degrees. Our pigmentation, which is the natural color of a person, is not a barometer of intelligence level. It is simply part of our genetic makeup with more or less melanin. I submit to you there are no genetic persons called back or white—these terms are made up through the purported description of skin and physical features. According to researchers, all human beings are 99.9 percent identical in their genetic makeup, while the differences in the remaining 0.1 percent could have answers to diseases.[60] Further, black and white terminology does not accurately describe the skin color, and the connotations of the words have brought much discomfort and pain. They were used perhaps throughout the history of the world in different ways, but never meant to truly describe a "race," for we are one human race. For instance, some of my research revealed that the term *white* was first used for Hispanics, and the term *Caucasoid* was actually used for Eurasians who came from the mountain region of Caucasus, located on the border of Eastern Europe and Western Asia. Yet US Census reports show *black* and *white*, even though genetically, there is not a white or black race. You will note I use "racial" throughout the book for common vernacular, but in reality there is only one race. I submit that it is now time to change the terminology in America. We know for a fact that the US Census has changed terminology of people groups throughout its history. For example, the term *mulatto* used to exist in America, but it is not used anymore. Asians were only added in recent decades. I submit to America that we can change the landscape of ethnicity by changing and eliminating the terms *black* and *white* as a reference to ethnicity. According to color expert Kate Smith, the term *black* began with a group of tribes who were known as the Proto-Indo-Europeans, and the words meant burn or gleam (perhaps from the sun), but for the purposes of our discussion, the term *black* as it relates to skin color began in the sixteenth century with the English.[61] Further, Smith believes that etymologists hypothesize that perhaps the word white also came from Indo-European tribes. The word was first used by the Anglo-Saxons or earlier barbarians as a term to identify those who were of fair complexion or light skin.[62] We do know from most reports, ethnic identification in one form or another began in the 1600s and started making a difference in the way people are identified. Before the change to ethnic identification, people were identified by geographical locations, but over time, the shift moved to facial features, skin color, and hair texture. I submit that America needs to shift ethnicity identification, as race identification is made up, limited, and misplaced.

Perhaps we can learn much from other nations and how they deal with ethnic relations. I met a New Zealander recently who became fascinated with the ideas I was proposing. I asked him how the people of New Zealand were classified. He stated that they were not called white. I found this fascinating. In fact, because he was fair skinned, he would be called European (although we know not all Europeans are of fairer skin). Other ethnic groups included the Maori (Indigenous Groups or Hawaiians), Pacific Islander, and Asian. He went on to tell me there was a term used by the Maori for the Europeans, *Pakeha*, or "white man," and that New Zealanders are called New Zealanders and not readily identified by their ethnic group. The only time they get into ethnicity is for their national census. I was speaking to another friend about the subject of the book and he referenced the Brazilian experience. Brazil has been heralded as a "racial democracy" because of the many colors of people that seem to get along well. Instead of the two polarizing terms America uses—black and white—Brazil uses up to ten classifications for ethnicities. The people get to choose their ethnic identification. As I was researching this subject, I was intrigued to discover that my ethnic classification would change based on the nation I would live in. According to my research, because I am considered well off economically and have fair skin and semistraight hair, I could technically be classified as white in Brazil. Seems like an incredibly complex system to identify people and put them in various classes. Ethnic identification in Brazil is based on economics and not necessarily the color of one's skin, although skin color matters. In Haiti, I would most likely be considered white because of my European ancestry. I have another friend from Holland who explained to me that despite the fact that there are people of different hues of skin colors, no one is called white and no one is called black. Yet, lest I paint a picture that racism does not exist in other nations, there are reports of those who reside in Britain and other European nations who display racism against those who are of African, Indian, Pakistani, or Middle Eastern descent. The problems seem to revolve around the same things that plague America with the racial divide along the lines of skin color.

I have met former National War College classmates and high-ranking individuals from both Nigeria and Ethiopia, among other nations. According to them, there is no mention of calling each other black because you live in Africa. You are Nigerian or Ethiopian and not black. In Africa, you are identified by your ethnicity or as African. I could go further, but suffice it to say that not all people identify the colors as we do in America. I am trying to make the case that change is possible because there is no law that states these are the set terms we must use. As I have stated, the US Census has changed throughout the years with differing nomenclatures. There was a recent Facebook discussion about those from Cape Verde debating about what ethnicity the nation would be. The debate revolves around being African, Portuguese, and European. Many Cape Verdeans believe they are not African, but are in fact Portuguese. Some deny their light-brown skin, while others say their brown skin matters and should not be discounted. It is an interesting debate only as it is relevant to our discussion about skin color and how many either deny or embrace their heritage of Africa. Why is this important? Because somehow the "world" has the perception that having brown skin makes one inferior. More importantly, many brown-skinned people believe they are inferior. Why is identifying that I have some African in my bloodline wrong? According to biological anthropologists or evolutionary scientists, the entire human race has its origins in Africa. Remember, Africa is not limited to one ethnicity as you can be African and Arab or have European features (South Africa) or brown skin. Also, note that Europeans can also be Arab or brown. Let me repeat myself: Pigmentation should not be equated to intelligence or success, good or bad, and it is time to rid ourselves of the terms *black* and *white* in relation to humans. We are all humans, and we make decisions in our lives that determine who we are and what we shall become.

INSPECTION AND SALE OF A NEGRO.

Slaves being auctioned and sold.

Let's go deeper. Those of African descent have gone through a variety of different names throughout the history of America. A review reveals that early blacks in America (1600s–1700s) were actually called Africans, because they generally came to America directly from Africa and generally through the Atlantic slave trade. According to some reports, the Free African Society in 1787, for example, stated in its preamble, "We, the free Africans and their descendants ..."[63] There were also the African Methodist Church and the African Baptist Church. Again, the name African was the term of the day. By the way, this is congruent to what my research has consistently shown. People groups were known by their region or geography and not by the color of the skin or facial features. As time went on, blacks were called "mulatto" or "colored" in the late 1800s and early 1900s. The term *mulatto* can have negative connotations but means that a person generally had one white parent and one black parent, while colored generally meant they were multiracial and could be considered free in some circles.[64] One has to question why the term *colored* was related to a person with brown skin but not to a person with peach-colored skin. It was nonsensical and another term to show a less-than status. *Mulatto* has an etymology from the word *mule*, or a hybrid from the mixture of a horse and donkey. The terms *mulatto* and *colored* are not limited to the United States and are found throughout the world for mixed ethnicities and often bestowed greater privileges than those granted to people considered black. In the United States, it should be noted although you were of mixed ethnicity, the majority ensured you did not get additional privileges, and in the end, you were still considered black. The term for identifying those of African descent then shifted to *Negro* from the 1940s to the 1960s. *Negro* actually means "black" in Latin countries. Dr. Martin Luther King referred to those of African descent as Negroes in his famous "I Have a Dream Speech." The term, though, came to be filled with negative connotations. That term went away with time, and the term *black* became the name of choice. There was great debate to perhaps go to Afro-American as an identification term as late as the 1970s. However, in the mid-1980s, African American became the name of choice. This name was announced by the Rev. Jesse Jackson as a more appropriate name. Recently, there has been a push to go back to the term *black*, with *black* meaning having some descendent from Africa. If America has changed the nomenclature or terminology of ethnicity in the past, what hinders us from doing it again?

There is no doubt in America and the world that whites have been the dominant ethnic group for much of recorded history. As I have stated, the word *Caucasoid* actually comes from the region of the Caucasus; can refer to people from Europe, North Africa, the Horn of Africa, or Asia; and is not limited to one color of skin. According to *Statistical Policy Handbook* (1978), the US Department of Justice Federal Bureau of Investigations classified whites as people having origins from Europe, North Africa, and the Middle East.[65] Again, the color of the skin was not used to identify the people groups, but it was the geographical region that was the determinant. The term *Caucasian* was coined by German philosopher Christoph Meiners in 1785 because of the region.[66] In the 1790s, it was Johann Friedrich Blumenbach, a German philosopher, who divided the world into five races based on skin tone, cranial measurements, and facial features: Caucasian as the white race, Mongoloid as the yellow race, Malayan as the brown race, Ethiopian as the black race, and Native American as the red race.[67] Over time, these classifications have been disputed and are not accepted at all. In fact, the five race classifications have been expanded up to twenty race classifications by some researchers. For instance, in the United States, the race classification has repeatedly changed over the years, such as when the 1890 Census listed white, black, mulatto (fifty-fifty mixture of white and African), Japanese, Chinese, Quadroon (25 percent African and 75 percent white), Octoroon (one-eighth African and seven-eighths white), and Indian.[68] I only show them here to give some insight into the origins of the term white. It is believed that Meiners and Blumenbach originally used the term *white* due to the paleness of the skin tone. My question is how did the peach-colored skin of some Europeans get confused with white skin, as in the color white? They then began to add intelligence and superiority claims, stating that white people had higher aptitude and that the darker you were, the less intelligent you were. Doesn't this sound familiar? This type of flawed thinking is what has stagnated America and the world over the years, and it still exists today. In 2010, the American Anthropologists Association, an organization that has been around since 1902, and now has eleven thousand members, recommended that the US Census eliminate race terminology because race has been proven not to be a real term as compared to ethnicity.[69] In a PBS report, race has been equally denounced and been described as a made-up classification that does not have any basis in fact because there is no single gene that separates or distinguishes one race from all members of another race.[70]

Interestingly, the phenomenon of being light skinned or white is not limited to the United States. As one examines the color controversy, it appears that the lighter complexion you are in most communities, the higher your status. How did being of dark complexion come to denote a negative concept? It appears that it simply started in part from 1700s through verbal tradition around the world, with no empirical evidence that the darker you are, the less intelligent you are. Even worse, the darker you were, the more you were deprived of human rights and even considered as a partial human. Perhaps it was developed through the colonial systems that were based on a caste system of field laborers who would generally be darker due to outdoor labor, and an aristocratic system with the lower class darker population working in the fields. A closer look at those of Asian descent, for example, reveals an estimated $18 billon industry of skin whitening in nations such as Hong Kong, Malaysia, Japan, Philippines, South Korea, and China.[71] Evidently, the lighter you are, the higher your status, as a lighter complexion represents more power from not working in the fields. Further, for many, a lighter complexion equals feminine beauty, racial superiority, power, status, and better marital prospects.[72] As I have stated, skin bleaching is a multibillion dollar industry around the world in places such as West Africa, India, Asia, and many third-world countries, with many taking the risks with dangerous bleaching drugs, such as mercury, hydroquinone, or corticosteroids, to achieve the status of lighter skin and thus a higher standing in their society.[73] Even within the African American community, there have been litmus tests over the years, such as the brown-paper-bag test, in which the individual had to be lighter than the bag to be a part of a sorority or group; the flashlight test, which measured whether or not a profile (feature wise) was Caucasian enough; or the comb test, which tested if one's hair was too coarse to fit in with those of lighter complexion or the Caucasian ethnicity.[74] It is simply amazing that a lighter skin color, in almost every culture around the globe, means you are more acceptable and of a higher status.

In early America, miscegenation (the mixing of different racial groups) often happened through white slave masters sleeping with their back slaves, creating mixed-ethnic people (mulatto) who then were further classified to ensure they were identified properly in the American class system. However, the mixing of these ethnicities created further division in those of African descent, with those of light skin, sometimes called Creole (mixed with African, French, or Spanish descent), being treated with domestic tasks during slavery rather than field work and gaining access to higher educational opportunities and economic opportunities during the Jim Crow era.[75] It also created anxiety for the white society, as those who could pass for white or those who were close to appearing white wanted to gain citizenship rights (I provide examples later in the book). In fact, this is when America created terms such as *quadroon, octoroon,* and *mulatto,* to name a few, in order to identify and ensure that classification as white in America was limited to some Europeans and did not include all Europeans.[76] I could provide more illustrations to further make my case, but may it suffice to say that this viewpoint of blackness being negative is not limited to the United States and is spread worldwide. Thus, my charge is to begin to attack this faulty thinking by changing antiquated terminology and eliminating terms that are not meaningful or appropriate. Of course, changing the terms is only the beginning, for the negative mind-set and consciousness of skin color need to change in America.

Professor David R. Roediger of the University of Illinois espouses what I have been proposing in that the construction of the white race in the United States and around the world was basically to build separation from and superiority over those of brown color.[77] Roediger goes on to state that it was not until the eighteenth century that the term *white* became the predominant term to classify those with fair skin, and according to author and legal scholar John Theranian, many Americans we would now consider white were not so considered at several points in American history. Those include Spaniards, Slavs, Jews, Italians, Irish, Afghans, Iranians, Greeks, Germans, white Hispanics, and Arabs.[78] Trust me; it was important to be white in early America and to have all of the rights conferred on a family. According to records, many early immigrants sued the United States to gain white status. You had to be free. One only has to look back in history to know that the Irish were not treated as true Americans early on in their arrival to the United States and were in fact treated as "white slaves." According to John Martin, author of *The Irish Slave Trade, The Forgotten "White" Slaves*, the white slave trade of the Irish was one of the most heinous in history. The Irish were not considered white and were sold into slavery by the British in the early 1600s by the hundreds of thousands.[79] The following is an excerpt from authors Don Jordan and Michael Walsh in their book *White Cargo: The Forgotten History of Britain's White Slaves in America*. In this book, the authors capture the horrors of the white slave trade that came to America in the early 1600s, actually before the African slave trade:

> They came as slaves; vast human cargo transported on tall British ships bound for the Americas. They were shipped by the hundreds of thousands and included men, women, and even the youngest of children. Whenever they rebelled or even disobeyed an order, they were punished in the harshest ways. Slave owners would hang their human property by their hands and set their hands or feet on fire as one form of punishment. They were burned alive and had their heads placed on pikes in the marketplace as a warning to other captives.[80]

Jordan and Walsh go to great lengths to explain how many attempt to term those in the Irish slave trade as *indentured servants*, but they say it is not accurate or complete; this was one of the most vicious acts carried out against a nation of people with scores of murders, rapes, and families destroyed. The Irish were duped into signing contracts as indentured servants only to be lied to, traded, and stripped of all rights. They were, in fact, slaves. Others confirm that many "mulatto" slaves came out of the union of the Irish slaves and the African slaves, as they also were brought to America during the same era. My position is that all slavery is wrong. Skin color does not determine slavery, but slavery is a result of hatred and utter ignorance, with one people group believing they are superior to the other. An example of modern-day slavery is found in human trafficking. Human trafficking, meaning the capture of one person to serve as a sex slave or perform manual labor, knows no limits or boundaries to the color of the slave's skin. In fact, along with East Asia and the Pacific, Europe is a haven for human traffickers today with more than eight hundred thousand people worldwide trafficked every year.[81] I highlight this part of American history so that we can understand that my proposal to change the terminology is not about one ethnicity against the other, but it is about ending the perceived superiority of one ethnicity and the perceived inferiority of other ethnicity. Remember, as I have stated, the Irish were listed as one of the groups in America who were not granted white status or full citizenship rights in the early centuries of America. Interestingly, it was not until the black and Irish battles in the streets of New York that the status of the Irish began to improve, and they slowly began to gain standing in the United States, including being listed as white. Again, this means that whiteness was not as much about skin color in America as it was about power, superiority, and position.

As I was doing the research for this book, it became clear that I was not the first person to take a serious look at and deep dive into the names we use for identification and the vast implications that can be found in them. It is time to take down the walls of racial names that divide us. I am ready to be called American with no hyphen. If you must go deeper to identify me, then you will find that my ethnicity is mixed with African, European, Hispanic (Spanish), etc. The bottom line is that my region of identity, geographically speaking, is now America. I am not African; I am American. I am not European; I am American. I am not Iberian; I am American. I have ethnic blood from the aforementioned regions, and I am proud of my diverse heritage and ethnicity, but I am American, and this is a plea for my identification to change to American.

It is obvious that America is on a new path of ethnic diversity. Today, with a US population of roughly 319 million, 62.6 percent (197 million) are considered white alone, not Hispanic or Latino heritage; 17.1 percent (fifty-four million) are considered Hispanic or Latino; 13.2 percent (forty-two million) are considered black or African American; 5.3 percent (seventeen million) are considered Asian; and 2.4 percent (7.6 million) of the US population have two or more ethnicities (mixed heritage).[82] I personally believe the 2.4 percent, or 7.6 million number, is quite low, given that mulatto (mixed heritage) was removed from the census in 1920 or so. Instead of identifying with their multicultural history, millions of people like me are limited to one ethnicity, and most of the time, that ethnicity is black if you have any shade or tinge of brownness in your skin. According to the census and to a study from the Pew Research Institute from 2008, European non-Hispanic white Americans will no longer be the dominant ethnicity in America by the year 2050 and will only make up 47 percent of the US population.[83] To put this in perspective, Europeans or whites dominated America with more than 90 percent of the population in 1950.[84] I was speaking to a white friend who told me her husband, who identifies as Hispanic, could not choose Hispanic as ethnicity on the US Census and had to choose white, even though he does not actually identify as white. America is changing quickly. Again, I am particularly sensitive to this topic, as I am of mixed descent. I recently took a DNA test from Ancestory.com and discovered that I am 56 percent African; 41 percent European; and 3 percent Asian, Polynesian, and North American Native Indian. I sensed that I was of mixed ethnicity early in life but did not confirm it until I took the DNA test. I was simply classified as black. My mom was very fair skinned and said she was often teased when growing up in the inner city of New Orleans. She had an Italian European complexion. In fact, she was criticized for being white when she was a child and made fun of. I am not a stranger to being called names, such as "yellow boy" or "pretty boy with the light skin and wavy hair." The term *high yellow* denotes you have some type of European descent in your bloodline; essentially, you are a mulatto. The criticism and teasing mostly came from people of the African descent community. As I grew older, most people thought I was of Hispanic origin and perhaps from Puerto Rico (my son is often mistaken for Puerto Rican). Specifically, my largest single region, according to the Ancestry.com DNA test, shows that I am of European origin with 21 percent from the Iberian Peninsula (which is mainly Spain and Greece). This is not uncommon in New Orleans and Louisiana, where many have Creole descent (which means mixed European and African descent). This is mostly French origin but also Spanish. It made sense that my mother was Creole but mostly European due to her fair complexion.

The first picture on the top left is my mother, Phyllis Neyland; top right is my aunt (mother's sister) Marguerite Williams; middle left is my father, Millard Neyland Sr.; middle center is my maternal grandmother, Irma Mellieur; middle right is my father-in-law, Larry Duplessis Sr.; left is my mother-in-law, Roberta Smith; and bottom left are my paternal grandmother, Beulah Haynes, and my maternal grandfather, Manual Ozen Sr.

While I never had a DNA test performed on my mother, I did get a test from Ancestory.com on my aunt, Marguerite Williams, and we confirmed what we already suspected—she was nearly 65 percent European. My maternal grandmother, Irma Mellieur, was basically European with a French father (Theophile Mellieur) and Spanish mother (Louise Leon); my maternal great-grandparents were pure Europeans (white) as far as I can tell. I never met my maternal grandmother, but you can clearly see she was European from the pictures. My maternal grandfather, Manuel Ozen, appeared to have European, African, and Latino descent. Our records show that his mother, Marie Josephine Relf, my paternal great-grandmother, was of Latino descent. Today I can make sense of all this, for when I see my children or myself, we all look like those people of mixed heritage—the ones who say they do not know how to identify themselves. Secondly, my mother was considered African American or black her entire life despite the color of her skin. In reality, DNA tests would most likely had proved that she was 65 to 70 percent European, such as I discovered with the DNA test for my aunt who was closest to her in age. As I stated, it turns out that we have an abundance of DNA from the Iberian Peninsula (Spain and Greece). My mom was often mistaken for Hispanic, Italian, or European whenever she traveled with me to different locations around the world. This brings back great memories, as my mother could not speak any other language but English and would be shocked when people would walk up to her and start speaking Spanish to her. The look on her face was priceless! Again, I have been mistaken for Puerto Rican more often than not. The actual response I hear most often is "I knew you were mixed with something!" I recently visited the Dominican Republic, and I could not convince them I was not from their country. Even though I have 41 percent European DNA, I am most likely considered African American in America because I am light brown and less likely European even though my largest gene pool percentage of a single region or ethnicity is from the Iberian Peninsula. Moreover, my second daughter, Shontae, is often identified as Middle Eastern or European-mixed, and all of our children have been told they look like they are of mixed ethnicity or from another country. Shon II, my son, is often asked if he is Puerto Rican as he has extremely curly hair, a thin nose, and a light brown complexion. Ashley, the oldest girl, has browner skin, but her look is very exotic and she is often asked if she is Latino.

My immediate family, from top left to bottom: Ashley,
Shontae, Shon II, Shon, and Madeline.

When I compare my kids with those who are from parents with different ethnicities (especially African and European), you hardly see a difference. Part of the reason my children are so diverse is my spouse. She has European in her ancestry as well as a maiden name of Duplessis. The Duplessis in New Orleans are known for their mixed heritage and strong European (French) and African mix with skin tone, facial features, and hair type. At the time of the publishing of this book, Madeline had not completed a DNA test to find out her true heritage. Madeline's father, Larry Duplessis Sr., had strong European features while her mother had strong African features. By the way, my father, Millard Neyland, had gray/green eyes. Oh, how I wanted those eyes when I was younger! His mother was half European and half African. We believe my paternal great-grandmother on my dad's side was a concubine to her European owner, and thus, my grandmother Beulah Haynes was born with mixed heritage (mulatto). I do not have much information about my great paternal grandfather (European) and my great paternal grandmother (African).

My grandmother, Beulah Haynes, lived in Gloster, Mississippi, and had beautiful long hair, light brown skin tone, and gray/green eyes. My paternal grandfather, Alfred Tennyson Neyland, had distinct African features with very dark skin; I never met him, as he was born in 1873, but he looked purely African in my estimation. I don't know much about his parents (my paternal great-grandparents). The name Neyland was most likely taken by my paternal great-grandfather, because he was almost certainly a slave and then a sharecropper in Mississippi. I have such a diverse history, and I am very proud of it. My diversity should not limit my status in America or the world. Perhaps it was my destiny to speak out on this subject, given my mixed heritage. I am not sure why I have this passion about this subject except I know I want to see everyone accepted for who they are and have equal opportunity for happiness and success no matter what their ethnicity. I believe America offers that opportunity.

Picture of Youth Drinking from Colored Only Water Fountain

In America, the so-called one-drop rule was once a sociological and legal term from the twentieth century to classify anybody with black blood, one drop or more, as black.[85] This is why many leaders in the past tried to hide their ancestry and pass for white if they had the skin tone. This was a significant law as again it perpetuated the negativity associated with being of a darker skin tone. In 1910, Tennessee and Virginia were the first states to adopt the practice, but it was not officially law until the Racial Integrity Act of 1924, when many states followed suit.[86] It was a strange time in

America, for along with the Racial Integrity Act, many other laws were passed in the late 1800s to prohibit interracial marriage and to maintain segregation. Some of the laws had varying definitions for who was black and who was not. Not all adhered to the one-drop rule, for that was considered unrealistic. Generally, most states would begin to set the rule at one-eighth blood (12.5 percent) to be considered black (octoroon).[87] The ultimate goal was to keep the oppression and to disenfranchise blacks from equal rights. Some leaders, such as Walter Plecker, publically stated that if you allowed mixtures of black and white, you would then bring the blacks up in status mentally and culturally because of the mixture, and the courts of the land upheld many of those laws and rulings in the early twentieth century.[88] In fact, Plecker, who was the registrar of statistics in Virginia, did not believe records should show mixing of ethnicities and made sure you were only classified as black, white, or Indian, so he had many records destroyed and reclassified people into the prescribed categories.[89] I have no doubt that, had my mom spoken French or Spanish, she would not have been considered black, but rather European or white. I would have been considered mulatto (multiracial) due to my skin tone. By the way, mulatto was on the US Census until 1930 when Congress removed it due to pressure from the Southern legislators. This removal led to the loss of a long history of the United States' mixed ethnicity ancestry.[90] Why was the one-drop rule and law so significant? It was a mechanism to hold back those who might be able to pass as white to ensure that no one who had African blood or ancestry would get the benefits of being a free white person in America. The white supremacy belief was alive and well in America, and many thought a mixture of the white ethnicity with any other ethnicity would mean that the offspring of those persons would be whatever the minority was—that is, black, Jew, Indian, or Hispanic. Interestingly, North American Native Indians would classify the offspring of a white and Indian as half-breed and therefore white; they could no longer have the privilege of being called American Indian—this was called hypodescent.[91]

There are a couple of interesting things to think about at this point. Why is a person who has mixed ethnicity (for this example, black and white equally) considered black? Can't they simply be considered mixed and neither black nor white? It is a system that was put in place over two centuries ago to continue the oppression, and we still follow that pattern today. I am always amazed at Hollywood when they run features entitled "Stars you did not know were black!" How does that sound? In other words, we want to set the record straight: these stars meet the one-drop rule; thus they are black, not white, because even though their mothers are German or French, their fathers are from Kenya or Nigeria, for example. To demonstrate the nonsense of our ethnic rules, look at the following example: mixed-ethnic Puerto Rican reggaeton artist Julio Voltio is considered black in the United States and white in Puerto Rico.[92] Further, most of the world and America realized that with all of the uproar about ethnicities and intermixing, there was not one "pure" white person in America. In an effort to counter antimiscegenation laws during the South Carolina constitutional convention in 1895, George D. Tillman stated, "It is a scientific fact that there is not one full-blooded Caucasian on the floor of this convention. Every member has in him a certain mixture of … colored blood. The pure-blooded white has needed and received a certain infusion of darker blood to give him readiness and purpose. It would be a cruel injustice and the source of endless litigation, of scandal, horror, feud, and bloodshed to undertake to annul or forbid marriage for a remote, perhaps obsolete trace of Negro blood."[93]

Miscegenation meant the bloodlines were intermixed, and it was a very complex issue in America, for it was evident that the bloodlines had been greatly mixed through the years. Thus, the only way to counter the widespread mixing of ethnicities was to create laws to counter the movement. The US Supreme Court upheld most of the laws when challenged until the 1960s following the Civil Rights movement. It is very difficult to identify people by their color of skin alone. For example, in 2002, Steve Sailer has written on research by Mark D. Shriver, a molecular anthropologist from Penn State University, who studied ethnic origin with about three thousand individuals in about twenty-five regions and found that on average, white individuals had 0.7 percent of black ancestry, 70 percent of whites have no black ancestry, while 30 percent of whites have 2.3 percent of black ancestry.[94] Conversely, Sailer found that the average proportion of white ancestry in blacks was 18 percent and about 10 percent had more than 50 percent of white ancestry.[95] In other studies, genetic specialists estimate that 58 percent of blacks have at least 12.5 percent white ancestry, while 19.6 percent of blacks have at least 25 percent white ancestry, and about 1 percent of blacks have at least 50 percent white ancestry.[96] My point in sharing this data is to show that, while we sometimes make a huge issue of ethnic differences in America, it is interesting that we are closer than we think with our bloodlines. Further, earlier Americans were most likely to be even more mixed, given that there were many opportunities for slave owners and relatives to intermix with slaves. Nor can we forget the Irish, as reported earlier, who were also slaves in some cases and indentured servants in the early 1600s and 1700s and often given to voluntary and involuntary intermixing of the ethnicities. America was birthed out of revolts against England for its unjust laws, taxes, and religious requirements. Yet at the same time as America decried the restriction on freedom placed on the colonies, there was a movement of restricting freedom of Irish and blacks. It was a paradoxical time in America that would continue throughout our great history. The antislavery movements begin to rise up from the very beginning of America when inhabitants other than the indigenous North American Indians set foot on our great land. From 1616 to 1865, black slaves kept fighting for their freedom, often with the help of white abolitionists. Massachusetts was the first colony to legalize slavery in 1641.[97] History records that there were uprisings by whites and blacks who wanted to end slavery before America was fully birthed. For instance, there was the burning of New York in 1712, where blacks and whites were charged with rebellion and banished or killed (eighteen blacks executed and nine whites killed).[98] Even when the oppression continued in pre-Revolutionary days, there were those of African descent who continued to demonstrate their intellect and ability to fit in society. For example, there was Lucy Terry, a poet and author, who was so articulate and gifted that people came from all over to hear her speak in the late 1700s.[99] Who could forget Phillis Wheatley in 1773, who was the third American woman to publish a poem and first African American to do so.[100] She was revered internationally, and even General George Washington praised her for her verse. People knew then that blacks were intelligent, but the narrative had to be changed to build the empire of oppression. Why has this battle raged for centuries? The cry for freedom and equal treatment has always been there. I need to emphasize clearly that, as our great nation was birthed, many Americans were fighting for freedom of all people, yet the color of one's skin was a major issue from the nation's founding. As America was birthed during the American Revolutionary War, few would remember or know that in 1774, the First Continental Congress banned trade with Britain for slaves and set out to abolish the slave trade by 1774. In 1775, General George Washington, who originally forbade free blacks from fighting in the war, reversed his stance and allowed free blacks to fight for a new America.[101] Specifically, in 1776, Philadelphia's Quakers (a religious group) forbade owning slaves; Delaware prohibited importation of African slaves in 1776; and in 1777, Vermont was the first of the thirteen colonies to abolish slavery. In 1777, New York released all free men from servitude, and in 1780, Pennsylvania and Massachusetts abolished slavery.[102] Don't ever let anyone tell you America did not have a conscience with regard to slavery. The forefathers and all Americans knew it was wrong, and men and women of all ethnicities fought and died for the cause more than a century before the Civil War. It was unfortunate that slavery continued in America until 1865 because of the economic benefits and the greed and bigotry of some.

Dred Scott

Think about the time when those of African descent were not considered "fully human" (only two-thirds human), according to the *Dred Scott v. Sandford* (slave owner) ruling—which began in 1847 when Dred Scott wanted to sue for his freedom in Missouri and fought ten years to finally get a hearing in the Supreme Court.[103] Scott was actually free in Illinois, a free state at the time, and he also lived in Wisconsin, which also did not have slavery. Dred Scott would be set free with his wife despite the Supreme Court ruling in 1857 as he was bought by the son of his former slave owner, but unfortunately, he would die only nine months later.[104] In

1860, blacks, or those from African ancestry, were considered not fully human and therefore could be treated as property or a commodity to sell or trade. According to the Supreme Court, they had no rights to sue in federal courts. Oppression of those of African descent was still high in the evolution of the new America, but the abolitionists were winning some of the battles to keep the Union stable. The Missouri Compromise of 1850 prohibited the spread of slavery in new territories and states but allowed for slavery to continue in the states that currently had legal slaves.[105] In response to the Missouri Compromise and to balance the tables, Congress passed the Fugitive Slave Act, which allowed for slaves to be hunted in the north or west if they ran away. This allowed slave hunters to track down perceived slaves for pay, sometimes capturing free men and putting them in chains in the south.

In the case of *Plessy v. Ferguson*, the US Supreme Court upheld constitutional segregation, justifying it with language that it called the "separate but equal" doctrine.[106] In 1896, Homer Plessy, who was classified as octoroon (seven-eighths European and one-eighth African), decided with the backing of prominent blacks, whites, and Creoles (French and African descent) to challenge the Louisiana State law in New Orleans that required blacks and whites to ride on separate rail cars, one for "whites" and the other for "coloreds."[107] Interestingly, despite being seven-eighths European, Plessy was not considered white but black, although he easily passed for white. The Supreme Court not only upheld segregation, ignoring the Thirteenth and Fourteenth Amendments, but it also basically set a precedent that told states they could set the laws how they wanted to without the fear of federal intervention. Plessy was arrested for not going to his car and would be fined. However, his case was not lost in the annals of American history, and it would serve as a major part of shaping American history with regard to racism. It would not be until *Brown v. the Board of Education* that the "separate but equal" doctrine was overturned in 1954.[108] In *Brown v. the Board of Education*, Olivia Brown won the landmark case in which the United States finally realized that segregated schools were wrong, and they could not be and never were separate but equal. On the contrary, the "separate but equal" laws and others like it only served one purpose: to suppress and disenfranchise a group because of the color of their skin. The ruling overturned *Plessy v. Ferguson* and found that the Fourteenth Amendment was violated by such laws.[109] Black and white were no longer legally separated in the United States after the ruling, but we know this decision was not easily accepted and led to many bloody physical altercations.

Many have stated that the leadership of John Brown, a white abolitionist, helped usher in a wave of change in America with regard to slavery. John Brown, who would work with other abolitionists like Frederick Douglas and Sojourner Truth, led an inflammatory attempt in 1859 to end slavery with a raid on the federal armory at Harper's Ferry.[110] Many of his followers, including his sons, would be killed, and John Brown would be publically hanged. Even though unsuccessful, many historians believe that John Brown's act to try to defeat slavery was the fire that led to Civil War just two years later. Another prominent person in American history during the Civil War was General Robert E. Lee, leader of the Virginia Army and eventually leader of the entire Confederate Army. It was most interesting that it was General Robert E. Lee, who did not even care for slavery, who would end up leading the South after turning down President Lincoln's offer to lead the Union. General Lee was loyal to Virginia, which seceded from the Union, but perhaps his heart was never in the war to defend the right to maintain slavery in the America. General Lee wrote to his wife, Anna,

> In this enlightened age, there are few I believe, but what will acknowledge, that slavery as an institution, is a moral & political evil in any Country. It is useless to expatiate on its disadvantages. I think it however a greater evil to the white man than to the black race, & while my feelings are strongly enlisted in behalf of the latter, my sympathies are more strong for the former. The blacks are immeasurably better off here than in Africa, morally, socially & physically. The painful discipline they are undergoing, is necessary for their instruction as a race, & I hope will prepare & lead them to better things. How long their subjugation may be necessary is known & ordered by a wise Merciful Providence. (Robert E. Lee, to Mary Anna Lee, December 27, 1856.[111])

It is clear that General Lee was torn between the institution of slavery and the status quo of the South. His own words show that he knew slavery could not last. He also acknowledged the moral and political evil slavery was, but his loyalty was to those of white ethnicity. It is also believed that he knew his wife and daughter had great success educating slaves and even helped some escape to Liberia.[112] I submit that this dilemma was common among the great leaders of our nation, but only a few had the courage to stand, for the scorn it would bring and the economic loss would be too great.

General Ulysses S. Grant (18th US President)

Yet another prominent leader during the Civil War was General Ulysses S. Grant. General Grant would end up leading the Union Army toward the latter years of the war as he quickly rose through the ranks in the four-year war. General Grant was considered a great military strategist. He defeated General Lee in several key battles, including the decisive battle, the Battle of Appomattox Court House, where General Lee surrendered, and the war ended. General Grant, the popular general and war hero, went on to become the eighteenth president and served two terms from 1868 to 1876. In 1875, he was key to the Civil Rights Act (March 1, 1875) that was signed into law and legalized equal rights for African Americans in education, transportation, and public accommodations. This act was later overturned by the Supreme Court in 1883, which cited that the Fourteenth Amendment only made federal discrimination illegal, but private citizens and organizations could still discriminate.[113] The Supreme Court rendered an incredible decision stating that the Thirteenth Amendment only eliminated the "badge of slavery" but did not prohibit racial discrimination in public accommodation.[114] This is why America struggled to find her footing in the late 1800s as lawmakers reversed everything they could with senseless and discriminatory logic to keep African Americans oppressed. Grant showed that he was a forward thinker, and he tried to keep the legacy of President Lincoln alive through further legislation. He tried to reconcile the North and the South, while ensuring the rights of blacks in the South and in America. We know, however, that upon the tenure of the nineteenth president, Rutherford Hayes, in 1877, the federal presence would be removed from the South, and the Jim Crow era (a system of racial oppression) would begin and erode what much of the war had accomplished.

Illustration depicting Civil War.

As we continue with a brief review of American history with regard to ethnicity, we must remember that the Civil War (1861–65) did equal the end of legal slavery in America, but it did not begin equal rights for all Americans. One cannot understand America without truly understanding the Civil War and the system of slavery. In a sense, one can say that blacks were free without freedom following the Civil War. According to new studies of the Civil War, more than 850,000 gave their lives in the bloodiest war in history on American soil.[115] Some try to argue that it was about the cotton industry and economics only, and while I agree the reason for war included the South's income source, mainly it was about the oppression of a people and the spread of slavery. The South did not want to give up the slave industry, although it did agree to end the slave trade. The North said it wanted to preserve the Union, and slavery was secondary. The South attacked federal property beginning with the first battle at Fort Sumter in April 1861, which would change America forever as the war would begin. In 1616, there were approximately eight hundred thousand African slaves in the United States, but by 1860, there were four million slaves. Congress technically halted the transatlantic slave trade in the early 1800s. It was the Constitution that counted slaves as three-fifths of a human for representation purposes. This gave the South an advantage in Congress due to a larger population representation. The Republican Party formed in 1854 as a revolt to new states gaining slaves and slavery beginning to spread out west. Perhaps the greatest president our nation would know rose out of the newly formed Republican Party and helped change the destiny of America forever. Sen. Abraham Lincoln lost the race for the Senate seat in 1858, but two years later, he won the presidency on the Republic Party ticket in 1860 in a four-way race with 39.8 percent, in part due to a split in the Democratic Party.[116] Our sixteenth president, Abraham Lincoln, was a great champion for the sanctity of all human life and was the key, along with abolitionists, for the change in America. Even then, he would first advocate against the spread of slavery, not necessarily its elimination. The South realized the direction President Lincoln was going and knew change would eventually affect them. Thus, the Southern states began to secede from the United States in rapid fashion from December 1860 to June 1861. President Lincoln was determined to not let the nation split and deemed the secession illegal. The Civil War was inevitable at that point, as both sides were moving further apart. After the Emancipation Proclamation was signed in September of 1862, more than 180,000 African Americans fought in the army, and another eighteen thousand served in the navy, with more than forty thousand giving their lives in the war to end slavery.[117] The Civil War ended on April 9, 1865, when Confederate general Robert E. Lee surrendered to Union general Ulysses Grant. Congress passed the Thirteenth Amendment of the Constitution on January 31, 1865, and ratified it on December 6, 1865, to officially end slavery or involuntary servitude in America.[118] Three years after the Civil War, the Fourteenth Amendment passed, which allowed for citizenship of all persons born or naturalized in the United States and the right of life, liberty, and property. In other words, all people in the United States, regardless of color, became citizens. In February 1870, just five years after the Civil War ended, the Fifteenth Amendment was ratified and allowed for voting rights of all male citizens regardless of ethnicity, color, or previous condition of servitude.[119] Despite the amendments specifically forbidding states from denying rights or abridging the Constitution, federal laws and state laws were not congruent with those constitutional amendments, and it would take ninety-six years before blacks were allowed to vote unencumbered. This is the call throughout this book. For the most part, framers of our Constitution and the amendments that followed were right and tried to get it right, but those who wanted to maintain a slave state in the United States found ways to usurp the intent of federal law to meet their own ends. Since the inception of our nation, there was always a movement to end the heinous practice of slavery, but it was a hard fought battle that could not be easily won.

The Reconstruction Acts of 1867 and 1868 eventually readmitted all of the eleven states back into the Union by 1870 and also divided the South (except Tennessee because it had already ratified the Fourteenth Amendment) into five divisions with army commanders over each section.[120] The purpose of the period was to readjust from the devastating destruction from the war and to restore the South into the Union and ensure its allegiance to the Constitution. Remember, the blacks who were free were economically, socially, educationally, and emotionally disenfranchised. Thus, it was easy to hold blacks back from gaining their legitimate and rightful place in America. Some blacks, however, began to win the state houses in the South and hold the majority in some of the State legislatures. Most of the Southern states, however, felt embarrassed and refused to give up their rights to slavery and slowly began to pass legislation that restricted blacks once again. Once President Lincoln was assassinated, it was difficult to institute the freedom and rights that were fought for in the South. In fact, President Andrew Johnson, Lincoln's successor, was perceived to be very lenient to the South, with limited Congressional intervention allowing the South to reinstate many of its egregious practices against blacks through Black Codes, which were designed to oppress the black community.[121] There were several black Senators and House members elected to state legislature, roads were restored, and the economy was once again growing in the South. However, when the South began pushing back and killing blacks in the early years following the Civil War and stopping white Republicans from voting in the South, many racist groups began to form. White supremacy groups, such as the Ku Klux Klan, were birthed in the South during this era. However, during the Reconstruction, soldiers from the Union intervened and kept the peace as best they could until, in 1877, they were removed from the South and "separate but equal" laws began to apply. The South came back in a fury to enact laws and intimidation tactics to keep blacks in a stagnant state and to undo the progress that was made in the Reconstruction period. It would take until the early 1920s and then the 1950s for substantial change to take place again in America. Imagine if the soldiers had not been pulled out in the late 1870s; I believe racial reconciliation would have moved further at a much earlier timeframe in America. I believe that if President Rutherford B. Hayes would have kept soldiers in place, the nation would have been more secure, and thus, the reversion back to the oppressive South would not have been allowed to take root. Apparently, part of the agreement for Hayes to become president of the United States and gain the needed electoral votes from the South included removing the troops from the South. Again, those who would keep the oppressed in a disenfranchised state found a way to accomplish the task through usurping the law. Without this collusion, the Jim Crow era might have never been born, and America would be so much further with regard to ethnicity relations.

Before we go on, let's examine the terms *black* and *white* a little closer to understand why I advocate loudly for change. As I have stated, I submit that these terms are a manmade creation meant to not only identify, but also to divide. The term *black* has negative connotations for the most part, and when examined closely, one will see meanings such as void of color, dark, evil, bad, and absent of light. *Black* is the opposite of *white*. Think about this statement: "It was the blackest day of my life when I found out my best friend died." What about "The business received a black eye with news of its loss" or "She is the black sheep of the family," referring to negative situations of a family member? Each of these terms could refer to a factual event or situation, for a black sheep is rare and stands out in the flock, and when you hit someone in the eye, you change the pigmentation with a bruise, and it turns black or dark. Here are a few other concepts to think about: blackmail; blackballing; black market; black list; devil's food cake (colored black); white-collar crime; white lie; knight on a white horse; doctor's lab coat, and angel food cake (colored white). Thus, in my estimation, one can easily see how the negative connotations with the black color in everyday language and the positive connotations with the white color paint a picture that being black is bad, while being white is good. The above are common uses of the word *black*, and thus, when they are used for a human, the human is then related to the tragic or malicious events, whether consciously or subconsciously. Likewise, the above are common uses of the word *white*, and thus, when they are used for a human, the human is then related to goodness or purity. The term *white* has connotations normally of purity, righteousness, holiness, and wholesomeness, and I believe today we realize that none of us fit neatly into those characteristics based on the color of our skin or based on the terms we call each other (e.g., black or white). Do you remember the old western movies? Those in white hats were the good guys, and black hats were the bad guys in most cases. This is significant in Western culture. What about Luke Skywalker in the *Star Wars* series: the more he was led to the Dark Side, the more his clothing slowly changed from pure white to completely black. These ideas seem simple, but they have deep meaning in our subconscious. If they make it to my consciousness, then they affect my psyche, and if my psyche tells me I am negative because of my brown hue, then I began to see myself as inferior and even live out the stereotype. Let's take it further: If you see someone walking in all-black clothing today, you may immediately think he or she is a goth or an outsider, especially if the person has on heavy black eyeliner and black lipstick. These terms with their meanings are ingrained in our society and in our psyches. Some may be thinking I am taking this color terminology too far, and black just means what it says, a dark color, not negativity, and white just means light skin, not goodness. Well, perhaps a case can be made for that in some instances. While there may be some exceptions, such as a market being in the black or a black-tie event, I believe I am on to something with color identification. For instance, I was watching the African channel on cable recently, and I noticed a similar conversation was being held about the Barbie doll complex that African children (African nationality) were dealing with. Many of the children, according to the report, felt they were not pretty because of their dark complexion. To counter this, a company in Africa began its own line of brown-colored dolls to build confidence in the African community. That is amazing in a country where the vast majority has a brown complexion! How could this concept of being brown carry such a negative connotation even when everyone around you is brown? Am I the only one who is puzzled by this? This is not new to America, of course, but it is interesting that this issue is a worldwide phenomenon, where people feel inferior due to the color of their skin, and it appears that the darker they are, the more inferior they might be perceived to be. Simply put, I do not believe that the color of one's skin should be the determinant of what one is called or how the status is determined.

If we call an Indian from India black, will this be acceptable? I submit the Indian will be very offended. Let me go further; what if I went to the Honduras and called them black because of their skin color versus Honduran? I saw an article online recently where a man from the Dominican Republic was offended because he was called black in the United States. He stated that he was not black, but Dominican. This is not an uncommon view around the world. Similarly, what if I identified a person of Middle East descent from Turkey, Iraq, Afghanistan, or Jordan as a black person since they tend to have brown-colored skin? It would not make sense because we know they are Middle Eastern and not black in our American vernacular. The color of the skin is similar, but they are not of African descent. Hence, I believe to term someone black because of their skin color is incongruent. We are identified by our descent and our regions. Therefore, if I am of a brown complexion, there is a possibility I have an African descent. Yet as I have demonstrated, I could have a brown complexion and be from India, Indonesia, or the Middle East, or even the Pacific. What if I called all people of Asian descent yellow? News headline reads, "A Yellow Person Was Given the Highest Honor Today by the Mayor of the City." That would be offensive to all people of Asian descent. It simply does not make sense to identify people by the perceived color of their skin. Thus, I submit the term *black* for a human is a pejorative term that was created to indicate disparaging and defamatory expressions. Over the years, America embraced the term as a part of society, and it became the norm. James Brown, the famed soul singer, coined the song "Say It Loud, I'm Black and I'm Proud" to give a sense of pride to black people. The song was released in August 1968, four months after the assassination of Dr. Martin Luther King. There are reports that the song was released to calm the people and build a sense of pride. Racial tensions were high following the assassination of Dr. King in April 1968 and there were violent riots taking place across the streets of America where mostly blacks destroyed property in their own neighborhoods and literally set major cities on fire. While the song did build a sense of pride, it also perpetuated the stigma associated with being black in America. Still today, we now know the term *black* is mostly associated with negativity and not positivity.

One of my friends of European descent, Angel, related a story to illustrate my point about negative connotations with color identifications and labeling. Her son, Aiden, eight years old, came home frustrated one day after school because his friend from Ethiopia was called a bad name. He told his mom he was upset because his friend from Ethiopia was teased. Angel asked Aiden to tell her what was said and why was it so upsetting. Aiden did not want to say the word, but asked could he spell it. His mother agreed and Aiden began to spell the name that upset him. To her surprise, Aiden began to slowly spell the word *black*. Angel, like most of us would be, was caught off guard and expected another word. She calmed Aiden down and asked him what color was he? Aiden said he was white. She then asked the question that I think defines what I am writing about. Angel asked Aiden if he felt uncomfortable with being called white, and he stated no, he did not. This example drives home why I think color identification has outlived its usefulness and was never effective. Aiden was offended by the term *black* but not by the term *white*. Without truly knowing, I suspect it is because kids under ten years of age mostly see in concrete terms and the term *black* generally denotes negative things, such as fear, scariness, darkness, or evil. Thus, Aiden believed that if you called his friend black, then you were associating the friend with a bad name. Conversely, Aiden had no problem with being called white because it represents goodness, light, and a sense of safety.

As I have stated, I know this is a radical concept, and it will be criticized by some, saying it could never happen. My friends have warned me that it will be difficult to change society; these racial terms are ingrained in American society and in some parts of the world. Further, some will say, "We need to be proud of our heritage, or the terms we have are set in stone for history and cannot be changed." But there were many who said that America could never change with blacks and whites living together in integrated neighborhoods, businesses, and society. Some have stated, "You can't give blacks voting rights or put them in society—you must keep them out of the mainstream, or America will be destroyed" or "Blacks are not smart enough to fly aircraft, lead the country, fight in the military, or serve as doctors, etc." By the way, history records that many of the same thoughts were said about women, Latinos, and Asians. These statements are made from fear, ignorance, and selfishness. I could go on, but I believe I have painted the picture that there were many who said we would not have made it this far, but we have, with regard to equal rights for all people. Why? Because we are Americans, and I believe we possess a unique capability to see the greater good for mankind. I hope my European ancestors are not offended by my comments, but imagine if I went around calling all Europeans by the color of their skin. That would be an interesting situation. Would I call them peach or light orange in some cases? Imagine the headline "A Peach-Colored Man Was Arrested for Assaulting Light Brown Woman." It sounds ridiculous because it is. Remember, I have endured those terms over the years and have been called yellow and orange. But it is no different from what we do today. For instance, headlines read during the hotly debated Ferguson case in 2015, "White Police Officer Kills an Unarmed Black Man." What is the difference in the aforementioned statements? Yet the latter is acceptable, and the former is not. How did we come to accept these ridiculous and archaic color terms, especially when no one is the color black, and no one is the color white? It has been ingrained in us as a nation to accept these terms (myself included), but I believe change is possible. Please note that we hold on to unconscious biases and stereotypes based on perceived color differences and what we have been taught. For example, a co-worker was sharing how his son, who is of European descent, was automatically placed as three point shooter on the basketball team before the coach actually assessed his skills. The coach made the decision based on the color of his skin rather than his skill set. In the end, my co-worker's son was eventually given a chance to showcase his skills as a point guard and has impressed the coach, team, and fans ever since. I could share many more anecdotes to show how this type of faulty thinking and stereotyping pervades our society across all ethnic lines. Limiting and judging one based on their skin color is nonsensical.

To further illustrate my point, since I am light brown or a bit yellow, as some may say, imagine if only my arm could be seen from behind a curtain on the surface of a white cloth. Along with my arm, imagine other arms (all shaved) sticking through the curtain on a flat table next to mine. For illustrative purposes, let's say there is a brown-skinned Hispanic person's arm, an Indian's arm, a Pakistani's arm, an Indonesian's arm, a Samoan's arm, and a Puerto Rican's arm. If you could see nothing but shaved brown arms from behind the curtain, could you tell which arm belonged to whom? Could you identify who is the so-called black? I doubt it very seriously. Just because one's complexion is a brown hue does not make him or her black, or African American, as we would say today. A Samoan would be offended if you called her black, because she had a brown hue, and the same could be said of the others in the example I mentioned.

Conversely, if I took persons of European descent, a Chinese, a Korean, and fair-skinned persons from Turkey, Vietnam, and Jordan and did the same experiment, only allowing you to see their shaved arms and displaying them through a curtain on a table next to one another, could you pick out the so-called white person, as classified in America? Again, I seriously doubt you could do it, because again, calling someone with peach-colored skin white does not make sense. Therefore, we must ask, why would we identify people by color if color does not tell us who they are? I have a friend whose skin tone would look as though she was pure African descent; however, following her DNA test, it was revealed that her Germanic descent was the dominant genetic code. This is my point— her skin looked African, but in reality, she was predominately European; thus, we cannot determine ethnicity based on skin color alone. If we called black people black because of their color, then wouldn't we surmise that all brown-skinned people should be called black? We know, however, that this does not make logical sense. It clearly demonstrates why using a color term for a person is incongruent with the world at large. I have tried to emphasize how bizarre it is to call people by color, yet we accept the terms *black* and *white* because they have been ingrained in our very consciousness for almost three hundred years. As a side note, please make reference to those I named in the example (there could be many more), who are all called by their region or national name. One would not say, "She was a black Pakistani or a brown Indonesian." Again, this would be insensitive and disrespectful. I have verified this with several of my friends from India and those from the Middle East and they said it was only when they came to America that the terms black and white became the norm for identification of people. I have also asked my friends who emigrated from nations in Africa if they were called "black" and not one said that was a common term in their nation of origin. Please see the back of the book for illustrations of both the above examples to demonstrate how ethnicity can be easily misapplied when comparing skin tones and complexions.

One misnomer, and innocently stated, I might add, is to call people with brown skin "people of color." I have been guilty of saying the same, but I am trying to train myself in this paradigm shift. The fact is that we all have color! Yes, it is true; not one of us is devoid of color. Again, this is a way to subjectively state the person of brown hue is different from others. My issue is that one's color has been used to breed hatred, unspeakable brutality, murder, bigotry, and disenfranchisement. Remember, this brutality I am referencing has been perpetrated against literally every ethnicity and creed. You may be wondering why I want to get rid of identifying people by color? It is simple; because color identification is an antiquated device that was devised in the United States and around the world to distinguish classes of people, divide people into ethnicities, and disenfranchise those of darker complexion. My research shows that it is a systematic teaching or training that espouses that the lighter you are, the more successful and powerful you are. Again, this is not limited to the United States. Thus, if I used terms that relate to one being dark and one being light, it makes it natural to associate those terms to also mean one person is superior to the other based on skin color. As I have demonstrated, the early scientists, without any empirical evidence, came to that conclusion. The inferiority lie, as we know it, has been perpetuated throughout the ages. Again, people of darker complexions were inextricably linked to lower intelligence, considered animallike, inferior, and untrainable. I am proposing we move to an America where we are all called Americans. As I stated earlier, we don't deny our heritage, or mixed heritage, as in my case (African, Hispanic, Asian, and European), but we embrace our identity as Americans. The most important thing about you and I is that we are, first, humans. Anthropologists have determined the human race is one, and the biological differences between all people are so minimal that they are hardly calculable.[122] Interestingly, many researchers suggest that the origin of the human race is from Africa (the "out of Africa" theory), with the earliest fossils of humans beings found there.[123] Thus, trying to prove that we are different is an unrealistic point, and saying that if you have African descent or brown skin color you are inferior is incongruent with the world as we know it. The bottom line is that race differences over time have slowly been debunked. I make this point only to show the importance of how the fabricated racial differences only divide us further. All humans are God's creation, and we should all have equal rights, no matter what hue of skin color we have. The "Statement on Race" from the American Anthropological Association in 1998 stated the following:

> In the United States both scholars and the general public have been conditioned to view the human races as natural and separate divisions within the human species based on visible physical differences. With the vast expansion of scientific knowledge in this century, however, it has become clear that human populations are not unambiguous, clearly demarcated, biologically distinct groups. Evidence from the analysis of genetics (e.g., DNA) indicates that most physical variation, about 94 percent, lies within so-called racial groups. Conventional geographic "racial" groupings differ from one another only in about 6 percent of their genes. This means that there is greater variation within "racial" groups than between them. In neighboring populations there is much overlapping of genes and their phenotypic (physical) expressions. Throughout history whenever different groups have come into contact, they have interbred. The continued sharing of genetic materials has maintained all of *humankind as a single species.*[124]

Dorothy Roberts, scholar and law professor, stated it this way: "A mountain of evidence assembled by historians, anthropologists, and biologists proves that race is not and cannot be a natural division of human beings."[125] Thus, I'm proposing to America, and the world at large, that we should move away from race identification, including these types of terms, and move toward referring to one another with a new terminology that will bring us together and unite us. Why can't we simply be known as Americans? Think about which person you know who is actually black or white. There is no actual human being the color black, and there is no human being white as in the color white. Go to the deepest parts of Africa or the northernmost parts of the Caucasoid mountains, and you will not find a person devoid of color or white like snow and meeting the definition of black or white. Admittedly, you will find people of very dark hue in some regions of the world as you would also find those of extremely light hue in other parts of the world, but again, no one meets the true definition of the color terms called black and white. Thus, we must understand that we are all basically shades of different colors. We see color based on the mixture of the three primary colors in pigment, which are red, yellow, and blue.[126] I'm spending time here to help the reader realize who we are as humans. When you realize that the pigmentation of your skin is only a few shades different from another person and comprehend that we are all people of color, perhaps we will demonstrate sincere love and care for each other as humans based on who the person is and not the differences in skin color or facial features. There is no doubt that we are humans on the inside for the organs don't matter. I remember when I was a kid, it was a big deal when a black person donated an organ to a white person. Today I don't see any restrictions on the color of the person donating organs to save a life! Somehow society has come to realize that this is not important. No one is a pure color in any sense of the word. When one reviews the basic primary colors that all other colors are formed from, you will find that we are all basically peach, light peach, yellow, orange, brown, tan, dark tan, or dark brown, but we are all human beings in God's eyesight. I recall a concert I attended many years ago that made an impact and shaped my views today. I was at a Mike Warnke comedy concert in South Dakota in the 1990s, and he asked how many white people were in attendance—of course, the majority raised their hands. He then asked how many black people were in attendance and those who felt they were of African descent raised their hands. He then went on to explain that none were white and none were black. Further, he went on to state that we're all people of color and he held up a piece of pure white paper bag and said, "Look at my skin color compared to this bag. I challenge anyone that is as white as this bag to come up here." He did a similar thing when he used the bottom of his shoe as an illustration to show what black looked like and how no one was truly black. Of course, no one could show that they were white as the bag or black as the bottom of the shoe. His illustration was poignant and timely. I did not consider the impact it would have on my views of the different ethnic groups over the years.

There are many more examples of how negative and divisive the terms *white* and *black* have been over the years. Who can forget the Clark Doll

Test that was conducted by Dr. Kenneth Clark and his wife Mamie Clark during a study on stereotypes with children and their perception of the value of their ethnicities in the 1940s?[127] The study was conducted to show how black children in Washington, DC, schools were influenced negatively by racism, prejudice, and discrimination. In fact, the case proved to be influential in ending segregation in schools and demonstrated that "separate but equal" was anything but equal in the education system; the Supreme Court used the results to justify the beginning of desegregation in American schools.[128] The study called for black children aged six to nine to answer several questions dealing with self-perception and self-esteem as related to the black doll versus the white doll. The results showed that most of the black children thought of the black doll as negative and chose the white doll as being prettier, nice, and better.[129] This was unbelievable. How could a six-year-old girl or boy believe that being black was negative at such an early age? I watched the experiment repeated several times on YouTube, and the results were astonishing; the children of all ethnicities mostly agreed (European, African, and Hispanic) with the early findings from 1940s experiment in that they overwhelmingly believed that black children were bad, dumb, and ignorant, while white children were smart, prettier, and good. What is the origin of the negativity and where does it begin? I submit that it begins very early in life from media, TV, video games, movies, billboards—in fact, almost every aspect of life. It is apparent that negative or positive imprinting begins at the beginning of life. Each of us is vulnerable to what we hear, see, or comprehend with regard to our well-being and our roles and disposition in life. For years, movies, some music, and many TV shows primarily showed blacks in negative roles, and when they were positive, it was minimal. Aside from outside of the community and home, one has to ask what was being taught inside of the community and home. Was there communication indirectly and directly that being of darker color is not good, not smart enough, not intelligent? One has to remember, the Civil Rights Act was only signed in 1964, and before that we had a racial divide across America due to Jim Crow (racial segregation in society) laws—almost one hundred years after the American Civil War was fought to end slavery and the first Civil Rights Act was passed, America was still segregated. It is amazing to understand the mind-sets of the time; those of African descent were still discriminated against in almost every aspect of life well into the 1960s and 1970s. Blacks were still the victims of gross, inhumane treatment akin to slavery, and thus, their self-image was severely damaged throughout the history of the United States. When put in the correct context, you begin to understand why so many people of brown skin saw themselves in a negative manner. Let's take if further: As I started watching YouTube, I found that many of the reports on the subject showed that as children got older, they began to form similar opinions and could articulate why they believed what they believed with regard to both negative and positive thoughts. Many of their beliefs came from racist statements from parents or relatives who told them not to mix with people with different ethnicities. This is what I have been trying to combat in this book. Covert racism is still prevalent in America. It is most likely to happen when people are with persons who look mostly like them. By the way, I must emphasize that the discriminatory thoughts and actions go both ways and are not limited to any ethnicity. The discriminatory statements also came from bullying of one ethnicity or the other. In other words, you have those of African descent ganging up on those of European descent or vice versa. When we lived in Hawaii, I can remember my kids telling me that there was a battle with the Samoans versus the whites. There was also a racist term for whites in Hawaii that was commonly used. Again, this is wrong and should not be tolerated in America. Any racism against any American is racism against all Americans. It is commonly known that when children of different ethnicities are raised together, those people are less likely to have discriminatory practices. Why does this happen so often? Think about recent reports in the media of twins who were born of the same interracial parents, but who look totally opposite in skin color. James and Daniel Kelley, for example, are literally full-blooded siblings, yet one looks of African descent and other looks as if he is of European descent.[130] This happened because their parents are Jamaican and European. Further, the Jamaican male most likely had European DNA, which allowed for one of his twin sons to get the dominant European DNA which mixed with his wife's European DNA. His brother got the father's African DNA and thus came out with a brown hue. Even though Daniel is European, family members and the community tried to make him African. Daniel was picked on and discriminated against for being white and was often thought of as a guest when outsiders saw him with the family. This is very common in many communities where one may look European, but their counterparts will insist that they are African. What's interesting is the fact that many don't believe they are siblings, and I can almost guarantee it is highly unlikely either child will discriminate based on skin color. We were recently in New Orleans and the exact same thing happened to us at a restaurant. The waiter, who seemed to have African descent, introduced us to his sister who looked totally European but was his blood sister. It was astonishing to see and experience. The young man went on to tell me that often when they are out with his family, his sister is considered a friend of the family.

Do you remember when *The Cosby Show* hit airwaves in the 1980s? America was fascinated with the show and made it the number-one sitcom for years. It was a counter to the entire previous majority-black sitcoms—it was a groundbreaking depiction of what was reality for many, but not known by the majority of Americans. It began to show that people of brown hue could become successful professionals and live in a home where everyone goes to college! Of course, this is not new to me, as I grew up in a different era where this was expected. Somehow, I never got the message that I was inferior or that people with different color were better than me or that they did not like me. However, this was new to many, despite individuals like Dr. Carter G. Woodson, a PhD from Harvard University in the 1900s who led the studies of blacks and their contributions to the world; Dr. Charles Drew, a medical doctor who was critical to the development of the blood transfusion; or Senator Hiram Revels, who was elected to the Senate in 1870. These are just a few examples of black leaders who were scientists, engineers, doctors, or political leaders, etc., in the early formation of our nation. Yet one hundred years later, the message was that blacks, poor whites, Hispanics, or women were second class citizens who did not have the capacity to perform acts of intellect or to take the lead in technical careers. The sad part was that not only did blacks, poor whites, Hispanics, and some women believe the narrative, but most of America believed the same despite the evidence. We know that history has proven overwhelmingly that all of the above groups had more than enough skills and have been critical to the success and growth of America. I could fill this book with volumes of examples of scientists, inventors, military geniuses, strategists, technicians, engineers, doctors, entertainers, politicians, chemists, and lawyers who made extraordinary inroads to defeat the myth that if you had brown skin you were intellectually inferior.

Women have had a most egregious history behind achieving suffrage in the United States and around the world. Somehow, mankind formed the opinion that women were second class citizens and not due the rights of men. Some would even point to the Bible for this concept, or other world religions, but I never have read that women were inferior in the sacred texts. In early pre-America days, women were mostly treated as indentured servants and used for labor in the fields, as sex slaves, and as domestic servants in the homes. Most women in the 1700s and 1800s were limited in what they could do in society, with black, Irish, and Swedish women serving as servants in the United States. Further, most women had limited rights and were treated as property of their men in many cases, they were basically trafficked. The women's suffrage movement began in 1848 to fight for women's rights, and in 1866, Elizabeth Stanton and Susan B. Anthony formed the American Equal Rights Association, composed of white women and black women, to obtain suffrage or the right to vote for all.[131] Again, it is interesting throughout history where people of like conditions come together and ethnic barriers or color of skin becomes less of a factor in their relationships. We saw this in early America with the Irish slaves and African slaves. Women were seen as inferior and basically as property in our society until key legislation was passed. It was not until 1871 when legislation and laws were passed to make beating women illegal.[132] As I was researching this data and the history of woman suffrage and maltreatment, I found it hard to believe that our great nation could not see the erroneous ways in which we treated humans, no matter what color or gender, that it somehow deemed as inferior. Women, just as men, were fighting for their freedom and moving for change. In 1655, Elizabeth Key Grinstead, a mulatto slave and baptized Christian, sued and won her freedom because her father was a free white Englishman.[133] After Grinstead and others won their freedom, the laws were changed in the colonies to limit the status of the child to that of the mother, regardless of outward appearance. This meant that if the mother was a slave of brown hue, that is what the child was destined to be, even if the father was a free white male. This move was meant to continue the oppression against women and children born to slaves, despite their skin color. This also had an economic benefit, as slave owners could increase the numbers of slaves they owned without having to acknowledge or support their illegitimate children. As America developed with industry and progressive jobs, women began to slowly change their roles from primarily domestic jobs to work outside the home. Job opportunities arose in department stores, schools, and clinics (as nurses only because physicians could only be men). Women would work in those fields until they were married. In early America, women were prominent in the movement to end slavery. Women such as Harriet Tubman, Sojourner Truth, and Harriet Beecher Stowe were key in leading the fight against oppression. It was not until the Nineteenth Amendment was passed in 1920 that white women could vote in elections; black women could not vote uninhibited until the 1965 Voting Rights Act.[134] In 1922, Rebecca Latimer Felton, a prominent women's leader in Georgia, became the first woman appointed to the US Senate.[135] Following the right to vote in the 1920s, women begin to set many firsts, such as Nellie Tayloe Ross, first female governor of Wisconsin, and Edith Warton, who became the first woman to win the Pulitzer Prize for fiction.[136] The barriers began to come down over time. In 1942, more than 150,000 women served in the Women's Army Corps during World War II.[137] By 1943, women demonstrated they could serve as pilots and formed the Women Airforce Service Pilots (WASPs) in a noncombat role to free male pilots for combat services.[138] Today women can serve as combat pilots and in almost every combat position in which a male can serve. All combat roles are now open to women. I remember shortly before I began my duty as a nuclear missile launch officer, we began to put men and women together in missile launch capsules, because women were now combat ready. This move made headlines, and many complained that a man and a woman should not be in the capsule for twenty-four hours together. My wife was very accepting and understood, as I did, these women were serving their nation and deserved that right, uninhibited. I could continue to write several pages on the many contributions of women who have made tremendous accomplishments in the United States. Today we should not be surprised by the great achievements of women, such as Hillary Clinton or Condoleezza Rice, who both served as secretary of state at one point in their illustrious careers. I could name the first women pilots, athletes, judges, military leaders, engineers, medical doctors, police officers, attorneys, entertainers, executives of some of the largest corporations, prosecutors, congresswomen, and senators. This list is not close to exhaustive, but it paints the picture that women today have come from indentured servants and slaves having little to no rights and lacking suffrage to rise to the highest government offices in our land. The reason I emphasize this is because women can do anything that a man can do. Certainly, we acknowledge bodily differences and physical strength differences, but these differences notwithstanding, women are not second-class citizens. Women are not inferior beings and are not intellectually challenged. You may be wondering why I am spending so much time here. It is simple; woman suffrage was similar to what I have been writing about throughout this book. No gender or ethnic group should be held back or treated as inferior because they are different from the majority.

As a young teen, I knew we were in a strained world with regard to ethnicity, but growing up in New Orleans, it was easy to see many different ethnicities get along and blend. I worked at a movie theater, the Loews State, in downtown New Orleans, and I worked very closely with the New Orleans police, who would ensure customers were safe and could watch the movie peacefully. Similarly today, the police would do that job when off duty to make more money to support their families. Naturally, one becomes close to those with whom they work. As it turns out, when on duty, one of the police officers I knew was chasing bad guys in my neighborhood. My family and friends were surprised when this white officer stopped to acknowledge me and speak. Most looked at me as if I had broken an unwritten rule: "Thou shalt not speak to white police officers!" I realized then that my mind-set was different, and I could not understand their displeasure with me. I soon realized that many felt the sting of or knew someone who had experienced unjustified harassment from the police and predictably linked all police officers as unfair and as the enemy. I make this point to emphasize that I grew up in era of change that I could not fully comprehend. I saw all people as equal and hadn't experienced the racism or prejudice that many in my community had. I never thought I was less than someone else because of my brown/tan color, and I believed I could be an engineer, a doctor, a scientist, or professional. I did not see limits to my potential. I excelled in academics in high school and, in fact, thought I would be an engineer one day. I even had an opportunity to attend West Point, but I was afraid to leave home. I was in the National Honor Society and attended special mentorship programs for science and engineering near the University of New Orleans. I was in the Math Club and a part of the Junior Reserve Officer Training Corps. I saw no limits but only opportunity. Again, in the late 1970s and early 1980s, America was changing, and I saw myself as a part of a great nation without thinking about skin color.

I am submitting again that America should begin a new quest that will lead the world as well. The terms *black* and *white* should be eliminated when referencing an ethnic group. I know this is radical, and I have been told by many that it is not possible. How can we simply change terminology that has been accepted for so many years—for over two centuries, in fact? Most that I have talked to from all ethnicities like the idea, but few believe it is possible. It will take a major culture shift in the middle of one of the most fraught times of ethnic relations I can recall in America. Perhaps this is the perfect time to launch this campaign. I submit that we are all *Americans* who happen to have divergent ethnic origins of Hispanic, Caucasoid, European, African, Arab, Native American, and Asian or Pacific Islander. After all, America, as we know it, was founded through immigration.

The indigenous groups, North American Natives, were essentially disenfranchised and dehumanized through what history calls the Indian Wars. In 1829, during his first inaugural speech, President Andrew Jackson promised

> to observe toward the Indian tribes within our limits a just and liberal policy, and to give that humane and considerate attention to their rights and their wants which is consistent with the habits of our Government and the feelings of our people.[139]

Yet approximately fourteen months later, the United States signed the Removal Act, which was designed to move all Native Americans west of the Mississippi, outside of America.[140] By 1832, the Native Americans started to form their own Cherokee nation apart from the United States and won approval from the US Supreme Court, but by 1838, thousands were killed during many battles for land and territory near the Cherokee Trail (passage through Oklahoma, Kansas, Colorado, and Wyoming toward the west).[141] These battles would repeat themselves over the next several years with the loss of thousands of lives, and Native Americans did not gain the right to be US citizens until the twentieth century. Much of the Native American land or nations would later become Native American reservations in the midst of the ever-expanding USA.[142] These were cruel and vicious times in the United States, during which the treatment of the indigenous groups was not something we look back on with pride. Great crimes of rape, false imprisonment, murder, and theft of land were perpetrated on tens of thousands; entire families and villages were uprooted across America.

Today no one denies these tragedies against humankind. Thus, America is made up of all immigrants, essentially, with the exception of the native inhabitants who now are a very small ethnicity in America. This proposal is not to denigrate who we are by deemphasizing our ethnicities, but to eliminate the divisive terms that hurt all. These discriminatory and divisive terms are used with all ethnicities—we do not need to list them at this point. It is interesting that we, as humans, are naturally inclined to be drawn to the differences rather than to see each other based on the content of our characters. I submit that America is ready for the change. I remember a recent commercial showing a mixed couple advertising Cheerios. The ad caused a lot of controversy and gained a lot of attention. Even though interracial marriages are becoming fairly commonplace today in America, there are still remnants who will fight the unity of ethnicities and lash out with hurtful, denigrating terms. It shows that America is not where we would like it to be yet. What is most interesting about the negativity toward the advertisement for Cheerios is that many Americans feel it is okay for people of different ethnicities to work together or participate in professional duties or athletics, but some in America are still sensitive to the intermixing of ethnicities. Many other interracial commercials and movies receive wide acceptance with little fanfare or attention. Sunday morning worship is still very much segregated in America. Friends and gatherings are homogeneous for the most part. In other words, I see a limitation to how far we will go with intermixing. This can be cultural, but it can also be the stereotypes that we all bring to the table. Let's face it; we have had racial stereotypes pushed on us for years. We put each other in these categories, and we are always pleasantly surprised when a person of a different ethnicity does not fit the stereotype. My point throughout this book is that we cannot put everyone into one category or another because of one incident. We must be open to both sides of every point of view. The reader will note that I will counter myself throughout this book while I make my overarching point. I try to see the issues from all angles, and I think that is what will help to unite America. With this in mind, let's transition to some more hard-hitting current examples that most of us are familiar with at the publishing of this book.

BUILDING A DIVERGENT AMERICA

We hold these truths to be self-evident: that all men are created equal; that they are endowed by their Creator with certain unalienable rights; that among these are life, liberty, and the pursuit of happiness.

—President Thomas Jefferson,
US Declaration of Independence

Independence Hall

I believe I have made it clear why I am bringing up the need for this change with regard to ethnic relations in America. The opening quote of this chapter has been noted as one of the greatest statements in the birth of America. It was actually edited several times to reach its final version. I do find it troubling that America had an opportunity early on in its history to shape the world by simply living out the words found in our US Declaration of Independence. In fact, in 1776, abolitionist Thomas Day pointed out the hypocrisy and irony of signing the Declaration of Independence on one hand and continuing the viciousness of slavery with the whip in the other hand.[143] Moreover, it is reported that more than a fourth of the declaration was removed because it spoke against slavery and many members of Congress, as stated earlier, owned black slaves, including Ben Franklin and President Thomas Jefferson.[144] There are many accounts of President Jefferson's preferential treatment to slaves, especially those who were thought to be his offspring. I have said it earlier; we had a chance to shape America early on, and many of our forefathers wanted to end slavery and begin a new America, but they were overridden by those who would hold on to the superiority of one ethnicity and could not find the courage to stand against this heinous crime. Not all signers of the Declaration of Independence were afraid to declare hypocrisy. In fact, William Whipple freed his slave, Prince Whipple, before signing the declaration, knowing that if he did not, he would be a hypocrite because the very document he was signing represented freedom for all and was not limited to the color of one's skin.[145] Others noted this apparent confusion in the quest for freedom from tyranny, yet continued the heinous practice of slavery. Again, English abolitionist Thomas Day wrote to the United States in a 1776 letter, "If there be an object truly ridiculous in nature, it is an American patriot, signing resolutions of independency with the one hand, and with the other brandishing a whip over his affrighted slaves."[146] I think that statement from Thomas Day says it all with clarity and accuracy.

I could not talk about color and ethnicity issues in America without referencing some of the major incidents that have rocked the nation in the last few years. Please note there are far more incidents than I have time or space to comment on; however, I will highlight a few cases that have caught national attention in recent years.

I will begin with the Trayvon Martin case in July 2013. I believe that this case was the prototype of what is wrong with America with regard to ethnic relations. First, we must realize that George Zimmerman, the person who shot Trayvon Martin in February 2012, identifies himself as Hispanic, not white, yet the term *white* was the focus of the news. A white man has shot a black kid! This began to spur huge ethnicity debates and demonstrations throughout America calling for justice. In fact, Zimmerman appeared to have African ancestry from his Peruvian DNA, along with German ancestry.[147] While thousands marched and demonstrated for justice as America waited for the trial to begin, I estimate that thousands of black young men, Hispanic men, and white men killed each other in the major cities of America. For example, according to the Uniform Crime Reports of 2012, a total of 6,454 blacks were killed by homicide, with 91 percent of known ethnicity of the murderers being at the hands of blacks (meaning out of 2,648 total killed, 2,412 blacks were killed by blacks), and a total of 5,855 whites were killed by homicide, with 84 percent of known ethnicity of murderers being at the hands of whites (meaning out of 3,128 total whites killed, 2,614 were killed by whites).[148] Between ages fifteen and twenty-four, murder is the number-one cause of death for blacks, the second leading cause of death for Hispanics, and the fourth leading cause of death for whites.[149] Of note from the Uniform Crime Report in 2012 of known ethnic murders, 193 blacks were killed by whites, while 431 whites were killed by blacks.[150] I want to highlight the fact that in 2012, more than twelve thousand blacks and whites were killed, with 87 percent being killed by their own ethnicity. This is where we miss it in America. There should be an outcry for the murders of all people of all ethnicities. The statistics clearly show that the greatest threat to each ethnicity is itself, yet that is not what is portrayed in the media. At this point, light bulbs should be going on in the reader's mind, and you should all be asking yourselves why we have been fed the opposite lines. Blacks are dangerous, and they want to kill whites, or whites are vicious haters, and they want to kill blacks. We are pitted against each other, when the truth is, each ethnicity kills itself at incredible rates. My point is that we should despise and fight against all murders with all vigor and diligence instead of focusing on the one national case that grabs the headlines because it was white versus black. These same ethnic crimes against humanity hardly made the national news. The question is, Why did we (Americans) generally ignore these many deaths and have all of the national media, pundits, talk, and news programs focus on this one case? The answer is simple, from my perspective—it comes down to the battle America has faced since 1775, the dilemma of dealing with ethnicity. How could the nation do very little in terms of a national outcry when thousands of blacks and whites would die on the streets at the hands of each other? To be sure, police forces and communities in each of these major cities have stepped up to try to curb the violence and insidious murders. Some cities held marches to protest against the gang violence and the crimes against humanity.

Given the above, the question remains, why was there not more of a national outcry and national task force to investigate and mitigate the violence in the streets with black young men and white young men killing each other? It is very much a phenomenon that has plagued America. Specifically, many leaders (of all ethnicities) will hardly speak out against the heinous crimes, such as young babysitters being caught in crossfire, innocent children killed by drive-by shootings, or mass murders on college campuses. Some of these crimes might catch the media's attention for a day or even a week, but it's when it is black versus white that the media dominates the airwaves with the story. In April 2014, Chicago had forty shootings in one weekend, with five dying of gunshot wounds.[151] These attacks are so heinous that innocent babies are killed and young teenagers who are simply relaxing inside of the house have been shot and killed. Black-on-black crime happens for many reasons, and I have my hypothesis, which I will share in later chapters. But remember, every ethnicity kills itself more than any other. It is part of the human nature of self-preservation and selfishness.

Before I go on, I can tell you my thoughts on the Trayvon Martin case, lest I will be seen as a sympathizer with George Zimmerman. First, I believe that young Martin should not have been killed. Second, I believe that Zimmerman was wrong for following Martin and not standing down as instructed by law officials. I believe he was looking for confrontation, and that is what he got. No one but Zimmerman and Martin knows what happened that dark evening (notice the term *dark* and its connotations) in American history, but it is clear that Martin would not have been killed if Zimmerman had followed the instructions of the law from the beginning. As a side note, Zimmerman has been arrested several times following the Trayvon Martin incident for a variety of charges, such as a high-speed chase, death threats, and violence and domestic abuse. Interestingly, all charges were dropped against Zimmerman, including restraining orders. While these incidents with his ex-wife, ex-girlfriend, and other individuals do not mean he murdered Trayvon Martin, they demonstrate the volatility and troubled history of this individual.

The incitement that comes from the view of black against white sometimes leads to a call to arms and violence. Many will use some of these cases to hijack the injustices and try to use them to their advantage to reach their agenda and achieve financial gain. Many leaders have spoken against the nearly criminal activities that have been perpetrated against blacks when it comes to the law. I believe we should speak out against the wrongdoing without indicting the entire justice system or all police officers. Unfortunately, some black leaders spoke out with carelessness and used words that could be interpreted as a call to rise up and fight back against those wrongdoers (i.e., the law). On the other hand, there are white supremacist groups speaking out and claiming they want to fight for a white America and go back to the way things were. Rush Limbaugh allegedly wants a white equivalent to the NAACP to ensure white rights and protect against "reverse discrimination." As you may recall, I do not espouse reverse discrimination, because all discrimination is wrong. If this rhetoric is true, it is the kind of language that can indeed incite ethnicities against one another. One of my closest friends happens to be white or as I say of European descent. He informed me that he often feels attacked for being white, male, and from the South. This should not be. The goal of racial reconciliation is not to make one ethnicity feel superior to the other. He should not be hated because he is white; he must continue to be afforded the same rights as all Americans. My goal is not to see anyone discriminated against economically, socially, or educationally because of his or her ethnicity.

Before we go further, perhaps it is important to review who has been killed in 2015 by police officers for a variety of altercations. According to "Killed by Police" tracking data, 39 percent of those killed by police were white, while 25.5 percent of those killed were black, 15.3 percent were Latino, and another 16.9 percent killed by police had no reported ethnicity identification.[152] As you have grown accustomed to, we must look at the raw numbers to put this in perspective. Given the data above,

323 whites, 211 blacks, and 127 Latinos were killed by police.[153] When I examined other studies by the FBI, these numbers were consistent over a five-year period, with an average of about five hundred killed annually in the 2000s by police, and the racial breakdown was similar. When viewed in these terms, one begins to see the disproportionate number of blacks and Latinos killed when juxtaposed with their population size of forty-three million and fifty-four million, respectively. The Latino community is roughly 25 percent the size of the white community, and the black population is 21 percent of the size of the white community. This means that proportionately and at the current rate, if the Latino population were the same size as the white community, 508 would have been killed, while more than eight hundred would have been killed in the black community in 2015. Remember, there are 197 million whites currently in the United States. This data is consistent throughout out this book—no matter the data source, when you dig deeper, the rates of crimes committed, victimization, and incarcerations are disproportionate to the size of the Latino and African communities. Again, any loss of a loved one hurts the same, no matter what your population size or your ethnicity, but it does help put things in perspective regarding why there is an outcry by those in minority communities against police tactics. Change is needed in America now.

America was confronted with yet another major development when Michael Brown, a young African American teen, was shot and killed in August 2014 by a European American police officer, Darren Wilson. There are two versions as to what happened on that fateful day. One account says the unarmed eighteen-year-old teen apparently put his hands in the air after he was shot the first time. He was shot a total of six times. However, another version is that the teen was the aggressor and instigated the encounter by hitting the officer as he sat in the car. Then the shooting ensued, and his hands were never up as to surrender. The encounter lasted all of ninety seconds, but it would impact America and ethnic relations greatly. Mass protests and vigils were held in Ferguson, St. Louis, and many major cities across America when the officer was exonerated by a grand jury and found to have done no wrong. It should be noted that it took months before the verdict was released, and the protests were integrated and not limited to ethnicity. There were many people from all ethnicities demonstrating for change in the justice department. While some from the political arena disagreed and thought that the protesting of the verdict was unnecessary and wrong, most Americans, Democratic, Republicans, and all other political groups, recognized that the protests were justified in that our justice system is broken and skewed to lean toward harsher punishments for blacks and Hispanics. I address these statistics and findings in the coming chapters. Further, there are some instances when police officers are given the benefit of the doubt because of the ethnicity of those who were injured or killed. Unfortunately, some of the protests turned violent and involved looting and vandalism. This type of behavior is never justified, in my opinion. A peaceful demonstration is one thing, but violence and stealing have nothing to do with peaceful protests for justice. During the same period as this tragic death of Michael Brown, no fewer than 150 young men were killed in New Orleans (my hometown) in 2014 and 156 in 2013.[154] Yet no major national rallies were held for those who lost their lives on the streets of New Orleans or other major cities. More than five thousand to seven thousand young African Americans lose their lives on the streets of the big cities every year, yet there are no mass protests, and in fact, an interesting article quoted that 324,000 blacks were killed by blacks over a thirty-five-year period.[155] Again, this is not to say that marches and rallies have not been held by the local communities and programs have not been implemented to counter the murders, but the dramatic nationwide protests are almost nonexistent in these cases. The local media does address these crimes, but no nationwide media is covering these crimes and the situation in America consistently. I simply believe that if the nation rises up together, we can make a difference and slow the violence down.

Interestingly, there were at least two major cases of violence in America that made national headlines in early 2015 and many more that do not. One case involved a New Yorker named Eric Garner. He was clearly choked by three police officers with unnecessarily extreme pressure. The gentleman was not a major criminal, and he cried out the now infamous words "I can't breathe!" His family stated that he made that statement about eleven times during the altercation. Garner clearly died due to the excessive force, and yet the investigation revealed that the force the police used was justified. Major protests began once again to highlight police brutality. I was happy to see that many major broadcasters also decried the not guilty verdict and called for reformation of police forces across America. The unnecessary violence has to be curbed. Let me be clear, as

I have already stated; the majority of police officers are not violent. They are good people who uphold the law. I have several relatives and friends who have served honorably on police forces around America, and I am grateful for their sacrifices and unwavering support of all communities in keeping law and order. However, there are a few who absolutely violate their positions and authority and abuse their power through excessive force. At the same time this case happened, there was yet another case in which a black police officer shot an unarmed black male during a routine stop. The white officer (his partner) also fired, but it was the black officer who killed the man while he was apparently surrendering and not making a movement of aggression toward the officers. The black male did have a terrible record of violent crimes and had recently gotten out of jail. Yet it appeared that the shooting was not justified. There was not an outcry of protests in the communities this time. No major marches were noted across America in light of this incident. I point this out to show the disparity in the reporting. Because there was no white versus black, the inciting foundation was not present, thus the lack of attention. As a side note, at the publishing of this book, Eric Garner's family was awarded $5.9 million in a wrongful death settlement with the city of New York even though no charges were filed against the officers.

Perhaps the pattern is found in communities where there is a huge problem with violence when blacks are the minority. Yet another horrific example happened on March 6, 2015. A young unarmed black teen, Tony Robinson, was killed by a white police officer. Robinson died when he was shot in his apartment following a confrontation with Officer Matt Kenny. Neighbors said they heard a disturbance inside and that was why the officer was responding. According to the Madison Police Department, the officer shot the teen after he was assaulted and the teen reached for the officer's weapon. Allegedly the teen ran into his apartment after altercations in traffic (causing distractions by jumping and running in front of cars and yelling). According to reports, the police officer chased him and made his way through the door where the conflict ensued and the teen was shot. A small crowd of demonstrators marched in the streets in March 2015. I understand why there was outrage because a person in authority may have misused his position to exact punishment. The crowd that night chanted, "Black lives matter!" I could not agree with them more, but *all lives* matter—no matter what color or ethnicity. And if we are really concerned with black lives, then we must come together and develop intervention plans to stop the mass killings, drug use, and violence in many black neighborhoods. I don't mean this to be insensitive, but it makes America as a whole look hypocritical when all we focus on are the white versus black incidents. What is America doing to stop black-on-black crime, white-on-white crime, and Hispanic-on-Hispanic crime? However, what is interesting is that I was speaking with my aunt in New Orleans, and she relayed that a young black woman, Walesha Williams, aged twenty-five, and her daughter, Paris Williams, aged eight, were allegedly shot by Dwayne K. Martin, who was Williams' boyfriend on the streets of New Orleans two days earlier on March 4, 2015.[156] No national news was made with the deaths of those young women (a mother and her daughter) at the hands, most likely, of another black person. Another woman was shot in this same incident but survived. This crime is egregious and outrageous, yet I don't see the outrage in America for this type of violence. This is my point given that we seemingly ignore the deaths of those two young women in New Orleans, but in Robinson's case, it became national headlines. I realize that it was because of the authority position of those who took the action (police officer), and it appeared to be an extension of oppression from the early years of America. I am also reminded of the sad fact that on that same Friday night of Robinson's death and the death of Williams and her daughter, perhaps a dozen more of all ethnicities were murdered across America. As a person who espouses love for all fellow humans, that brings me great sadness, but I recognize it is life as we know it in America and around the world.

Digging deeper into the Madison incident reveals interesting facts. The uncle, Turin Carter, of the slain teen, Tony Robinson, spoke about the incident, noting that Robinson's family was multicultural. He also stated that Robinson could not easily fit into communities because of his multicultural heritage and even said one could not simply say that Tony was black because of his mixed white heritage. He pointed out that all ethnicities should come together to fight the injustice facing all Wisconsinians. Thousands of multicultural protesters were in the state capitol's rotunda. He made a great statement that police are not all bad and that most are good. He supported police officers and said they are necessary in our society. In fact, the chief of the Madison police officers apologized and asked for peace during the protests. The chief even supported the protests. Again, protesting is a part of democracy if done with decency and dignity. I applaud the police chief for allowing and supporting the protests.

The apparent misbehavior of the police officers is not limited to black on white. In San Bernardino, California, a white male was viciously beaten by white deputy sheriffs following a stolen horse chase. Francis Pusok was badly beaten by the police officers and his family has filed a lawsuit.[157] Ten officers have been placed on administrative hold while the investigation continues. The FBI also got involved in the incident to examine whether or not Pusok's civil rights were violated. Of note, Pusok has been known to be aggressive and has a criminal record, but the beating appears, at least on the surface, to have been over the top. The media covers these types of events, but in my opinion, the coverage doesn't last long because the cases don't breathe the energy or gain the viewership ratings of black versus white; thus, the revenue is not being brought in, because the viewers are not there. Therefore, could it be that money is an important part of what is covered and what is not covered?

As I was thinking of the large number of blacks killing blacks and Hispanics killing Hispanics, and whites killing whites on the streets of America weekly, I could not help but reflect on early-twentieth-century America where white-on-white crime was at an all-time high in the 1920s and 1930s due to the same type of issues. There were gang wars over territory and selling of illegal substances—at that time, it was mostly alcohol that had been prohibited by the Eighteenth Amendment to the Constitution. This is happening today as well. In the roaring 1920s of America, gangs controlled prostitution, gambling, alcohol distribution, black market drugs, and other criminal activities.[158] These gangs would line up enemy gang members and simply shoot them dead, sometimes as if they were in a firing squad. It was a dark time in American history, with ruthless killing of one another and low regard for life. This sounds familiar to me today and rivals the inner cities where blacks, Hispanics, and some whites are killing themselves over gang territory and drugs. The gangs of the 1920s and 1930s were known as public enemies because their warfare would often lead to innocent civilians dying in their battles, and they would also conspire to kill police officers.[159] This was the era where now famous criminals such as Al Capone, Bonnie and Clyde, John Dillinger, Machine Gun Kelly, Kate "Ma" Barker, Legs Diamond and Dutch Schultz, and

Pretty Boy Floyd were viewed as celebrities by some Americans because they lived lavish lifestyles in the midst of the Great Depression.[160] I have listed the famous gang leaders that were household names, but the FBI has estimated that in Chicago alone, there were more than 1,300 gangs by the mid-1920s, and more than twelve thousand people were killed yearly in America through the mid-1930s.[161] Again, this was mostly white-on-white crime. Think about this for a moment—it is eerily similar to the annual murder rates in the suburbs and inner cities today, yet any senseless and criminal activity that takes a life gives one great pause. From 1921 to 1938 or so (seventeen years), more than 204,000 humans were killed. Today the raw number of murders per year is very similar to murder rates in the 1920s and 1930s when you combine murders of European descent, African descent, and Hispanic descent each year (eleven thousand to thirteen thousand).

Major crimes and massacres are not limited to a particular ethnicity. I believe the senseless taking of lives comes down to ignorance and acting out of selfishness. In Waco, Texas, in May 2015, nine white bikers were killed in gang-like warfare. It appears those Bandidos Motorcycle Clubs were fighting against the Cossacks. The battle resulted in 170 arrests following the incident, with many of them being held on $1 million bond each. How could this happen in America in 2015? The shooting left the town in shock. Allegedly gang members from the Bandidos and Black Widows subsequently made threats to retaliate against police for allegedly shooting fellow gang members. Police believe that this battle was over territory with the Bandidos not allowing other gangs to ride in Texas. Further, the 170 who were arrested appear to be under investigation for a variety of gang-related activities, including drug sale and transportation of those drugs. Police found more than three hundred weapons in the aftermath. I want the reader to understand what we are up against. There should be a national outcry against this type of activity in America. These were basically people of European descent killing other people of European descent. This happens frequently in America, and we simply let it blow over. I hope I am making it extremely clear that all murder is wrong and must be addressed in America. Unfortunately, the media ratings are found in white-versus-black crime, so that is what the focus is on, and thus, this type of story doesn't last long in the eye of the public.

Often, when we think of a book that addresses ethnicity, we think of the minority as the only target of unjust treatment, but in reality, all ethnicities can face mistreatment and racial discrimination. The horror continues in America when whites or people of European descent are targeted for simply being white. There was a movement in recent years where it became a game to hit a white person or kill a white person for no reason. Do you remember the knockout game? This is where you simply go down the street, and you punch someone in the face to see if you could knock them out with one punch. This is the vengeance I am talking about. These are hate crimes against humanity. A white college student and aspiring baseball player from Australia, Christopher Lane, twenty-two, was running one morning in Duncan, Oklahoma, and was allegedly killed for no reason at all by two young black teens, Chauncey Luna, James Edwards, and one unidentified (one who was half white or white)—it was a random killing just because they were bored.[162] This is heinous and wrong. Hating another person because of the color of his or her skin is simply unacceptable. What about the elderly white World War II veteran, Delbert Belton, who was killed with heavy-duty flashlights by two black teens in Seattle?[163] The young black teens beat the veteran for no reason. Again, this is a clear example of a hate crime, in which one ethnic group feels superior over another and believes the other ethnicity is the enemy. These types of events have gained national attention from time to time, but they simply fade away after the controversy is over, further dividing the ethnicities.

Yet another event came to the forefront at the same time as the shooting in Wisconsin in early 2015. The president of Oklahoma University (OU) had to apologize for disgraceful remarks by the mostly, if not all, white chapter of the fraternity Sigma Alpha Epsilon (SAE). They were spouting off a self-made song in which the lyrics went something like this: "There will never be another N SAE. Hang them on trees; they will never sign with me." This event took place on the fiftieth anniversary of the march on Selma, March 7, 2015, and with a clear reference to segregating SAE and lynching blacks. The OU chapter made the video on a bus on its way to an event. The OU president has removed the chapter from the campus as an organization, but there is no word of punishment for the individuals, some of whom can be clearly identified on the video. Masses of OU students and others came to the center of the OU campus to protest in silence. The song was clearly rehearsed and practiced by SAE. The national SAE chapter leaders spoke out and also disagreed with the comments, of course, and decried these types of racist statements. Some OU students said this has happened repeatedly, but rarely is it caught on video. Another student said this is just a sample of what goes on, but they believed the incident was not surprising, for they alleged it happens all the time in these environments. This is the covert racism and discrimination I have been speaking about. Someone stepped up and filmed the offensive and racist actions and turned over the video. That is the only reason it made headlines and the only reason I am writing about it. How often does this happen in America in 2017? I believe it is rare, but it still happens covertly in a myriad of environments and within many organizations. These organizations are not inherently racist, but there are some within the stated organizations that are racists. Further, the organizations are mostly segregated and fueled by the white versus black mantra that often dominates our society. Again, it is the negative connotations unfortunately associated with being black: "Blacks are less than" and the "I am better than you" connotations associated with being white. When the two thought patterns collide, we breathe continued racism and hatred between the ethnicities.

Let's dig deeper. The video from the OU students demonstrates why I believe the N-word must be considered a no-go by all. I am not concerned about what ethnicity you are—the word should not be used. The word is still incendiary and has a vicious meaning linked to it. I will address this in the coming chapters. I cannot leave this story without pointing out that protests we saw in Madison, Wisconsin, and at the OU campus are beginning show the solidarity I am writing about. We are Americans. The makeup of the crowd is increasingly multi-ethnic, as it was in Ferguson, New York, and other major cities around the United States. This is an important sign, because even the Selma March of 1964 was made up of one-third whites and other ethnicities—the changes that were made in America could not have happened without the ethnicities coming together. Change is possible in America when we all come together to exact this change. We must end the divisive terms of *black* and *white*, not to mention the racial slurs associated with all ethnicities.

In another stunning situation in our American postsecondary education system, the president of the University of Missouri resigned in 2015 amid a racial crisis. Student athletes and others began calling for the resignation of the college president due to allegations of inaction over a series of racial incidents, including racial harassment and threats. President and Chancellor Tim Wolfe resigned amid pressure from students and faculty alike due to growing frustrations and anger for his inaction or indifference toward a racist environment on the campus.[164] Wolfe stated that the frustrations were "clear" and "real" for the campus, with a black student population of only 8 percent out of the more than thirty-five thousand students.[165] White students make up approximately 79 percent of the student body. President Wolfe went on to state, "We stopped listening to each other," and Jonathan Butler, a graduate student, went on a hunger strike to protest the racist actions and inaction of the president.[166] In fact, Butler was seen by many as the leader of the movement. Just as stunning, the top administrator of the Columbia campus, Chancellor R. Bowen Loftin, put in his resignation for the end of the fall semester of 2015.[167] A key component to turning the tide was the football team's thirty students of African descent, who stated they would not play the rest of the season unless the president resigned. In fact, in an unexpected turn, the entire team, with the support of the coaches, said it would not suit up until the president resigned. It was a strong demonstration of what can be done when people come together. It is believed that if the team did not play the following weekend, the university could have lost over a million dollars in revenue due to contract obligations.[168] Students of African descent were allegedly called the N-word in open forums on several occasions, and someone allegedly painted a Nazi swastika in feces on a fraternity house as a symbol of hate. Interestingly, there was also solidarity from students of all ethnicities, European descent and African descent coming together. However, I submit that true healing and reconciliation will only take place when racism is directly confronted. These are young people (millennials), and these incidents show that America still has a long way to go. I know America is tired of claims of racism, but the fact is, the former president, Tim Wolfe, confirmed that racism existed on a major campus in America and needed to be dealt with. The scenes eerily reminded me of the 1950s protests, but the one difference is that America has the courage to root out those who will not learn how to disarm themselves from past racial prejudice and discrimination.

Despite the above, I was encouraged by a story that swept the world headlines in 2015 when three Americans stopped a would-be terrorist from carrying out his potential massacre on a train in France. What a dramatic feat of heroism to watch, as many lives were potentially saved from the gunman who showed the intent to deadly harm with an AK-47 assault weapon, nine magazines of ammunition, a Luger pistol, extra ammo, and a box cutter.[169] Of course, what stood out to me was the bravery of these three men who risked their lives while traveling in France. Americans Anthony Sadler (a college student), Spencer Stone (an airman) and Alek Skarlatos (an Oregon Army National Guardsman) were honored almost immediately by France for their heroism with the French Legion of Honor (France's highest honor).[170] These men were not the only ones trying to stop the terrorist; French American Mark Moogalian was shot when he first tried to wrestle a weapon from the terrorist.[171] Moogalian would also be recognized by the French government. Additionally, British passenger Chris Norman also helped tackle the terrorist and received the Legion of Honor. Just as interesting to me was the terminology these men were called.[172] One was of African descent and the other two were of European descent. But they were not referred to as black or white when they stopped an armed terrorist in France. No, not even close. The headlines all around the world read, "Three Americans Stop Terrorist Threat." Some might say this is not significant, but I disagree because it illustrates what I have been advocating. We need to address Americans as Americans and not as white or black. Further, not one of us who saw the images of the American heroes thought about them being from different ethnic backgrounds. Instead, we thought about how three American childhood friends came together to stop a terrorist's plot for destruction. As a side note, did the headlines say that a white French American and a white British man also helped thwart the terrorists attack? No, of course not, for they were identified by their nation, not by the perceived color of their skin.

However, when the divisive rhetoric continues, we support lunatics who act maliciously against ethnicities. This can happen by a black killing innocent whites or whites killing innocent blacks. Take, for instance, in a display of pure evil and mass murder, in 2015, where Dylann Roof of Charleston, South Carolina, killed nine innocent black worshipers in Emanuel African American Episcopal Church. As he shot the innocent worshippers after attending Bible study, he is quoted as stating, "I have to do it. You rape our women and you're taking over our country. And you have to go."[173] What a ridiculous statement. But in many ways, this vision of reality has been portrayed in the media in our society over the years.

Note that this statement is a very common complaint dating back to the Civil War and was one of the calling cards of the KKK. There has been a negative psychological bombardment of who whites are and who blacks are, both of which are stereotypical and wrong. But it is these kinds of stereotypes that constantly divide us. The pastor of the church, who was also a state senator, was killed. Even more eerie is that the twenty-one-year-old Dylann Roof had sat with the pastor through the one-hour Bible study and then proceeded to execute the nine innocent individuals, whom included two other pastors and a recent college graduate. Dylann Roof was a wolf in sheep's clothing. Obviously, this young man is deluded and acted as a terrorist for his own twisted cause. This was purely and simply a hate crime where the shooter espoused white supremacist rhetoric, including clothing and videos that were antiblack and anti-American (defacing the flag and American values). It is interesting to note that this is still happening in America, and it is not the 1950s or 1960s. This person killed for racial purposes. He was a loner and outcast in society who had confrontations with the law. The saddest part of this tragedy is that, once again, the event became politicized. However, it was great to see the prayer vigils held in the city and the unity of people of all ethnicities coming together. It was meaningful for me to see the hundreds holding hands across racial and ethnic lines and standing strong. There were marches and prayer vigils across America to decry this heinous, senseless act. My heart was warmed to see thousands show up to the memorial services and see thousands of all ethnicities march throughout Charleston. This is what America can be. This crime meant for hate may be the catalyst America needs to break racial gridlock, yet it will undoubtedly be used as leverage for hate groups as well. President Obama eulogized those who lost their lives, and he focused on God's grace. In fact, he sang a moving rendition of "Amazing Grace" that dominated the airwaves, and his speech was one of hope and reconciliation.

As a result of this violent act in South Carolina, national attention was given to the Confederate flag and whether it is time to pull down the flag from federal buildings in the South. Roof could be seen on social media as holding the Confederate flag and stepping on the American flag. This is what racial hatred spews—a disrespect for America. They know that America represents acceptance of all. Why do you suppose white supremacist groups or black supremacist groups do not have the American flag as their symbol? I submit that it is because they realize that their ideals and the ideals of America are not congruent. Over the years, people have called for the Confederate flag to be removed due to its link to slavery, white supremacy, and oppression. However, you have others with a different view who state that the Confederate flag honors the fallen who died in their fight to protest unfair tariffs and to not allow the North to invade their land. Some of my close friends and I disagree on this particular point. Those who support the flag see it as a part of Southern culture. I cannot see a true explanation that counters the fact that the South did not want slavery to end and feared that Lincoln would not only stop slavery from spreading west, but would eventually forbid slavery in the United States of America. Remember, the transatlantic slave trade was already restricted by 1880. The Loyal White Knights of Pelham, North Carolina, of the KKK planned a rally following the murder of the innocent churchgoers on South Carolina state grounds to protest the removing of the Confederate flag. The group's leader said that Dylan Roof should have targeted rappers and not churchgoers.[174] This is the kind of violent rhetoric I am referring to; hate begets hate. Think of the insensitivity with the statement to say that the shooter could have "done better" by changing his target, which intimates that the shooter did okay but could have improved. Most who hold on to the Confederate flag and lobby for its continued use don't even realize that it was not the original flag; there were three official flags of different designs during the four-year Civil War.[175] Very shortly after the Civil War, the flag was easily identified as a divisive symbol. Even General Robert E. Lee, commander of the Southern Army, declined to be a part of any ceremony representing the flag. When invited by the Gettysburg Battlefield Memorial Association to an event in which the Confederate flag would be displayed, he is quoted as stating, "I think it wiser moreover not to keep open the sores of war."[176] History does not support the concept that the war was fought for purely economic reasons, as several of the seven seceding states (Georgia, Mississippi, and South Carolina) mention slavery in their decree for secession, as does the Confederacy's constitution. For instance, the declaration of the state of Mississippi, in the first line, read, "Our position is thoroughly identified with the institution of slavery—the greatest material interest of the world."[177] They called slavery the greatest material interest of the world! Another interpretation is that Mississippi needed slavery because it made the state rich. Another fact that most will miss is that the Confederate flag only truly resurfaced as those of African descent began to fight for their freedom in the mid-twentieth century, around 1948. Each step along the way, the flag would be raised, along with national outcries advocating for segregation and Jim Crow laws to continue in the United States. For thirty-nine years, from 1961 to 2000, the Confederate flag flew atop of the state capitol building in South Carolina before being moved to the flagpole next to the capitol.[178] In my opinion, no matter where or how it is displayed, the Confederate flag elicits a reminder of a time in our history that was particularly shameful. I submit to America to let the Confederate flag go. Removing the Confederate flag would serve as a great sign of hope in America, indicating that we are moving to a new era in our nation. Thousands across America from all ethnicities have come out to support removing the flag from all federal buildings, and many states have banned the flag from their license plates. Former governor and former presidential candidate Jeb Bush has called for the Confederate flag to be removed, along with former South Carolina governor Nikki Haley and many high-profile Republicans, including former presidential candidate Lindsey Graham.[179] It is time for change in America. On July 10, 2015, the Confederate flag was officially removed from South Carolina state grounds as a result of state legislative action that overwhelmingly supported the change. As one might imagine, not everyone agreed, but it is time for change in America. Indeed, it is time to come together as a nation. As a side note, a photo went viral across America because it showed a black police officer, Leroy Smith, coming to the aid of a distressed white supremacist who was overcome by the extreme heat during a KKK rally of the Loyal White Knights to maintain the Confederate flag on the state capitol building in South Carolina.[180] According to reports, the officer provided first aid and ensured the individual's safety. The photo went viral, and the officer is to be commended for moving beyond the racial divide. This is what America can become when we find the courage to stand. Humanity knows not color of skin, and compassion is not limited by ethnicity.

As the controversy continued from the shooting of the innocent victims in the church, yet another sign of hate began to manifest itself in June 2015 with the burning of six African American churches in rural Southern states. In the first few days following the shooting, these churches were burned to the ground. Not all fires were found to be the result of arson during the investigation, but common sense tells us this is not a coincidence. Why are black churches or houses of worship targeted? Remember, throughout the history of America, the black church has been the symbol or power base for social change, racial justice, and civil rights, and thus was a target to stop any momentum toward that end.[181] Of note, more synagogues and mosques are targeted in America than black churches, but it does not deter from the fact that this is happening as a part of the racial divide and controversy in America. Who can forget the bombing in the Sixteenth Street Baptist Church in Birmingham, Alabama, where four little black girls lost their lives, and twenty were injured in a terrorist attack to stop the civil rights movement in 1963? Interestingly, it took decades for justice to prevail for all of the perpetrators of this crime—Robert Chambliss was convicted to life in prison in 1977, while Bobby Cherry and Thomas Blanton were indicted in 2000 and convicted to life in prison, and the fourth suspect, Herman Cash, died in 1994 (thirty-one years later) before facing trial.[182] The taking of innocent lives on American soil—killed by other Americans in a terrorist act because of their skin color—is unacceptable. There was national outcry over this hate crime, and once again, with the loss of lives, it galvanized America and moved her one step closer to realizing that we needed to come together. According to Jack Levin, a professor emeritus at Northeastern University who has studied hate crimes for the last thirty years, "It isn't unreasonable to speculate that at least some of the black churches are acts of arson, especially coming in the aftermath of the horrific massacre of nine people in a black church."[183] The point is that America must confront these types of horrific acts meant to intimidate and divide. Remember in the 1990s, when there were a major rash of black church burnings? They led to then-President Bill Clinton forming the National Church Arson Task Force, which revealed that most of the crimes were committed by one person, Jay Scott Ballinger, a self-proclaimed "missionary of Lucifer" who was against all churches and Christianity, but somehow targeted largely black churches and teens who were looking for the thrill of burning down churches.[184] As it was then, we will probably find that most of the burnings are not ethnicity-related and were accidental, but some will be directly related to the racial divide in America and are meant to stoke the fires of division and show a sign of supremacy.

In another example of maliciousness and mistreatment of individuals because of ethnicity, a South Carolina police officer, Michael Slager, was arrested without bail, charged with murder, and fired for shooting a black male, Walter Scott, in the back five times as the man tried to run away during an arrest.[185] The charge came almost immediately, within three days of the incident. The man was pulled over for a broken rear light on his car. The officer tried to stun the man, but it did not work, and it appears that Scott then resisted arrest and tried to run away. He was shot with his back to the officer with no weapons or no aggression toward the officer. Unbeknownst to the officer, the incident was caught on video camera. The camera is what allowed the police department and the city to swiftly react. The police report allegedly stated that the man tried to grab his weapon and the officer feared for his life. It is clear that the officer's report did not line up with the video filmed by a bystander. The media pundits pointed out that the line the officers use are the same—that they feared for their life and the person they were arresting reached for his or her weapon or did something with his or her hands. The officers also reported that they tried to save the man's life, but the video shows that the officers, one black and one white, simply stood around for a few minutes and then another officer came on the scene and performed medical treatment, but by then, it was too late. The camera also shows a possible attempt to plant an object (possibly the Taser) by the dying victim. There was a protest in South Carolina; however, it was a small and peaceful crowd, perhaps due to the swift reaction from law enforcement.

As I have demonstrated, 2014 and 2015 were volatile years with ethnic relations between the police and those of African descent. Yet another police officer, State Trooper Sean Groubert, a police officer in South Carolina, shot a man in the hip when he approached for a traffic violation at gas station. The man was of African descent and the police officer was of European descent. The officer drew his weapon and told the man to show his registration. The man got out of the car with his hands held high, and the officer told the man to get his registration. When the man turned to reach for his registration in the car, the officer fired three shots, hitting him once. You can hear the man asking what appears to be, "I was just getting my license. Sir, why was I shot? All I did was reach for my license. I'm coming from work."[186] The officer stated, "Because you dove in your car head first, then jumped out." The officer's web camera showed the man was compliant with the officer's request and did nothing aggressive. Luckily, the man survived the shooting. The officer was fired, arrested for aggravated assault, and charged with assault and battery of a high and aggravated nature, a felony that carries a penalty of up to twenty years in prison, according to a news release from the South Carolina Law

Enforcement Division.[187] What needs to be explored more in our society is the aggressive nature of the officer in question. Was he on high alert because of the color of the man he was stopping? Why did the officer feel threatened? By the way, the officer has pleaded not guilty and posted bond. These are the types of things that need be addressed directly. Sometimes the officers are exonerated in these cases, but not always. Again, I am simply overwhelmed by the number of incidents that are happening monthly in America, where violence and shootings target those who appear innocent. In most cases, the victims suffer unjustified homicide. There is simply not enough time and space for me to capture them all, but may the examples that I am capturing be sufficient to illustrate the problems America faces.

The cases above are not always typical. In some situations, police officers seemingly move on without any repercussions. For instance, in February 2015, New York Police Officer Peter Liang was indicted and suspended without pay for shooting and killing an unarmed African American, Akai Gurley, in a darkened staircase in a housing project.[188] Akai was with his girlfriend, and they were taking the stairs because the elevator was not working. The lights were broken in the stairwell. According to reports, the officers were patrolling with their weapons drawn and flashlights in hand. Akai was reportedly going to surprise his mother for Thanksgiving with a visit to Florida the following week. I must admit, I had not even heard of this case until I saw that an officer was indicted for shooting an unarmed man. The media has not made this an around-the-clock issue; thus, the case is not widely known. Although the trial has not been completed at the publishing of this book, it is an indication that the process can work.

In yet another case, an African American police officer, Braheme Days, shot an unarmed African American, Jerame Reid, as he was exiting the car with what appears to be his hands up, according to the police cam video.[189] Officer Days' partner, Roger Worley, a person of European descent, also appeared to fire at least once. Reid had an egregious criminal record, there was a gun in the glove compartment, and evidently, he had been arrested before by Officer Days on charges of obstruction, resisting arrest, possession of narcotics, and failure to appear in Millville Municipal Court.[190] I have not heard of anything of mass protests for the actions of this officer. Again, the original video (police camera) seems to show that the man should not have been shot. The police officers, Days and Worley, have been suspended pending the investigation. Again, no mass protests were held for the officer's conviction. The media covered it as a blip on the screen only briefly. The incendiary tone of ethnicity was not there; however, the crime is very similar to other high visibility incidents. This helps make my point very clear—it is not necessarily the loss of life that has called the mass protests, but the idea that a white officer allegedly abused his power to kill a black person that grabs national headlines. The terms *black* versus *white* will constantly bring up a divide and depict racial inequality, thus my push to eliminate those terms as antiquated and out of date.

Perhaps no incident I followed on the news more clearly depicted why I am calling for a full review of our justice system than the case of a young person, seventeen-year-old Laquan McDonald, of African descent, who was killed by the police on the streets of Chicago in October 2014.[191] It was hard to watch. The police officer, Jason Van Dyke, was on the scene less than thirty seconds with other police surrounding the young teen, when he fired sixteen bullets into the teen in approximately thirteen seconds.[192] The police officer, of European descent, was locked up and charged with first-degree murder for the shooting incident when the video was released. Of course, the police officer claimed that he thought his life was in danger and that the teen was lunging toward him. The teen was allegedly on drugs (PCP) at the time and was wielding a small knife. However, the video shows he was walking down the middle of a major street with the knife pulled and actually moving away from the officer, not confronting him. Even when the teen was on the ground, the officer continued to shoot. A video released in November 2015, one year after the incident, showed the heinous shooting of a young man who could have easily been handled by other means—even if Tasered or confronted physically by the host of officers on the scene. The only person I saw on national TV who would support the officer was the defense lawyer who spouted the same rhetoric that the officer feared for his life and the teen was coming toward him with the knife. However, every major broadcast I saw had the opposite opinion and equally condemned this act, whether Republican or Democrat. When the video was finally released, there were major protest marches for justice on the streets of Chicago, with calls for key officials to be removed. Why was the video held for a year? The FBI was reportedly investigating and wanted to keep release of the video limited so as not to cause bias during the investigation.[193] There is much controversy surrounding the release of the video, and it is these types of actions that build the case for corruption and cover-up. It was not until a judge ordered the video released that is was shown to the public. Let me be clear; I am not saying the marches are not needed in these types of cases, but why not march every weekend for the vicious crimes of those of African descent killing those of African descent? Even though we did not see the video until November 2015, the family saw the video in April 2014, and the city paid the family $5 million in damages.[194] The family did not want the video released but stated they understood the significance of its release. Every time I see this play out in America, I am frustrated, because it is like a broken record that won't move forward. We need to change it—the results won't change until we change! How can we march for justice in the case of an officer killing a person, but not in the case when children are killed doing homework or lured into a life of crime? As a nation, these subjects cannot be off limits. We must speak up together as one. Of note, I was once again happy to notice across the nation, the marches were not made up of one ethnicity. The crowds were indeed diverse and very peaceful, for the most part.

A deeper dive into the number of police officers indicted for criminal activity shows the number is higher than one might think. It is actually similar in some cases to America at large. As I was doing my research, I could easily see that police officers are human, and, unfortunately, just as the human race, there will be that element or percentage who are criminal and who have evil intent. Police have been charged with a variety of crimes, such as brutality, sexual misconduct, fraud, theft, illegal shootings, wrongful arrests, drugs, wrongful raids, bias, misuse of a Taser, perjury, animal cruelty, and, yes, murder.[195] Let's take a close look at the National Police Misconduct Reporting Project (NPMSRP) of 2009, which showed the following numbers:

- 3,445: Unique reports of police misconduct tracked by the NPMSRP
- 4,012: Law enforcement officers alleged to have engaged in misconduct
- 261: Law enforcement leaders (police chiefs or sheriffs) who were cited in those reports
- 4,778: Alleged victims of police misconduct cited in tracked reports

- 258: Fatalities reported in connection with alleged instances of misconduct
- 15.05: Reported incidents of misconduct tracked per day on average, or a report of misconduct every ninety-six minutes
- $198,943,000: Reported costs in police-misconduct-related civil litigation, not counting legal fees or court costs
- 980.64 per 100,000: Estimated average 2009 US police misconduct rate (PMR = officers implicated per 100,000 officers)[196]

Police officers are not above the law, and this report demonstrates that law enforcement is held accountable. I could fill many pages of this book with examples of police officers found to be corrupt and lying about felonious acts they had committed. Unfortunately, many of their victims have not lived to tell the truth or to see them captured. In fact, it is not uncommon for lawyers to open up cold cases, or those that were closed, in order to pursue justice against law enforcement officers for wrongly incarcerating young men (mostly of African descent) and depriving them of their livelihood and prime years. Justice has been served in many cases. You may be wondering if these officers are in fact convicted and do they serve prison time. The NPMRP, again in 2009, reported the following when juxtaposed against the 2008 US Department of Justice, the FBI Uniform Crime Reporting (UCR) statistics, and the 2004 Bureau of Justice Statistic Criminal Sentencing Statistics:

- 1 out of every 266 (376.5 per 100k) police officers were accused of a violent crime. Per the UCR, 1 out of every 220 (454.5 per 100k) citizens were accused of a violent crime in 2008.
- 1 out of every 1,875 (53.3 per 100k) police officers were accused of homicide. Per the UCR, 1 out of every 18,518 (5.4 per 100k) citizens were accused of homicide in 2008, while 1 out of every 4037 (24.77 per 100k) officers died in the line of duty in 2009.
- 1 out of every 947 (105.63 per 100k) police officers were accused of sexual assault. Per the UCR, 1 out of every 3,413 (29.3 per 100k) citizens were accused of sexual assault in 2008.
- 33 percent of police officers charged in 2009 were ultimately convicted, while 68 percent of citizens charged were ultimately convicted in 2004.

- 64 percent of police officers convicted were actually sentenced to spend time in prison in 2009, while 72 percent of citizens convicted were sentenced to incarceration in 2004.
- Law enforcement officers were sentenced to an average of 14 months in prison when sentenced to incarceration in 2009, while citizens were sentenced to an average of 37 months in prison when incarcerated in 2004.[197]

Finally, the NPMSRP reported in 2009 that 45.9 percent of the officers involved in misconduct had adverse effects on their career, including serving prison time on an average of fourteen months.[198] These reports demonstrate that officers are not simply committing random acts of crime against innocent citizens without any repercussions. Even as I write this book in early 2015, the Department of Justice has released a report stating that the Ferguson Police Department does have a propensity to use excessive force against blacks and tends to arrest them disproportionately as compared to whites. Further, blacks are arrested more frequently for petty crimes. Again, most in America believe that the police forces in our major cities do in fact need an overhaul. Perhaps it begins with sensitivity to the communities in which they serve, and, again, seeing all people in a different light. In other words, most of the alleged abuse probably comes from situations where the police force does not understand the culture it is dealing with or has preconceived ideas of a person and their status based on the color of their skin or how they are dressed. Not only did the Department of Justice discover a pattern of abuse by police officers in Ferguson, it discovered defamatory and racial slurs against blacks and President Obama on the official Ferguson computer data base. Although the Department of Justice stopped short of pressing charges against the officer in the case or against the Ferguson Police Department, this is a prime example of what I referred to earlier in the book when I spoke of covert racism in America that infiltrates almost every facet of society. Remember, this is only one department; how many more are just like it? I hope I am starting to connect the dots that all of the abuse and inflamed hatred between ethnicities can be traced back to nomenclature and preconceived notions of who a person is. Dr. Martin Luther King said it best when he stated that we should strive to live in a nation where we don't judge our fellow man by his skin color, but by the content of his character. Again, I must emphasize that most police officers are honorable and do a great service to our nation. However, what gives the entire police force a bad reputation are the actions of a few rogue officers. A headline-grabbing incident recently happened in Virginia, where an honor-roll student, Martese Johnson, at the University of Virginia, was severely beaten and bloodied.[199] The images went viral. Johnson was severely beaten during an arrest. Allegedly, he was attempting to enter a bar while underage. Police were called and said he was drunk in public and using a false ID. The governor's office requested an immediate investigation for the alleged abuse. In this case, the young college student was African American and the police officers were of European descent. Again, these types of incidents stoke the public's ire and further divide the nation. However, once again, the protests were multicultural. This continually demonstrates that America is coming together in many instances despite those who want to divide America. One of the newscasts correctly reported that these incidents are not limited to European-descent police officers arresting African Americans, but there are clear cases of overreaction from European-descent police officers when dealing with European-descent Americans. The real key is to try to help police officers understand the communities they are dealing with and perhaps gain better training on dealing with unique situations at the lowest possible level. Again, the police officers are very much aware of the above and have this type of training continuously, but it only takes a few disingenuous officers to taint the system. We also must keep in mind that America has witnessed heinous, brutal behavior by law enforcement during the Jim Crow laws and segregation in America.

Another incident that captured the nation's attention involved Freddie Gray, an African American male, who died shortly after his arrest in Baltimore in April 2015. Six officers who arrested Gray were suspended pending investigations. Early on, the ethnicity of the officers was not immediately known, but the video showed at least some were of European descent.[200] I point this out because it shows how quickly the nation would think that all officers were in fact white; hence, the massive protests ensued. Freddie Gray's spine was nearly severed with an almost eight-inch gap. According to the police, he was arrested for "making eye contact" with the police and then running from them.[201] According to most estimates, Freddie Gray should not have been arrested. He was in great pain as he lay on the ground and was virtually dragged to the police truck. After being placed in the truck, police say he was not restrained. Somehow during the trip to the police station, he was further injured. There were reports that the injuries could have been self-sustained when Gray banged his body and head on the truck walls, but that was refuted. From my perspective in watching the footage, it appears that Gray was in great distress before being placed in the police van, and no footage shows what happened prior to Gray being shown in handcuffs, facedown. Gray died in the hospital and police officers admitted they did not get him to the hospital soon enough. Mass protests began to form with the outcry for justice and to decry police treatment of those of African descent. The protests were positive in the beginning, but after about the seventh day, the protests turned from peaceful to violent, with fires, looting, injuring of police officers, and destruction of the neighborhood. These were purely criminal actions, with individuals destroying their own neighborhoods to show their pain and frustration. Businesses were shut down and many burned. I don't believe any acts of violence by the rioters are justified. The stories continue to pour in across America, and the intensiveness grows between the ethnicities. I must admit, it was painful to watch our beloved country go through that night, and I felt deep sorrow for the community, the people, and even the rioters. I was also angry that a few rioters could come in and destroy what was otherwise a peaceful democratic demonstration. It was good to see congressmen, clergy, and other leaders coming out to quell the unrest. Thousands of National Guard soldiers had to be called in, and a curfew had to be set. Even when the protests were in the peaceful stage, I did note that on the news broadcasts, you could see some of the protestors getting rough with news agencies, grabbing equipment, and yelling profanity into the cameras.

What makes the Freddie Gray case interesting is that it sparked a nationwide response in many other major cities, such as New York; Minneapolis; Washington, DC; Boston; New Orleans; and Philadelphia. Even more interesting was the racial makeup of the crowds of these protests against police brutality. From my perspective, the crowds in many of the peaceful marches were overwhelmingly white and Hispanic. Of course, there were some arrests as usual, but for the most part, they were peaceful marches and demonstrations. Again, it showed me that America is willing to come together on these issues. I observed that the media did not emphasize the multicultural makeup of the crowds and the signs of unity across America and across the often hard racial lines. Surprisingly, or perhaps in a planned public relations move, the prosecutor released charges against the officer on the Friday following the Monday riots. All six officers were charged with varying degrees of crimes, from second-degree manslaughter to criminal neglect. However, the most interesting part of the release was the racial makeup of the six officers. Indeed, three were white, while three were black, including one female. I was not shocked, but I am almost certain the majority of Americans were, for we had all grown used to the same story line of "white officer kills black citizen." At the publishing of this book, all officers have been exonerated. But the charges showed that there was a shift toward accountability, and once again, the video camera was crucial in bringing these actions to light.

At the same time as the Freddie Gray incident, there was a report of a white male, Richard Fletcher, who was nearly beaten to death by up to fifty young black teens in late April 2015.[202]

The teens were reportedly fighting each other and jumping on the man's car, essentially vandalizing it, when Fletcher came out to ask them to stop it. They quickly attacked him and beat him viciously, causing Fletcher severe damage and putting him in critical condition with broken eye sockets, a broken nose, and broken ribs. He was near death. The teens were charged with attempted homicide and a variety of other charges, and Richard Fletcher's hospital bill was reportedly somewhere between $200,000 and $400,000.[203] This is America, and we must treat Americans as humans with dignity and grace. These types of crimes only make a blip on the radar screen. Senseless violence and ingrained prejudice continue to force our nation down the road of racial divide. It is amazing how the color of our skin evokes so much disrespect, bigotry, and hatred for the other, one way or another. I must also note the media barely covered this, and there were no major marches in America due to this vicious beating of Richard Fletcher. Many will say it is because the European ethnic group in America is the majority; thus, there is no need for an outcry or demonstration. I submit that this is not a justifiable explanation. All hate crime is wrong and should be considered wrong by all Americans. Any offense against one American is an offense against all Americans.

Richard Fletcher was wrongly beaten and battered and almost lost his life; likewise, in March 2015, in Queens, New York, a white male out with his girlfriend was threatened with the phrase "I am going to kill you, white boy." He was cut from his ear to the middle of his throat by a Hispanic male.[204] Thank God the cut was not deep enough to kill the man, and he survived. What is interesting about this case is that it happened without almost any national attention. There is no apparent motive in this case other than that it was a pure and simple hate crime. Police treated it as such as they launched their investigation. These are the types of senseless crimes that make one question whether or not we will ever move past racism and discrimination. Once again, there was limited media coverage, there were no mass protests, and there was essentially no justice, as the suspects, a Hispanic couple, have not been caught.

In a similar case on the Fourth of July 2015, a mob of black teens viciously attacked a white male, Christopher McKnight, for allegedly bumping into a black dude while getting on a bus in downtown Cincinnati, Ohio.[205] It was certainly a gang beating, causing McKnight severe but not life-threatening damage. The original report filed by a junior white officer called it an antiwhite crime, but that report was debunked by Cincinnati Police Captain Mike Neville, who is white. He asked for caution before jumping to the conclusion that this was a hate crime or ethnicity-related incident. However, a few days later, Cincinnati Police Chief Jeffery Blackwell called the incident a hate crime and asked federal prosecutors to pursue charges.[206] The beating was caught on camera and posted on social media. According to reports, the onlookers simply cheered and watched one man, an American, get beat down by three other Americans. How can this disrespect for one another, seemingly because of ethnicity, continue? Again, there were no major rallies or domination of the news airwaves with this story. I only found out about it as I was researching another story for the book. I didn't see any mass marches calling for justice and these types of crime to stop. Again, I find this type of behavior particularly troubling because individuals are cheering on the dreadful crime against humanity. Please keep in mind that these things took place on the Fourth of July—a day when we are supposed to celebrate freedom in America and togetherness. In yet another incident of racial hatred in America, Darren and Hayli Franke of Spring, Texas, a white couple, were hosting their friend, a black person, over the Independence Day holiday. They woke up to a horrific surprise of finding racial slurs, including the infamous KKK symbol, painted on their white truck.[207] If this doesn't shock you, nothing else will. This happened in America in July 2015, again during a time when we should be celebrating the freedom of our nation and respect for all Americans, but there are some who still want to see the racial divide in America due to the color of the skin. The couple's vehicle was spray-painted with racial slurs and graffiti in a neighborhood that was surprisingly multicultural. In a demonstration of true American resolve and solidarity, people of all ethnicities in the neighborhood came together to help clean the vehicle. Frankly, I believe America-at-large is tired of these types of actions. We have seen this behavior far too many times. I am noticing a pattern with the American people when racial demonstrations and hatred are carried out. The American people are stepping up and demanding that this hatred ends by showing solidarity by holding prayer vigils, engaging in marches, speaking out in legislative forums, taking legislative actions, cleaning neighborhoods, and, yes, cleaning vehicles. This is why I believe America is ready for change with regard to the names by which we identify one another: no more black person, and no more white person—simply American. America, we can do this together!

In July 2015, yet another police officer was killed when shot in New York. Unfortunately, some will turn to this type of action due to the incitement of ethnicity against ethnicity and citizens versus police officers. When this type of rhetoric is spewed, it creates an atmosphere of boldness for the criminals to attack police officers, often unprovoked. On the other hand, in New Orleans in 2015, there was a special feature honoring an officer with the Purple Heart for his valor during duty where he was shot three times but survived. The officer was shot while directing traffic in what seemed like an ambush by someone who had a vendetta. When I was growing up, I remember my dad would slow down his car if he saw a police officer coming near his car even though we were not violating the speed limit. I remember encouraging him not to slow down because he was not violating any laws, but it did not persuade him. It took me years to figure out what was going on. It was because of what he had seen as a youth. The apparent misuse and abuse of power he had witnessed caused him to respond the way he was responding. For him, it was a reaction to protect himself based on his experiences. It was extremely odd for me at the time, and I could not comprehend it. I was totally secure in driving on the highway at the speed limit. This demonstrated that one's experience and context determines the reaction to the stimuli. My father was responding from a past of threat based on perceived inequality, and I from a place of safety and equality.

In August 2013, John Geer, a white male, was shot dead by Adam Torres, a Hispanic or Latino police officer of the Fairfax County Police in Virginia.[208] Geer had a confrontation with family members and his common-law wife called the police. When the police responded, a fifty-minute encounter began with, in my opinion, unorthodox moves by the police. Why would you stand and talk with a person who has his hands above his head for over fifty minutes? He was not drunk or belligerent at the time of the police's arrival. He had to ask several times to scratch his nose. It was on his last request to scratch his nose that he was shot. His father and common-law wife had to witness this, in my opinion, senseless shooting. It appears to me that if you have three or four police standing on a front porch, pointing weapons at the suspect, you would have ordered Geer to step out of the house with his hands up and then go down to his knees. Then you would simply handcuff him and arrest him. This was clearly an unnecessary shooting, and the other arresting officers admit that Officer Torres overreacted, saying Geer was not a threat to them. There is a major lawsuit by Geer's common-law wife, and an internal investigation is underway.[209] According to the article, Officer Torres was known for anger issues and had been subject to other internal investigations for other alleged misconduct with regard to arrests. I must admit that I had not heard of this incident until I started researching crime in America and altercations with police. Once again, the media did not capture this act, and it almost went unnoticed. We must ask ourselves if this would have been the case had the roles been reversed. Most Hispanics would say the same would have happened without much media attention if it were a Hispanic killed, but if it were a black person being shot by a white police officer, you would have major coverage from the media. There is certainly an imbalance in what the media decides to emphasize. I point out this story for two reasons: First, we must know that all life is valuable, and it should not be decided to be ignored based on the ethnicity of the person; second, I want to point out how we in America have decided which stories to push and decry when all life is valuable no matter what skin tone one might have. All lives matter, despite what the ethnicity may be. In mid-2015, Martin O'Malley, Democratic governor of Maryland, said that very statement—"Black lives matter, white lives matter, all lives matter"—at a conference dealing with criminal justice and police brutality. He was booed and heckled by the audience.[210] This illustrates my point of the divide that continues to grow in our nation. Of course, all lives indeed matter, and we must come together as a nation to send the message to every ethnicity. Governor O'Malley apologized and understood how the mostly black, politically liberal audience could view his comments as insensitive. I could not disagree more. That is exactly the issue: All lives matter! Yes, I am not going to get caught up in the rhetoric stating that if I say, "All lives matter," I am somehow disrespecting the rallying cry for justice. No, that does not diminish my struggle as outlined in this book, but on the contrary, it is call for justice for all people and an acknowledgment that, indeed, all lives matter, all humans matter. I will address the justice system and its practices against minorities in the coming chapter, but make no mistake, believing or stating that all lives matter does not diminish one ethnicity but calls for respect and dignity to all people. By the way, the Black Lives Matter movement has gone on to disrupt many political events in 2015. While attention should be brought to the injustices and discriminatory practices of those who uphold the law, attention must also be brought to the heinous crime of self-genocide through murder.

Take the case of the nine-year-old boy Tyshawn Lee, in 2015 who was lured into an alley on Chicago south side and shot by gang members allegedly because of his father's involvement in gang warfare.[211] This crime was simply outlandish and inhumane, and no words can describe the pain the family must be experiencing. This was a young black youth cut down in the developing stages of his life, allegedly by another black person. An innocent young man was killed or assassinated, allegedly because of his family ties to a gang, and the father is not cooperating with the investigation. Yet this cowardly act takes place weekly in our inner cities with hardly any change in the aftermath. I could add a new story to this book almost weekly concerning another drive-by shooting with another young life randomly taken on the streets of America. For instance, in October 2015, fifteen-year-old Kiyon Evans died of gunshot wounds to the legs and torso, and in September 2015, fourteen-year-old Tyjuan Poindexter was killed in a drive-by shooting in Chicago.[212] The community must speak up and take to the streets in protest and demand protection by law enforcement. Witnesses cannot protect those who commit such atrocities. If everyone comes together, we can thwart the threats if we speak up together and unite. The gangs would have to shoot the entire neighborhood. It is time to put fear aside and step up, or continue to face the killings of innocent children. As the police officers indicated, someone knows who carried out the crime against this innocent young man on his way home from school. I also noticed that there were no major rallies, no Black Lives Matter rallies. This is where the rallies need to take place, for it is the far greater crime destroying the population of those who have African descent. Are we going to keep making excuses for why such killings take place? It is madness to blame this type of killing on slavery and oppression of the government. I will not be silent concerning the great offenses that rob children of their selfhood and a chance to develop—it is time for America to change.

Thus far, I believe I have shown that ethnic relations are clearly not where they need to be in America, even though we have come a long way, and there are many Americans who are ready for change. There are signs of hope in America all the time. There are those who will complain about discrimination working both ways. There are continued reports that talk about the police targeting blacks and how awful our police officers are. May I make a plea to the reader at this point to understand that, again, the large majority of officers risk their lives for us daily, and most are honorable and not corrupt. There are an estimated 1.2 million officers in law enforcement, and the vast majority are upholding the law. Many who jump quickly to blame the police for being overly aggressive, especially to people of brown skin color, must understand the hazards the officers face in defense of citizens in America. A case in point is the incident in Arizona where a white police officer responded to a domestic violence incident. His body camera recorded a heinous crime against him. As he was talking to the white male suspect, the police officer was suddenly shot six times and killed by the male. The male then shot himself. Note, the officer had not drawn his weapon, and when the officer asked if he could check the man for weapons, the man pulled out a revolver and murdered the officer in cold blood. These are the tragedies we face in America, and this is why some officers are overly aggressive. Be mindful that I am not justifying the crimes against humanity, but trying to paint a picture from all views so that perhaps we can understand why these are tense times in America.

To further illustrate the state of America in 2015 with regard to ethnic relations, let's examine recent headlines that literally captured the fact that there are some who want the escalation to continue. For instance, the FBI arrested two men who were white supremacists planning to start a "race war." According to the FBI, Robert Doyle and Ronald Chaney, who ascribed to a white supremacist version of the Asatru faith, were planning to shoot or bomb the occupants of black churches and Jewish synagogues.[213] Yes, in 2015 in America, this is what is still arising, despite the progress made over the history of our great nation. It is pure ignorance to want to kill others who are different just because they are different. Further, a radio station affiliated with the Black Lives Matter movement had a host who called for an ethnic war with the murder of whites, stating on air, "It's about to go down, it's open season on killing white people and the c-word."[214] Really, this is happening in America. How can we support such hate speech and rhetoric? There have also been questionable signs at some of the rallies that seem to advocate killing police officers. This is unacceptable, and America must stand up. Further, four white supremacists allegedly tried to end a Black Lives Matter rally in Minneapolis, Minnesota, by firing shots into the crowd of marching in protest of the killing of Jamar Clark.[215] Allen Lawrence "Lance" Scarsella III, twenty-three; Nathan Gustavsson, twenty-one; Daniel Macey, twenty-six; and Joseph Backman, twenty-seven were the alleged shooters. They injured at least five in the process.[216] The protesters were on their ninth day of protests due to an incident where twenty-four-year-old Jamar Clark, black, was killed by white officers in Minneapolis during an arrest. No charges had been brought against the officers at the time of the rally and a grand jury was reviewing the case. These incidents did not make a lot of headline news. Yes, this happened in the open public—white versus black yet again. My daughter mentioned to me as I was writing the book that she could not believe she was seeing the events that were unfolding before her very eyes across America—she thought the ethnic fighting was history and over with. Again, I submit that America needs to come together and get rid of these hateful actions by first eliminating how we address one another. It is not black against white. We are the same human race, as I have demonstrated in this book.

As you might imagine, this kind of data with regard to death by ethnicity causes America to be further divided along ethnic and political lines. This also causes some to want to begin an all-out war against other ethnicities or the police. These are the worst things that can happen. As Dr. Martin Luther King so often illustrated, hate cannot drive out hate, but it has to be with love for our fellow humans that we find a new way forward. The following scenario demonstrates what I am espousing. In December of 2014, a raged and deranged African American male, Ismaaiyl Brinsley, killed his girlfriend, and then murdered two innocent police officers in New York before ending his own life.[217]

The police officers, Wenjian Liu (Asian) and Rafael Ramos (Hispanic) were killed at close range as they were sitting in their patrol car. The man posted on Instagram that he was going to "kill pigs" in retaliation for Eric Garner's death.[218] This type of violence is senseless, and innocent, honorable police officers were needlessly killed and taken from their families. Now, this person was certainly an anomaly, but how many have thought similarly, but have not taken action? I am grateful that more violence has not erupted, but it is a reminder that America must continue the transformation of unity that has happened over the past fifty years.

The police are wrongly targeted, and I believe it's in part because of our ongoing racial tension in America. Here is yet another example of the horrific attacks against police. In early 2015, a twenty-five-year-old police officer, Brian Moore, was shot dead responding to a routine traffic stop, the third New York police officer slain in the line of duty in five months.[219] He was white and the perpetrator was a black male, Demetrius Blackwell.[220] Just one week later, two officers were killed in a routine traffic stop. Officers Liquori Tate (black) and Benjamin Deen (white) were ambushed at the traffic stop by at least three men and one woman, all black.[221] Officer Tate was being trained by Officer Deen because he was a new to the force. He had recently graduated from the Police Academy in June 2014; he wrote, "I graduated the Police Academy today. I am now a Police Officer. I would like to thank God, the Police Academy, the Police Department, my family, friends, and loved ones."[222] All four of the alleged shooters were arrested: Curtis Banks, twenty-six; Marvin Banks, twenty-nine; Joanie Calloway, twenty-two; and Cornelius Clark (age unknown), and all black. I only emphasize the ethnicity of the officers and the alleged perpetrators to show the unjustified violence against our officers of the law. These officers, in my opinion, were exactly what this book is about; they were not simply black and white working together, as happens across America every day, but two officers, two humans, serving the community with honor and dignity. In fact, Officer Deen had been recognized for being the Hattiesburg Officer of the Year in 2012. This only heightens the tension in America between the police and certain communities. Think about the families who were destroyed by these heinous acts of violence against these officers of the law, who were in the line of duty and trying to protect the very people who assassinated them. There are no justifications for the actions. Period!

In May 2015, yet another police officer, Kerrie Orozco, who was white, was killed in the line of duty days before her maternity leave in Omaha, Nebraska, by a black man, Marcus Wheeler, during a shootout.[223] Her baby was born prematurely, and she was about to take leave to ensure the baby would get needed care. Police were hunting Wheeler because of another shooting. Officer Orozco was a seven-year veteran working the North Gang Suppression Squad. This type of disrespect for officers causes instability across America. According to the FBI, violent crimes against police officers were up by 89 percent in 2014 (fifty-one) as compared to 2013 (twenty-seven, record low).[224] More than sixty-three officers have died in 2015 in the line of duty, with sixteen officers dying by firearms.[225] This is not what our nation needs. There should be a national outcry of outrage because of this treatment of our law enforcement. Yet again, it is a blip on the radar screen when one of our officers is killed in the line of duty, similar to the military members dying for their nation. I submit to America that we must respect all lives. Violence against police officers must stop.

Even as America cries aloud for the violence to stop, it continues against our law enforcement officers. In the summer of 2015, a New Orleans veteran police officer, Officer Daryle Holloway, black, was shot in the head with a .40-caliber weapon. He had just arrested Travis Boys, black, searched him, and had him handcuffed, but somehow Davis allegedly had a weapon and fired the fatal shot.[226] Officer Holloway had over twenty-two years on the force and was killed the day before Father's Day. These types of crimes are senseless and continue to show the disdain that can arise for police officers. Officer Holloway was a true hero whose life was cut too short. He was instrumental in saving lives during Hurricane Katrina. Thankfully, Boys has been recaptured and is in police custody. Of note, I could go on with many more stories such as these, with officers being killed while performing their duty, but it would take pages to capture them all. Again, the attacks against our police officers are cowardly acts against those who would protect our families and America. This is why the negative rhetoric against police officers cannot be tolerated. CNN showed a vehicle in one city that had "Kill a cop" spray-painted on the side of a trailer. I believe these and other types of language incite those who are perhaps unstable to commit the unthinkable crime of police murder.

Another officer was tragically gunned down in Memphis, Tennessee, in 2015 at a routine traffic stop. Police Officer Sean Bolton, white, was killed when he stopped to check out a car that was parked illegally.[227] As he approached the car, a struggle ensued with the passenger, and Officer Bolton was shot several times and rushed to a hospital, but was later pronounced dead. Both the driver and the suspect fled the scene, and it is suspected they were making a drug transaction when Officer Bolton interrupted them. The suspect, Tremaine Wilbourn, black, is on the run and there is a $10,000 reward for knowledge of his whereabouts.[228] Wilbourn has been deemed armed and dangerous. The police director, Toney Armstrong, black, made a moving plea for assistance to catch the suspect. But he went further and stated, "We say so often … do black lives matter? And at the end of the day, we have to ask ourselves, do all lives matter—regardless of ethnicity, creed, color, economic status, what profession that person holds? All lives matter …This is just a reminder of how dangerous this job is."[229] As you know, I highlight the ethnicities of these individuals to make my point so there is no room for confusion on what we are dealing with.

Listen, those who state that they own the "Black Lives Matter" slogan and claim that any other phrase is offensive are totally missing the point of coming together as Americans. All lives matter, and that is the bottom line. I saw a grandmother lament over the Black Lives Matter movement, calling them hypocritical because they are silent about the hundreds killed in the streets of our cities every month. Black brutality is what kills the most blacks, just as white brutality is what kills the most whites. The same is the case for Hispanics, as Hispanic brutality is what kills Hispanics. The point is that all lives matter, and we need to speak to the murder problem across America. Yet another woman, Peggie Hubbard, spoke out on YouTube and on Fox News because she was extremely distraught at hearing about a nine-year-old black girl's death from a stray bullet in Ferguson, Missouri, during a drive-by shooting. Black Lives Matter chose to ignore the death of Jamyla Bolden, instead marching in support of an alleged criminal (black) killed in a shootout with police during an arrest.[230] Hubbard made great points about the high black-on-black crime rate, disrespect of society, and heinous violence against one another and disrespect of the police officers. No protests from Black Lives Matter, no outcry in America, no major media coverage, just another life, a young American, snuffed out by senseless violence in the inner city. Hubbard was angry and lamenting the pointless and sad death of Jamyla, who was killed by a stray bullet from a drive-by shooting while she was in her bedroom doing her homework.[231] When will the senseless killings stop? This young girl was robbed of her future by a shooting that was most likely over a simple dispute or drug deal gone badly.

The bloodshed is not limited to young, innocent children, but violence against police officers continues to highlight the state of America. In 2015, a state trooper, Steven Vincent, white, stopped to help a stranded motorist, Kevin Daigle, white, whose vehicle was in a ditch in Louisiana.[232] There had been reports of a driver who was driving erratically. When Officer Vincent arrived, the vehicle that matched the description was stranded in the ditch. Officer Vincent was apparently shot with a shot gun when he approached the stranded vehicle. Officer Vincent would eventually die of gunshot wounds in the hospital. Apparently, another unnamed individual who was living with Daigle was allegedly shot and killed as well.[233] Police are still trying to determine why the incident escalated between Officer Vincent and Daigle, but it is clear that the respect for the police forces across America is lacking. Sadly, Officer Vincent left behind his son and wife and two brothers who are also in law enforcement. This type of killing is so egregious to me it pains me to type it. When sheriff's deputy Darren H. Goforth, white, was refueling his vehicle, he was shot in the head, execution style, by an allegedly mentally ill black man, Shannon Miles.[234] After Deputy Sheriff Goforth went to the ground, the alleged shooter stood over him and continued to shoot him to ensure he was dead. This behavior, as you would imagine, divides our nation and sends us further apart. Miles was found incompetent to stand trial in 2012 for an assault and sent to a mental institution for six months. Deputy Sheriff Goforth was a father of two and a husband. From all accounts, he was a very courageous police officer who was shot for no apparent reason. The alleged shooter appears to have singled out Deputy Sheriff Slogan simply because he was a police officer and possibly because of his skin color. Yet another apparent murder of a police officer happened in Fox Lake, Illinois, when Lt. Charles Joseph Gliniewicz, white, was apparently killed in the line of duty as he was conducting a foot chase to apprehend three men, two white and one black.[235] There has been a massive manhunt at the time of the writing of this book, to no avail. But the fellow officers stated that they refused to stop searching for the alleged perpetrators of this troubling shooting. Officer Gliniewicz was a father, husband, youth volunteer, and an army veteran. While at the time of this incident, fewer police officers had been killed in America in 2015 than in 2014, it is particularly worrisome when police officers are killed randomly with such ease and disrespect for the law. Although I left this story in the book, as we approached publishing, there was breaking news that Officer Gliniewicz had actually staged his death and committed suicide in an apparent attempt to end his ethical and criminal troubles.[236] Evidently, Officer Gliniewicz had been stealing from the police department for several years, laundering money meant for mentoring young people as future police officers.[237] Imagine the immediate judgment we all felt against the alleged perpetrators of this crime. I wanted to highlight why all of these stories involving law enforcement are so volatile and why we must be careful before jumping to judgment either way. This incident only highlights that there is corruption on all sides of the law and by all ethnicities.

Many from both sides will argue about whether or not police are justified for their sometimes excessive force due to examples outlined above. There are even laws that allow officers to be more aggressive in high-crime areas. Thus the alert meter is high, and chances for violent endings rise in certain neighborhoods. The question we need to deal with is, what do the statistics show with regard to shootings and or killings by police in the line of duty? Secondly, many question whether or not blacks are targeted more than whites by police officers. According to the *Guardian*, from January 1, 2015, through May 31, 2015, law enforcement killed 234 whites (50 percent of total killed), 135 blacks (29 percent of total killed), and sixty-seven Hispanics (14 percent of total killed).[238] Further, the analysis revealed that blacks are more likely than any other group to be killed when unarmed, with 31.9 percent of all killed being unarmed compared to 25.4 percent of Hispanics killed when unarmed and 15 percent of whites killed when unarmed. The FBI has a site that maps blacks killed by police, and it provides interesting statistics on this subject. In the study from the FBI, as of June 2015, 284 blacks were shot by police, with an approximate average of 25 to 30 percent being unarmed.[239] What does this data communicate to us? The raw data in terms of numbers shows that more whites are killed yearly by police than blacks and Hispanics. Yet the data clearly shows that even though the black population only makes up 13 percent of the total US population and Hispanics make up roughly 16 percent of the population, blacks and Hispanics are disproportionately killed by police. Remember, the white population is roughly 197 million, Hispanics are approximately fifty-four million, and blacks are approximately forty-three million. The study also revealed that more minorities are killed when unarmed. Although nonwhite Americans make up 37.4 percent of the population, 46.6 percent who are killed by police are minorities, and 62.7 percent of all unarmed people killed by police are minorities.[240] Again, the data shows without a doubt that if you are a minority and unarmed during a confrontation with the police, you are at greater risk than nonminorities of being killed. This has to be acknowledged and addressed by law enforcement departments nationwide and by the US Justice Department.

I was not surprised by the headlines when I read that in late 2015, a white officer shot and killed an unarmed white teen in Seneca, South Carolina, in a Hardee's restaurant parking lot. Most of America is unaware that this has been happening, but as I have shown in my research above, whites also face many challenges with law enforcement, perhaps just not as frequently as blacks. Zachary Hammond, white and nineteen years old, was shot to death during a drug investigation bust when plainclothes officer Lt. Mark Tiller, white, was attempting to arrest Hammond.[241] Police were actually after Hammond's girlfriend, Tori Martin, white and twenty-four years of age, a suspected drug trafficker. Police are saying that Officer Tiller acted in self-defense when Hammond proceeded to drive off, and Officer Tiller thought his life was at risk. The family is demanding an investigation and has hired a lawyer to represent them. A small amount of marijuana was found in the car. Officer Tiller is on administrative leave while the investigation is underway. No charges have been filed against the officer as of today; however, the Black Lives Matter group has been calling for a mass protest in honor of Zachary Hammond to rally against police brutality. The group is outraged that more people are not decrying this alleged crime by police.

In yet another heinous action, a white police officer was caught on film relentlessly punching Cindy Hahn, a white woman, in the head in 2013; and Hahn has since sued the Carlsbad, California, Police Department and several officers.[242] She stated that she was simply asking the officer a question about an alarm that had gone off at a nearby car. When Hahn asked if everything was okay, the same police officer asked her. "Is this your car?" and to mind her "expletive" business.[243] Hahn then claims that the same officer pulled her over for not wearing a seat belt and started punching her in the head as another officer held her down and yet another officer simply held back onlookers. Hahn is suing because she said she has memory loss and brain trauma. I place this here to highlight that police brutality knows no color limits. This type of tactic must be stopped. Luckily, Hahn survived the attack and lived to continue her life with her children. There are other stories related to this incident, but space would not allow me to capture them all.

Perhaps one reason for the clearly disproportionate incidents with blacks and Hispanics and police officers is due to the perceptions of what a black or Hispanic person will do when confronted. If the narrative in America is that a black or Hispanic person is aggressive, belligerent, violent, and basically a criminal, perhaps it causes the police to be more aggressive than normal. Let me make it clear that this is a false narrative. There is no doubt that there are some blacks and Hispanics who are violent, but that can be said for whites as well. It has taken years to build a negative perception of the black and Hispanic person. Years of stereotypical images in the media and the belief that blacks and Hispanics were not intelligent and were violent in general have taken its toll. This again is a false narrative. As it is a false narrative that whites in general want to harm blacks and hold them back. Certainly, history has shown this has happened in the past, but today is a new day, and it is time to go forward. As I have demonstrated throughout this book, blacks and Hispanics would not be, could not be, where they are without the help of white Americans. The false narrative that whites, blacks, and Hispanics only divide against one another along with other ethnicities is wrong and must change.

The Latino community has also protested the law enforcement killing of three men within one month in early 2015. These killings have seldom made national news, and there have not been any nationwide protests. Antonio Zambrano Montes was killed in Pasco, Washington, in early February 2015; then Ruben Garcia Villalpando was shot to death by a police officer in Grapevine, Texas, in February 2015; and Ernesto Javier Canepa Diaz was killed by police in Santa Ana also in late February 2015.[244] What is amazing is that all three men were unarmed and still Mexican nationals.

In Zambrano's case, police say he was acting erratically and actually ran toward the police while throwing rocks. Ruben Villalpando was shot during a stop on the highway when police thought he was the suspect in another burglary, but that proved to be untrue. Allegedly, Villalpando would not remain still and his actions were perceived as running away. Canepa Diaz was killed when stopped because, again, he was suspected as being part of another crime. The theme is the same, though, in that each of these young men was unarmed; although Canepa Diaz had a BB gun in his vehicle, he was not holding it during the shooting. As you can imagine, each of the families are suing the police departments for wrongful deaths. No arrests or charges were made of police at the time of this writing.

Consider the Hispanic ethnicity with the vicious crimes against one another. Something that is not often talked about is Hispanic-on-Hispanic crime that happens in America. These crimes, with the same ethnicity killing itself, are often underreported, as I pointed out earlier with white-on-white crime. I submit that it is underreported because there is not enough controversy to drive up the media attention. Let me give you some alarming statistics. In 2014, the murder rate for Hispanics in the United States was 5.73 per one hundred thousand, while the rate for whites was 2.52 per one hundred thousand.[245] Again, this is more than double the number of whites by Hispanics; think about the per-capita rate. These numbers are the raw numbers, but there are only fifty-four million Hispanics and 197 million whites in America; thus, the proportion of Hispanics dying from gun violence is incredible. Let me say I emphatically support gun rights, and my call for reconciliation means that people must change, not the guns. However, I do call for common sense gun reform to prohibit those with a mental illness or terrorists affiliations from obtaining weapons and a means to enforce the prohibition of automatic weapons on the streets of America. Remember, not only is this book about ethnicities reconciling, but it is about humanity finding a way to love unconditionally and to respect one another by stopping the violence in all ethnicities. It is about helping one another and not destroying one another. It is my hope that life is valued more in America, no matter which ethnicity we are referring to. Let's keep digging deeper with those of Hispanic descent. More than thirty-eight thousand Hispanics were killed with guns from 1999 to 2010, with more than two-thirds dying due to gun violence.[246] In 2011, FBI data also showed that 41 percent of Hispanic murder victims were under the age of twenty-four as compared to 40 percent of black murder victims and 22 percent of white murder victims being under the age of twenty-four.[247] Black murder rates are extremely different from what we are discussing here. They are simply incredible and hard to even fathom. I don't want to shock the reader, but according to the Violence Policy Center, in 2011, blacks were killed at a rate of 17.51 per one hundred thousand, and the national homicide rate was 4.44 per one hundred thousand.[248] Let's examine the numbers closely again for victims of murder: whites, 2.52 per one hundred thousand; Hispanics, 5.73 per one hundred thousand; and blacks, 17.51 per one hundred thousand. I wanted the reader to see this side by side. Further, if we were to average this out annually, this means out of the 197 million white population, on average, 4,925 whites are killed each year—0.000025, or .00, percent. Out of the fifty-four million Hispanic population, on average, 2,865 are killed each year—0.0000595, or .01, percent. Finally, out of the forty-three million black population, on average, 7,004 are killed each year—0.0001751, or .02, percent.

Ethnicity	National Homicide Rate	Annual Homicides
Whites	2.2 per 100K	4,925K
Hispanics	5.73 per 100K	2,865K
Blacks	17.51 per 100K	7,004K

Table Depicting National Homicides in 2011
(Violence Policy Center)

The disparity found in those proportions speaks volumes for what is going on in America. While I speak out against all murders and violent deaths due to homicide for all ethnicities, the deaths per year for blacks and Hispanics are eroding their populations. America, let's rise up to stop this violence against all population groups.

America has constantly had difficulties with immigrants throughout its history, and it was not only limited to blacks and Hispanics. Think about the ghettos in early America that were created for Italian American immigrants who were treated with disdain and disrespect when millions came to America in the late 1800s. They were discriminated against in housing, employment, economic exploitation, sometimes with violence.[249] In fact, one of the largest mass lynching in US history happened in New Orleans in 1891 when eleven Italians were lynched by a mob who thought at least nine of them had murdered Police Chief David Hennessy.[250] Following the lynchings in New Orleans, hundreds of Italians were arrested under the false pretext that they were all criminals. In Tallulah, Louisiana, a vigilante mob lynched three Italian Americans shopkeepers along with two Italian bystanders because they treated blacks with equal status in their shop.[251] I could go on about the terrible treatment Italian Americans received at the hands of American citizens. Most had to do with the erroneous links to mobster and criminal activity. Of course, there was an element of criminality in the Italian ethnicity, as there is with all ethnicities. White supremacist groups, such as the KKK, targeted Italians for violence throughout America and tried to ensure the supposed dominance of Anglo-Saxon Protestantism and defeat the spread of Catholicism.[252] The media has also been culpable throughout the years of portraying Italians with negative stereotyping of the men as low in intelligence and as gangsters, and the women as promiscuous.[253]

A full appreciation of how America has transformed requires a review and a reassessment of the social and academic climate that prevailed in the Western world and especially in North America before 1926 when Black History Month was established. It is important to recall that, between 1619 and 1926, African Americans and other people of African descent were classified as an ethnic group that had not made any contribution to human civilization. Within the public and private sector, African Americans and other peoples of African descent were continually dehumanized and relegated to the position of noncitizens, often defined as fractions of humans. African Americans were considered subhuman and subjected to denigration and humiliation. The family was fractured, and there were limited economic or educational opportunities. It is estimated that between 1882 and 1968, 3,446 African Americans were lynched, with most of the lynchings taking place between 1882 to 1920.[254] That means on average, forty-six African Americans were killed by lynching each year. By the way, the term *lynch* came from two Americans in the late 1700s, Charles Lynch and William Lynch, who were known for punishments and extrajudicial trials that eventually led to the so-called lynch law.[255] These were horrific crimes perpetrated against any ethnicity. Today the same African-descent ethnicity is killing itself at an alarming rate, given the size of the population. Specifically, the average over the last five years shows that more than six thousand died each year in violent inner city crimes. In May 2015, Baltimore had the highest murder rate since 1972 or in forty-three years, with forty-three young men killed on the streets of the city, and yes, almost 100 percent were killed by black-on-black crime.[256] Forty-three! That is an incredible tragedy and a sad number. Not to be outdone, in May 2015, Houston murders were up 40 percent from May 2014, and the Milwaukee murder rate was up 103 percent in 2015 as compared to 2014 at the same time.[257] Lives lost in the midst of violence. Most of the crimes seem to revolve around drugs and turf wars. Interestingly, in May 2015, both Dallas and Los Angeles showed a decrease of murders by 17 percent when compared with 2014 at the same time. There was an outcry by the Baltimore Police Commissioner—"All hands on deck"—that made headline news. What we did not see was an immediate rally and marches across America or in Baltimore for the vicious killing in the streets. There was no call for a tougher crime crackdown or any groups proposing interventions. Isn't it amazing that when we believe there is racial involvement in an incident (black versus white), it becomes a national phenomenon, but with forty-three dead, there is no rally or action. In fact, that same report happened in Boston, with violent crime and murder rising in many of the major cities across America.

The struggle for freedom was long and arduous, yet it happened. We must also remember that it was with the help of many European Americans, who were critical to transformation of America. I will repeat it again: Without the aid of European Americans and other ethnicities, African Americans could not have made the struggle to freedom. Every step of the way, European Americans were part of the catalyst to change. In fact, according to the Tuskegee Institute, 1,297 whites were lynched between 1882 and 1968, most often because they were seen as sympathizers with blacks.[258] Note that these numbers on lynching do not include Mexicans, Chinese, Italians, and others. On another note, in 1918, Republican Leonidas C. Dyer introduced what was known as Dyer Anti-Lynching Bill, but it was blocked by southern white senators.[259] Blacks and whites working together can effect change again, and in fact, the change I am advocating for cannot happen without the nation—that is, all Americans—coming together to fight through the old paradigm. It will once again take all people. We have to take action—change will only happen when *we* change. For instance, although we have already spoken about this case, the news concerning the murder of Michael Brown (young African American killed by a European American police officer) was interesting because the pundits on both sides of the debate agreed that this kind of incident happens every so often and gets major attention, but nothing else changes. Justice is either brought to bear or not—most would argue that justice is hardly ever brought to bear in these types of cases. The media makes a valid case that these events don't often lead to change. It is my desire that America will change through changing how we identify one another. When we can learn to identify one another, not by the color of our skin, but as Americans who may be from one heritage or another, true change will begin to manifest itself.

THE COURAGE TO STAND: A NEW AMERICA

Jackie Robinson, 1945, Brooklyn Dodgers, Major League Baseball

What is most interesting to me regarding taking down barriers of ethnicity and prejudice is the impact of sports, the military, and entertainment. This will not be an exhaustive review of those areas, but I thought I would highlight just a few examples. I have already alluded to the fact the military has been instrumental in bringing reconciliation to America, and later in this chapter, I write about the historical Tuskegee Airmen and what they had to face. My career could not be what it has been without the barriers being broken by giants who have gone on before me. Let's turn our attention to sporting events. When we participate in or attend sporting events today, our hearts and minds are far from the racial tensions that once dominated sports. There is something that changes when people of different ethnicities can come together to accomplish a mission. I do recall watching sports as a child and taking note that there were people of different colors playing together, whereas I grew up in an almost all black neighborhood. Who can forget Jackie Robinson, the first black in baseball's major leagues in 1945 with the Brooklyn Dodgers? Jackie Robinson had to face many barriers himself; he was taunted, called vicious racial names, and faced death threats from fans around the league.[260] Robinson's sacrifices crossed over from the athletic world into society. Further, we cannot forget the sacrifices of Jessie Owens, who in 1936, demonstrated in the Olympics at a time when people with brown skin color were considered inept that the color of one's skin did not make him or her inferior. Owens would ruin Germany's Adolf Hitler's erroneous racial views by winning four gold medals, breaking three world records, and resoundingly leading the United States to defeat Germany in the Olympic games.[261] All Americans were proud of Owens and what he did for America, yet when Owens returned home, he would have to face hatred and segregation in his home state of Alabama. Another group that many don't recall is the first team to have all blacks start in an NCAA basketball team in 1966. Texas Western, under the leadership of Don Haskins, made history and won the National Championship that season, even though they faced racial discrimination throughout the season and dealt with obscenities from the crowds that were antiblack and waving Confederate flags during the season and the championship game.[262] Think about Henry "Hank" Aaron, who in 1974 broke the major league's all-time home run record that had been previously held by the great Babe Ruth, with hit number 715.[263] Aaron received death threats throughout his run to the title as home run king because much of America was not ready for a black to lead in this category. Note, this was only ten years after many major civil rights laws had been passed. Similar to Jessie Owens, Joe Louis, in 1938, knocked out Germany's Max Schmeling in 124 seconds during a period when Nazi Germany was a rising power, and the match pitted democracy versus fascism.[264] It was an American victory received with joy and jubilation throughout the land, and for a moment in time, the color of one's skin didn't matter, albeit briefly, because it was an American who beat a German. In modern times, Tiger Woods, still arguably one of the top three golfers of all time, broke many racial barriers through golf, including showing that those of African descent could actually play the game of golf, even though some golf courses still restricted blacks from playing or joining until the 1990s.[265] I could go on with stories concerning Ernie Davis, the first black Heisman Trophy winner, from Syracuse, or Michael Jordan, who would break down many barriers for blacks in the advertising world, or Althea Gibson, the first African American woman to win the grand slam in women's tennis. It is interesting that these pioneers have a similar heritage in that they were cheered by fans during the games, yet despised, hated, discriminated against, and dehumanized by many in America following the games. Yet they also built many bridges with regard to ethnicity relations, and they helped others to see them positively despite the color of their skin.

Jessie Owens, 1936 World Olympics

I submit to you that these brave men and women shaped America through sports or entertainment and showed that we could go forward as humans. Despite all the barriers that were broken in every sport one can think of, I still remember reading stories about Venus and Serena Williams, speaking of the vicious taunting they had to deal with when they were early in their careers in the 1990s, a full forty and fifty years after many barriers were broken. They recall the name calling, harassment, being called the N-word, and other vicious terms, especially at the Indian Wells tournament, where one man said he wished they were still in 1975 so he could "skin them alive."[266] They were constantly harassed by some who thought they should not be playing the game of tennis.

All these incidents show the power of hatred. Even when these tennis stars had won Olympic gold for America, they were not considered American enough because of the color of their skin. Again, how could this be in the 1990s in America? Even in the National Football League (NFL), the stereotypes that blacks were not intelligent enough to lead teams still persisted in the late 1980s and early 1990s. At one time, it was doubted that blacks had the intellect to play quarterback in the NFL or to lead the team as an executive or as coaches in one of the major professional sports, only because they were a different color than the majority of Americans. Make note of this, because this was thirty to forty years following the time when blacks had to prove that they had the intellectual capacity to fly fighter jets and sophisticated aircraft or navigate large ships across the seas. Not only that, blacks were scientists, engineers, surgeons, general officers in the military, and holding high offices in Congress, yet their intellect was still questioned. How could there be any question about the color of one's skin qualifying him or her to play a game? Even in the early 2000s, it was a big deal in America for a black coach to lead a team into the playoffs or to win the Super Bowl. Again, I found it fascinating that we were still emphasizing the ethnicity of a coach or manager at a time in America when blacks had demonstrated excellence at every level and profession if given equal footing. Again, this is the discriminatory reference to whether or not blacks can be intelligent enough to coach a team to the highest pinnacle in sports. These have been headline stories—really! I actually find it insulting, more than anything else. It is amazing when one stops and thinks about that this is happening in our life time, not the past. From political office, astronauts, top scientists, chief executive officers, engineers, to neurosurgeons, blacks have shown the capability and capacity for great intellect at every level. Thus, I am baffled when ethnicity is emphasized as a discriminator in the performance of careers that are considered intellectual. It is time for America to move beyond the primitive ideas of ethnic division, where a person is considered inferior due to having brown skin. I personally believe America is still facing stereotypes with regard to ethnicities in almost every area of life, and it must be confronted.

Tuskegee Airmen (Planning Strategy)

As I said earlier, the military, like sports, was important with regard to demonstrating the intellectual capability of blacks. In fact, it was the military that led the way for racial integration in America. Groups such as the Tuskegee Airmen made a huge impact on the notion that African Americans were not intelligent enough to fly planes, with their complex and technical operations. Who among us can forget the famed Tuskegee Airmen of the 332nd Fighter Group and the 477th Bombardment Group, who broke the color barrier as pilots? Before 1941, blacks were not allowed to fly for the military. The Tuskegee Airmen regiment was formed to test whether the belief that blacks could fly combat aircraft was true or not. The training took place in Tuskegee, Alabama; hence their name. The Tuskegee Experience was formed by the Army Air Corps to train pilots, navigators, bombardiers, maintenance, support staff, and instructors.[267] The contributions of African Americans were considered inadequate, and African Americans were considered incompetent, not having the ability to fly the technical aircraft or to perform highly technical skills. Although serving as a separate division in the military and segregated, the Tuskegee Airmen proved the naysayers wrong and demonstrated what had already been demonstrated throughout history—all men are created equal, and their ability is not directly tied to the color of their skin or racial origin. The Tuskegee Airmen were instrumental in defending American bombers critical the war. The Tuskegee Airmen ended up flying 312 missions from June 1944 to April 1945, losing sixty-one of their own aircraft during combat missions, shooting down 112 enemy aircraft, and only losing an incredible twenty-seven bombers during those missions.[268] Although the Tuskegee Airmen were not the first to demonstrate to the world the intelligence of African Americans, they were pivotal in a time when discrimination and prejudice was rampant throughout most of the United States, and they changed the nation's perspective on what people of brown color could do. Additionally, even though no Tuskegee Airmen earned ace status, shooting down at least five enemy aircraft, many of them shot down at least four aircraft, and together they were awarded ninety-six Distinguished Flying Crosses. Of note, as you read consistently, change in America cannot happen in isolation, it must be America that changes and challenges the paradigms. For instance, the Tuskegee Airmen were not all black, but early on, many of the trainers and commanders were white. They supported blacks flying and wanted them to succeed.[269] Interestingly, the same argument was made for years in sports with regard to playing quarterback, directing/producing movies, coaching a team, running corporations, performing surgery, or producing records. In each of these instances, I actually witnessed much of history in the making as barriers were broken because African Americans were given an equal chance. I could not figure out why these firsts were such a big issue early on, but I soon learned why they were. These were milestones because America, 125 years after the Civil War, still did not totally believe African Americans could actually do everything European Americans could. Invariably, the milestones centered on the intellectual capacity of the African Americans.

While many of us can recall the Tuskegee Airmen, most do not know about the Golden Thirteen of the navy. In 1944, thirteen black enlisted candidates would become the first commissioned and warrant officers in the navy.[270] While not as famous as the Tuskegee Airmen, the Golden Thirteen serve as a reminder of the resilience needed to change the landscape of America. Each of the thirteen graduated, but only twelve were actually commissioned or graduated to the warrant ranks. However, they could not yet work on naval combat vessels and were limited to shore duty. Before they were commissioned, blacks were simply not allowed to serve in the officer ranks. They were relegated to labor duty. These men once again displayed excellence as they graduated with outstanding academic scores and served as valiant navy officers. I can remember news reports as little as two years ago with some European Americans rejecting treatment at major hospitals from African American doctors or nurses. Again, it is the subtle racism that still exists in America. I believe it is because of the polarizing way we view each other. I remember when we used to say that eleven o'clock on Sunday morning is the most segregated time in America—well, not much has changed—the majority of churches across America are still segregated on Sunday morning. I submit that not much has changed when it comes to intimate friends with the older generation. How could this be in 2017? It is because we still have polarizing terminology for one another—*white* and *black*. However, the millennials, like my children, are much more open to multiculturalism, and it will only continue to change for the better. My children also have an advantage because they grew up in the military. My son Shon's best high school friend was John, who was white. They were literally the best of friends until Shon went off to college and John joined the navy. John would walk into our house unannounced, and Shon walked into John's house much the same way. Both families accepted the boys and never did ethnicity come into play to hinder their friendship. Today they stay in contact, visiting one another occasionally, but I am not sure if they are as close as they were. In another case, an executive in a large corporation in America, who happens to be African American, has posted the heinous hate e-mail that is going on behind his back. The reason he found out about it was because another executive was trying to protect him and forwarded the e-mails he was receiving. The racist language that was used was a step back into the dark ages. But why was this happening? Some in America are not ready to accept equality for all, and in this particular case, the white executive believed that the black executive did not deserve the job. His goal was to ensure the black executive would not survive in the corporation. I will say it again: America has come a long way, but we have a long way to go.

You may not be convinced, but a good friend of European descent who was in the military shared a nice anecdote concerning the lingering racism that still pervades our society even in 2017. Her daughter was in a new school and started integrating with all of the kids, but she became fast friends primarily with girls of African descent. After a school session in which they were all sitting together again, a school administrator went over to her and told her, "You need to watch who you keep company with!" My friend's daughter was astonished, because the girls were not a criminal element and had done nothing wrong. She quickly realized she was in the Deep South, and this was a message from the teacher to maintain segregation and not get too close to friends who don't look like her. The problem was that my friend's daughter had been raised in a military community where we accept all people generally and are more likely to integrate racially in our personal lives, not just professionally. This was a shock, and her daughter refused to comply with the instructor.

On the other hand, there is the New Black Panther Party (NBPP), inciting violence with vicious hate speech through a rhetoric that calls for abolition of capitalism and a new unity for US blacks.[271] The NBPP on its website says it is against oppression of black and brown people who are basically fighting for their rights.[272] Further, the Southern Poverty Law Center classifies the NBPP as a hate group that is antiwhite, anti-Semitic, and espouses black supremacy.[273] These are the nonsensical positions I am fighting against in my book. Any group that feels it is superior to another group because of the color of its skin is confused and heading in the wrong direction. These views often espouse violence against the other groups that are seen as inferior. This rhetoric is hurtful to a strong America and counters unity and hope. It keeps us mired in the dark ages of racial injustice. The NBPP also faced charges for alleged voter repression and intimidation because some members showed up in Philadelphia with nightsticks in the 2008 presidential election. The NBPP members were arrested, but they did not face trial because the Justice Department decided to drop the charges.[274] Finally, the NBPP is criticized by the original Black Panther Party, that states that they do not espouse hatred for any other group, but love and respect for the black race. The NBPP has leveraged their legacy, with no real connection, for its own political gain.[275]

Another reason the terminology needs to change is that there is a growing multiracial population in America. In fact, in 2012, the Census Bureau estimated that 50.4 percent of all American children under age one is a minority.[276] The 2010 Census Bureau reported mixed ethnicities at 2.9 percent, but this number appears extremely low because many mixed ethnic people don't even know they are mixed.[277] In fact, we must remember that the mixed-race category was only recently added back to the census;

it was officially forbidden as an identification in the 1930s. Today there are still many who don't accept mixing of ethnicities because they believe it is wrong. Some even believe it is a sin according to the scriptures. Of course, there are no scriptures that forbid mixing of ethnicities except in the Old Testament, which dealt with the Israelites being set apart from pagan nations in order to preserve their focus on God and not turn to other gods. It had nothing to do with skin tone or ethnicity. For instance, Moses, the Hebrew leader of the Israelites in the Old Testament who led them from slavery, married Zipporah, who was of dark skin. Solomon, the third king of Israel, was known to have wives and concubines of all ethnicities, which did eventually turn his heart from God, not because the color of their skin, but because they worshipped other gods. Interestingly, the Bible says Noah had three sons, and they were evidently of different complexions and perhaps ethnicities. I spent time here to eliminate the scripture as a source for believing ethnicities should not mix. If mixing of ethnicities were a sin, how did Noah have children of mixed heritage? The essence of this section is that there is no medical or biblical reason to justify races not mixing. All of us are human, and the organs are the same for all humans. Everyday organ transplants have eliminated any claims that an African American organ cannot work in a European American's body or vice versa. Try telling a dying patient that we cannot give you an organ that came from someone of a different ethnicity! Ethnic hatred is really a human element and disposition that has nothing to do with the color of skin, but everything to do with the condition of the heart. Here is another critical question. What do you call a person of mixed ethnicity? Are they black, white, Hispanic, Asian, or other? I have noticed that, like me, if you have any brownness in skin, you are automatically black, even if you are half-white and half-black or Hispanic. Who made those rules? Is it the color of one's skin that determines it, or is it what society has established? Why isn't President Obama considered white? Clearly, if it is based on his biological ethnicity, he has both European and African DNA. The reason is simple: We have bought the notion that our skin color alone determines our ethnicity, and some have also accepted that certain colors are less intelligent or undesirable. This is why the ethnicity discussion is so complex. As stated earlier, it wasn't until 2000 that the US Census started allowing a mixed ethnic category again. Stop there for a moment. Take this in: It was almost a century before the US government allowed those of mixed heritage to begin to have an official category again. We must open our eyes to the truth. The reason ethnic mixing or categorizing was prohibited was to keep the ethnicities separate and, thus, preserve the social structure! A perfect example of the ethnic identification misnomer is what happened to me in the Pentagon recently. I saw a person who looked very African standing in the Pentagon, and I, like the average person, thought he was African until he opened his mouth. His language and accent were clearly Middle Eastern. I imagine he was Pakistani or from another region within the Middle East. Now, imagine for a minute if I had interacted with him and assumed he was African American—that most likely would have been insulting to him. Further, he would quickly have told me he is a Pakistani and not African. This is why identifying a person primarily by the color of skin cannot be the basis of determining who someone is. Another friend shared a story of how an instructor was trying to prove that ethnicities are made up and not truly a depiction of the genetics of a human. The professor picked random persons from his class of Kenyan descent, Irish descent, Finnish descent, and Asian descent and an African American. He then asked the class who, via DNA and genetics, they believed was the most similar. After hearing random answers, the professor explained that the closest genetically would be the Kenyan and the Finnish because of the origin of their DNA despite their geographical separation and clear differences in skin tone, hair type, and facial features. I think I have clearly made this case with my examples earlier in the chapter as well.

Dr. Carter G. Woodson, African American historian, author, journalist, and founder of the Association for the Study of African American Life and History

It was this kind of climate and the sensational, racist scholarship that inspired the talented and brilliant African American scholar Dr. Carter Godwin Woodson to lead the search for the truth and institutionalize what was then referred to as Negro History Week. A Harvard trained PhD, Dr. Woodson dropped out of mainstream academia to devote his life to the scientific study of the African experience in America, Africa, and the world. Under Woodson's direction and with contributions from other African American and white scholars, Negro History Week was launched on a serious platform in 1926 to neutralize the apparent ignorance and deliberate distortion of black history. Meetings, exhibitions, lectures, and symposia were organized to highlight the scientific study of the African experience throughout the year in order to give a more objective and scholarly balance in American and world history. During this era in the United States, racism was brutal and vicious. Those of African descent were humiliated in advertisements, writings, books, media of all sorts, and ridiculed for lack of intelligence and "bad" hair. Who could forget the minstrels and blackface characters that portrayed blacks as dancers, always smiling, with no intelligence or aptitude, basically as animals or property?

This is where we created our Jim Crow terminology, which grew into of a collection of denigrating views, laws, and treatment of blacks from the 1870s following the Reconstruction to the 1960s.[278] Jim Crow was not a person, but a character that represented minstrel shows, which, through song and dance, gave a negative portrayal of those with brown skin. Jim Crow was almost exclusively in the Southern states following the Civil War, with rigid antiblack laws and a system designed to oppress. Further, the education system did not support equal opportunities for learning, for it was only fifty years earlier when Africans were not allowed to read in the South—it was illegal to teach slaves to read. Teaching in school during that time reinforced the belief that those of African descent were unable to learn, as well as inferior in every manner thinkable. When I think about what early Americans of African descent had to endure, it is no wonder there is the incredible low self-esteem in the mid-nineteenth and early twentieth centuries. One only has to Google the offensive and egregious images that show the struggles those of African descent had to endure— signs stating, "Colored only," "I won't attend school with a Negro," or "We wash for white people only." There were signs that put Mexicans and Negroes in the same category as animals: "No dogs, Negros, Mexicans."[279]

It was a horrific time in American history and around the world, with some blacks treated as animals and placed on exhibition or in cages. For example, in the early 1800s through the early 1900s, blacks were often exhibited as oddities, especially if they had deformities, such as Saartjie "Sarah" Baartman (Hottentot Venus) from the Khoisan tribe of South Africa, who suffered from steatopygia (large fatty deposits in the buttocks). She was displayed in London and in Paris for her excessive buttocks and large female genitalia with purported elongated labia (although never on display).[280] Sarah does not appear to have been a slave, but a servant with limited rights who received a diminutive amount of pay for being on display. She died early in life in relative poverty in France. Other famous cases include the image of a young African girl in Brussels, Belgium, apparently being fed bananas while the large European crowd gazed at her, or many Africans on display at "Negro villages" in France and in the United States at world fairs, the Savage Olympics Exhibition, or exhibitions by PT Barnum and other exhibitors.[281] Make no mistake: this type of inhumane treatment was not limited to blacks but was extended to many people of different ethnicities who had deformities and were displayed in exhibits around the world. In the case of Africans, many of the exhibits were meant to continue to highlight the savagery, lack of intelligence, and inhuman status of the African in contrast to European superiority.

Here are some examples in the United States that continued to promulgate the false narrative of the superiority of whites and inferiority of blacks: A black male could not extend his hand to a white person, for it might be considered as the black saying he was equal with a white; a black male could not offer his hand to a white woman, for that could be considered rape; blacks and whites could not eat in the same restaurant unless there was a partition that separated them, hence "Colored to the rear"; and blacks had to sit in the very back portion of the bus.[282] We have indeed come a long way, but there's much work ahead. This behavior is sad and reprehensible to even type, but I must report it so we can never repeat this type of unthinkable behavior again. The Jim Crow system was definitely a systematically denigrating process in which Americans were relegated to despicable conditions. Whites were considered superior in all ways: intellectually, morally, and civilly, and any intermixing of the ethnicities would result in "mongrel" offspring that would destroy America.[283] Some would hold to those same ideas today, which is why I am sharing them—the battle continues.

Signs depicting separation of whites and coloreds

I want to end this section with a brief table on some of the rules that dominated the Jim Crow South. These rules were despicable, but they were part of the law of the South. This information was compiled by the Martin Luther King Jr. National Historic Site Interpretive Staff:

• Burial. The officer in charge shall not bury, or allow to be buried, any colored persons upon ground set apart or used for the burial of white persons (Georgia).
• Buses. All passenger stations in this state operated by any motor transportation company shall have separate waiting rooms or space and separate ticket windows for the white and colored races (Alabama).
• Child custody. It shall be unlawful for any parent, relative, or other white person in this state, having the control or custody of any white child, by right of guardianship, natural or acquired, or otherwise, to dispose of, give or surrender such white child permanently into the custody, control, maintenance, or support, of a negro (South Carolina).
• Education. The schools for white children and the schools for negro children shall be conducted separately (Florida).
• Libraries. The state librarian is directed to fix and maintain a separate place for the use of the colored people who may come to the library for the purpose of reading books or periodicals (North Carolina).
• Teaching. Any instructor who shall teach in any school, college, or institution where members of the white and colored race are received and enrolled as pupils for instruction shall be deemed guilty of a misdemeanor, and upon conviction thereof, shall be fined ... (Oklahoma).

Table illustrating some of the laws in the Jim Crow era
in America's South.[284]

Not only were blacks facing citizenship issues in early America, it is reported in the case of *US v. Bhagat Singh Thind* in 1923 that Asian Indians could not be citizens of the United States, because even though they were Caucasian, they were not white as their European descendants.[285]

The Fourteenth Amendment of 1868 made blacks citizens of the United States and of their state of residence; they became persons, no more slaves, and they could neither be sold nor killed by any owner. We must look at the facts that surround the division in our nation. When you see the protests that arise because of the shooting by police officers, we must consider that, in reality, the majority who are killed annually by police officers are of European descent. This is why this book is not about one ethnicity being persecuted more than another, but it is really about the nation coming together to remain the greatest nation on the planet. I am pushing for reconciliation in America. All people are valuable and all deserve freedom, protection, and their right to pursue happiness. We are a special nation, and I make no apologies for that. God has blessed America tremendously and we must live and treat each other in that way. It is time for America to move away from ethnic identification and see Americans as Americans, not as a color description. As I have stated, some think that blacks are the most violent in our society, and thus, that is the explanation often presented when justifying the greater intensity by police officers in high-crime areas. The problem with this on the surface is that it lumps all blacks into a category, and they are immediately perceived as a threat. It reminds me of the *Terminator* movies when Arnold Schwarzenegger was a robot who could sense if the individual he was facing was a threat or not. If they were a threat, he saw them in red, with all the data, and if not a threat, they were seen as green. That is what is happening in large part to blacks, in my opinion; they are seen as red immediately, identified as a threat based solely on their skin color. Perhaps this thinking comes from movies, music, media, television, and other venues in which blacks are often portrayed as violent. In fact, I will tell you during the black exploitation, or blaxploitation, film era of the 1970s, I often wondered if that was truly how all black people lived. Further, the black music genre consistently perpetuates the symbolism and glorification of violence. There is no doubt that the numbers indeed point out that blacks tend to commit more violent crimes than any other ethnicity, proportionately or per capita. Remember, blacks do not commit the most violent crimes in America as far as the number of crimes in a given year; that distinction is held by whites (I will cover this in later chapters). However, the violent crimes blacks commit proportionately cannot be denied or blamed on past racism, which is a real fact in history. The crime rate may be linked to poverty (we discuss this more in the coming chapters), but there still has to be accountability and responsibility in each community. Somebody has to stand up and tell the black community that you are killing and being killed disproportionally according to your population size. We cannot be silent. A recent study showed that between 1980 and 2008, blacks committed 52 percent of homicides and whites committed 45 percent of homicides.[286] Remember, homicide is only one type of violent crime. Again, on the surface, one might argue that there is balance between ethnicities, but this is a disproportionate number of murders compared to the number of people in the nation. Whites make up 62 percent of the population, while blacks only account for 13 percent of Americans; thus, blacks are disproportionally killing others and are disproportionally the victims of murder. In the same period, from 1980 to 2008, whites were victims 45.3 percent of time and blacks were victims 52.5 percent of the time.[287] Just as noted above, it is indeed interesting that with a population of only 13 percent in America, it is hard to justify being the victim 52.5 percent of time in all crimes in America. That would make anyone question feeling safe if you are of African descent.

In a similar study from 2013, the FBI reported that 38 percent of murders were committed by blacks compared to 31.1 percent of murders committed by whites and 29 percent of murders committed by persons of unknown ethnicity.[288] Even if you divided the unknown ethnicity murders evenly between whites and blacks, the result is the same; blacks are disproportionally, according to population size, involved in violent activity in America. This does not make all blacks violent, just as it does not make all whites violent, but it speaks to a higher propensity of blacks to be violent given the population size. I believe the facts are in, and the truth is that raw numbers of murders and victimization would almost depict both black and white as about the same rate, but it is just as clear that, because of the population differences, one can make an argument that blacks have demonstrated more violence consistently and proportionally since the 1980s. Notice I did not say blacks are more violent, but blacks proportionally demonstrate more violence than the rest of America.

In similar fashion, an analysis of the New York Police Department's "Stop and Frisk" law has revealed interesting numbers about who is more likely to carry a weapon. In 2012, the New York Police Department found a weapon in one out of every forty-nine stops for whites, one out of seventy-one stops for Latinos, and one out of every ninety-three stops for blacks.[289] This statistic has most likely gone unnoticed and has little impact on society despite it showing the opposite for potential violence. Further, I have shown that each of the major ethnicities in America is likely to be violent at the same rate when referring to raw numbers. Yet the perception in America is still that blacks are more violent as a whole. I will say that those blacks who commit violence certainly make a case to society at large to that effect. Their actions portray blacks as uncaring and violent in general. Likewise, the likelihood of finding drugs or contraband in New York when individuals are randomly stopped will also surprise the reader. In 2012, police found that they uncovered contraband in one out of every forty-three stops for whites, one out of fifty-seven stops for Latinos, and one out every sixty-one stops for blacks.[290] Again, these are the raw numbers; they must always be juxtaposed against the population size. Remember, whites make up 197 million of the population, and, all things equal, their numbers should be higher. If these numbers are compared to the population size, it will show that blacks and Latinos carry more contraband than whites per population size. One then must question that if the raw numbers are equal across all ethnicities for weapons, drugs, murders, violence, why is it that blacks are singled out for being a violent ethnicity? Is it only because of the population size, even though raw numbers are equal between whites and blacks in most categories? I am simply trying to call attention to the obvious. The disparity in the perception lies in who has controlled the perception over time and who has exacerbated that perception over the years. It makes one wonder if the stereotypes are an extension of the Jim Crow era. I submit that these perceptions are systemic. Now is the time for America to stand and say no more! We are all Americans, and there are law breakers across all ethnic lines, because that is the nature of humans.

There was a special on the History Channel in which a test was conducted to prove that Americans of all ethnicities—black, white, Hispanic, etc.—will more often shoot a black person who is perceived to be carrying a weapon more quickly than a white person who is perceived to be carrying a weapon. Interestingly, this reaction was consistent among both civilians and police officers. Similarly, I saw an article during my research in which police were a part of an experiment where a white male and a black male were walking down the street, both legally carrying AR-15s. In the two undercover scenarios, which used two sets of cops, the white man is confronted by police in a conversation but is eventually allowed to move on; however, in the second scenario, another set of cops orders the black man to lie face down. The police draw their weapons and aim them at the man.[291] The scenarios had several flaws. First, two sets of cops meant there would be two different reactions to the same stimuli; second, the black man's weapon was at his side, whereas the white man's weapon was behind him. Despite the flaws of the program, there are significant differences when one analyzes it from the human perspective. It is clear that the black man was treated with a much more aggressive style than was the white man. Again, as I have pointed out earlier, the statistics demonstrate that blacks are more likely to commit more crimes against blacks than against any other ethnicity, including law enforcement. The disproportionate number of violent crimes by blacks put police on high alert more often than not. Despite the high crime rates by blacks against blacks, it is interesting to note that whites are apparently more likely to commit mass killings in America than blacks, which could cause concern with someone white walking down the street with a large weapon (as in the experiment). No one understands this phenomenon of why whites more than blacks kill in mass, except we know that it leaves many innocent dead and many families mourning in the wake of their loss. Again, we in the white community (and I identify with that, given my ancestry)must come to grips with this inclination to mass violence and take responsibility, just as I have encouraged the black community (and I identify with that, given my ancestry) to do so. Further, according to the FBI, from 2004 through 2013, 511 police officers were killed feloniously by 540 offenders, with whites as the offenders 52 percent of the time and blacks as the offenders 43 percent of the time.[292] When the numbers are looked at over a longer period of time, there are not many changes. In fact, the FBI found that from 1980 to 2013, 2,269 officers were killed feloniously by 2,896 offenders, with whites as the offenders 52 percent of the time and blacks as the offenders 41 percent of the time.[293] Digging deeper, these statistics tell us three important things. First, in terms of raw numbers or actual police killed, whites kill more police than blacks. For instance, whites killed 1,506 police officers from 1980 to 2013, while blacks killed 930 police officers in the same period. Second, as I have pointed out earlier, in terms of proportionality, with blacks making up only 13 percent of the population and whites making up 62 percent of the population, they should not be even close statistically to killing the same raw number of police officers, but the fact is, they are. That means police will more likely feel more fearful and threatened when dealing with a black male than a white male. A closer examination reveals that if blacks had the same population as whites, approximately two hundred million, and killed police at the same rate they have from 1980 to 2013, 4,750 police would have been killed by blacks—that is basically five times the rate of whites. I know these are harsh statistics, but they must be dealt with. Blacks have to confront ourselves (and again, I identify with that, given my ancestry) and ask when the violence will stop. In this case, I can also ask when whites (I have to count myself in this group as well, due to my ancestry) will stop the violence against police.

Third and most importantly, the families of those who are killed are not wrapped around the statistics, for these are human beings; they simply know their loved one was killed in the line of duty while trying to protect each of us, and now those families are forever changed. Therefore, let me emphasize again that any crime against police officers is absolutely wrong. There is no justification, whether only a few in one ethnic group carries out the heinous crimes or a larger number does. The lives are taken, and that is what matters most. With over 1.2 million police officers sacrificing and putting their lives on the line daily for our safety, there is no reason I can think of to injure or shoot a police officer.

There should be mass protests in the streets of all major cities every week, given the heinous crimes that happen on the streets of America, especially in our inner cities. Most of the crimes are not across racial lines but are with each ethnic group killing itself. Thus, the call is for all Americans, no matter what ethnicity, to begin to take responsibility for the activities going on in each community. We can no longer simply point the finger and exclaim that the viciousness is a result of oppression in the 1700s and 1800s. I have literally watched guests on media talk shows justify the crime based on an oppressive America, versus saying that it the individual's responsibility to change and live with dignity. It is the family that must take responsibility for rearing a child with love, respect, decency, and honor. Men must step up and be the leaders of their families. We have too many absentee fathers in America. We need to rebuild America through rebuilding core values that we all agree upon, those values that our great nation was founded on. Where can I find those values? We find those values laced throughout the words of our US Constitution and Bill of Rights. Words such as *freedom, respect, pursuit of happiness, equality,* and *justice for* all are words we should stand on and live by. These are the core values we as Americans must strive to live by. We cannot continue to blame each other for the moral condition of our nation. We must look at ourselves. Change will not happen overnight, but change is inevitable; it must happen if America is to remain a great nation. The largest room in the world, as my old sensei would say, is the room for improvement.

Rachel Dolezal, a white female who portrayed to the world that she was black, poses an interesting case. Her story dominated the airwaves for weeks because it was so unique. It was almost unheard of, but I am certain it has happened in the past. Many did not have a problem with her wanting to be a part of the black ethnicity or to be identified as such, but the problem focused on the belief that she allegedly used her ethnic identification as a means to gain access into funds and job positions such as a leader of a chapter of the NAACP. Clearly she was of European descent, but for whatever reason, she felt she could no longer identify with the European ethnicity. Her parents pointed out that she was white, and the controversy forced Dolezal to quit. Likewise, another white female, Andrea Smith, professor of Native American studies at the University of California, portrayed herself as Native American or Cherokee.[294] But an investigation revealed that she in fact was not Cherokee, but white. As a professor and researcher on Native American studies, Smith believes that she is Native American no matter what her DNA says she is because she can identify as them. What is most interesting about both of these cases is that both women felt they identified with an ethnicity other than their own. Further, they both believed that they had to deceive others to fit into the ethnicity they identified with. However, it does me no good to fake my ethnicity in order to fit in. I would submit that the women should have only had to support the ethnicities without faking their identifications.

In another instance, I remember one of my relatives accusing the white police of only stopping blacks on the highway as we were taking a trip down the interstate. This conversation came up when a police officer pulled in behind me as we were going down the highway, Interstate 10. I did not slow down or fear other than the natural response—"Was I speeding?" I did not think about the color of the officer as compared to my color. I asked my relative why he would think this. I had traveled the world and never experienced, except on one occasion (while traveling throughout Europe and being apparently mistaken for Muslim), overt discrimination from the police. But my relative was responding from their perception and proceeded to state that the white officer behind me would pull me over. The officer never did pull me over, but I understood the perspective of my relatives. They grew up in an oppressive time when they were in fact stopped for being the wrong color, that is, of brown hue. As I was writing this section, I could not help but reflect on the time when I traveled in Italy. Because I was not in the sun as frequently as in the South, my skin tone was lighter, given my European heritage. Combine that with letting my hair grow a little longer and curlier, you have the perfect description of a person of Muslim affiliation from the Middle East. In fact, I was stopped three consecutive weeks in the Italian airport and asked for additional identification. I was picked out of the crowd of hundreds each time, when the police would confront me with their dogs in tow. I simply showed my military ID and was allowed to proceed after getting my bags. I was conducting counseling training throughout Europe, training chaplains and chaplain assistants to deal with impending air force manning reductions. I must admit that when I was stopped on the third occasion, I was quite frustrated and tired, and I did speak forcefully. I asked, "Under what grounds are you constantly stopping me, a United States officer serving in your country to aid in your protection?" The officers looked at each other and spoke in Italian, then simply waved me on. I was disappointed, but at the same time, I understood that I might have fit the description of a terrorist and they may have been getting credible tips of an impending plot—let's face it, I was traveling for three consecutive weeks, and of course, I stood out in the European crowd. I am not being sarcastic, because there are people who want to do us great harm because of skewed religious views. In that case, I wanted to cooperate, but it did get frustrating, as I stated. Remember, not all Middle Easterners are terrorists; in fact, the vast majority are not. To confirm how easily I can be mistaken for being Middle Eastern and/or South Asian, I share this quick anecdote. I was on a cruise with Madeline in the Caribbean, and I was going on a scuba diving equivalent excursion. I noticed that a mother of two who was on the excursion with her husband, most likely associated with the Muslim faith or perhaps from the Middle East or South Asia (she was wearing her hijab), kept looking at me in a strange way as we were riding on the small boat to the diving location. Finally, after a very awkward ride to the diving site, she spoke up and asked if she could take my picture, for I reminded her of her younger brother who had just died of cancer in Pakistan (Pakistan is considered to be a part of South Asia and has also been included with the term, Middle East gave her permission, of course, and she sent her two young daughters to also take pictures with me. That was a sad moment, yet joyful, because I brought a smile to her face in the midst of her grieving, but it illustrates how one's ethnicity can evoke two extreme responses. Unfortunately, some police officers still give cause for concern when they pull you over. Consider the case of Sandra Bland, who was arrested from what initially appears to be an overly aggressive confrontation with a Texas State Trooper, Brian Encina, in Prairie View, Texas.[295] She was pulled over for not using her turn signal when changing lanes. Instead of a simple ticket or warning, the state trooper became angry and aggressive because Bland also seemed somewhat aggravated by the stop and engaged in the confrontation with the state trooper. The situation escalated after Officer Encina checked Bland's license and registration and he threatened to Taser her. He demanded she get out of the car and stated he was arresting her (although there did not seem to be a cause). The officer became very aggressive, yelling, and begin tugging at Bland. This was truly unnecessary, and the escalation was out of hand. Once out of the car, after a slight tussle and yelling, you can only hear of the violent arrest and altercation. Some unclear footage from a cell phone shows Bland on the ground, and you can hear her complaining about her face being pushed to the ground and her arms hurting. Three days later, Bland was found dead in her cell. The jailers allegedly did not comply with the required hourly checks, and even though Bland had indicated she had attempted suicide in 2014 because she lost a child, they did not take precautionary measures, such as removing items that could be used to commit suicide. Bland was trying to raise the $5,000 bond to get out of jail but was unsuccessful. According to reports, she did not eat, was emotional, and cried consistently during the three days. This was simply an unnecessary death that is still surrounded by mystery. The initial autopsy showed that indeed Bland died of suicide.[296] The officer was placed on paid administrative leave. This case made national headlines because of the aggressive manner of the arrest for a seemingly routine traffic stop, the fact that it was a white officer arresting a black woman, and then the tragic ending. Bland was charged with assaulting an officer, but it is clear she did not assault the officer in the beginning of the altercation. The officer's report has been questioned for inaccuracies and disparities with the officer's camera. The family questioned whether Bland actually killed herself; they believe that foul play could have caused her death. Bland had just accepted a job at Prairie View A&M University, her alma mater, in Prairie View, Texas.[297] Prairie View is an area that is still known for its racial divide; there have been tensions between the ethnicities in recent years with allegations of discrimination from law authorities.[298] At the publishing of this book, Bland's family was paid approximately $1.9 million for damages.

In yet another instance, a white police officer, James Frascatore, aggressively arrested former tennis star, Jeff Blake, mixed ethnicity (mulatto), while he was waiting for a car to pick him up and take him to the US Open.[299] Blake, once the world's No. 4 ranked tennis player, was seemingly minding his business and calmly checking his phone, leaning on the pillar outside of a Hyatt Hotel in Manhattan. Undercover Officer Frascatore ran up to Blake and started the aggressive arrest; he did not ask questions or ask for identification—Blake was mistaken for a person who was illegally selling cell phones. He aggressively tackled Blake to the ground, pushing his face on the ground and kneeing him in the back. Luckily, Blake did not resist arrest, and he survived the encounter, though he suffered a cut lip and a bruised leg—he was released after fifteen minutes. Officer Fascatore has been reassigned while the internal investigation is pending for his behavior and tactics. By the way, Officer Fascatore has been accused of aggressiveness in at least five other cases.[300] The New York City Police Commissioner, Bill Bratton, and Mayor Bill de Blasio publicly apologized for the incident. Police Commissioner Bratton went on to explain that in the past year, more than $29 million has been spent on police training to help them curb this aggressive style of policing. He noted a department violation in the delay of filing a report on this incident.[301] Blake, who was actually on his way to the US Open for corporate appearances, has vowed to speak out on this issue and has already stated that what happened to him was not uncommon at all. He also acknowledged that most police officers are not like Officer Fascatore. I wonder how this case would have turned out if the officer had treated Blake as a professional and a human being, by walking up to him, asking for identification, and explaining to him why he was questioning him. Officer Fascatore would have most likely apologized for the inconvenience and walked away after seeing that he had the wrong person and most likely would have been embarrassed. That is what should happen, but it doesn't. Go back to my earlier points that all too often police confront those of brown hue in a more aggressive manner, generally speaking, with regard to stops, arrests, and questioning. It is important for me to also highlight that it is a vicious system with many people of brown hue, disproportionately to society, showing aggression. In other words, each disposition, the police and those of African descent, becomes a cause and effect in this example—it is not linear but circular. They play off each other in a vicious cycle. I am not making excuses for aggressive police behavior, but I am trying to shed light and identify possible causes. I'm not making excuses for those of African descent who would disproportionately show aggression when compared to society at large. Slavery, heinous as it was, or poverty, does not justify the behavior that I see today by our young men of African descent. I discuss this later, and I will show the crime rates as they relate to poverty. I will show how poverty affects everyone, not just people of one ethnicity or another. We need respect and unconditional love for one another, and I devote an entire chapter to this later in the book in order to create a real difference.

Again, these kinds of examples only show that the mind-set of ethnicity is entrenched in American society. When the average minority sees this type of aggressive behavior in a routine traffic stop, it makes them fearful of the police, rather than trusting the police. Again, I trust and believe in the police officers who protect us. There are some, however, who will make these types of aggressive moves unnecessarily and cause distrust for all police officers. I personally believe one of the greatest things to happen in America is the intermixing of the ethnicities. I know that this is easier for me to state, given my heritage. The reason I believe that it is beneficial is because it will change the landscape of America. As I have already pointed out, there are many who believe that by 2050, America will no longer have any one ethnicity with more than 50 percent of the population. This means that adults in the near future will most likely marry other ethnic groups or intermix, and thus, through generations, dilute the purity of any one group. This means my vision of an America where everyone is known as American first will become closer to being achieved. The division by ethnicity will become much harder to endorse. Remember that in the first few chapters I have shown how the intentional division, separation, and distinction of ethnicity has been the main catalysts for prejudice and discrimination in

America. Of course, there are some who preach sermons of hatred against this type of intermixing. It is amazing how the color of one's skin makes such an impact in our lives.

I have several friends with the disease of vitiligo; in fact, my dad developed it in his later years, and it covered parts of his body. Vitiligo changes the pigmentation of one's skin from brown to very fair, as if they were Caucasoid. With the change in color, a change in how one is treated often follows. It seems that the lighter one's complexion is, the more society as a whole is likely to embrace or disdain you, according to your viewpoint. I was reading an article online where a man, Luke Davis, who has the disease of vitiligo, began noticing that he was treated differently while living in Britain. He went on to report that he received a job as at a particular establishment, and he later found out that it was the color of his skin that got him hired. He went on to state that management pulled him aside and assured him he did not have to worry about blacks being hired at his establishment.[302] Luke said he did not accept the job once he was told that. Do you think this incident took place in the 1960s? No, it was in 2009! This is blatant racism based on the color of skin. Of course, the management did not realize they were actually talking to and had hired a black person. This is why I am so adamant that we must deal with this issue as Americans. This madness must stop. We can become the generation of change. This establishment would not have hired this man if his skin was a different color. It is so ingrained in our society that one color is better than the other or inferior to the other. Again, this happens on both sides of the color spectrum and with all of the colors in between. An associate and I were discussing the book during my writing and research stages, and she shared with me how her child, who is white, had recently commented that he was glad "Daddy and you are not black, because you would be dirty." Where did that thought come from? I know it wasn't the mother or the father, but perhaps it is what we subliminally teach in society at large. The mother quickly explained to her child that being black does not mean dirty and how we are all different just as if you had a bag of Skittles—they have different colors, but they taste the same. This is why I believe it is time for America to do something different and take the risk to change how we describe one another. I am not trying to take away the meaning of black or white, but I am saying let's not identify humans as colors. Do we call Chinese yellow or Indians red or Egyptians brown? Of course not;

as I stated, it would be offensive to label them with a color designation. Let's begin to reconcile through changing the nomenclature we use to identify the ethnicities—in fact, let's get rid of so-called races altogether and recognize the human race as one. Now is the time to move forward as Americans.

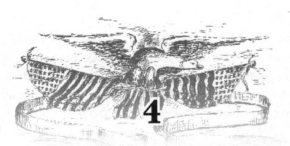

4

ELIMINATING DIVISIVE
LANGUAGE AND THOUGHTS

Their cause must be our cause too. Because it is not just Negroes, but really it is all of us, who must overcome the crippling legacy of bigotry and injustice. And we shall overcome.

—President Lyndon Johnson,
address to Congress, March 15, 1965

President Lyndon Johnson Addressing Congress in 1965

Perhaps one of the most devastating things we can do in America is label each other with derogatory names. Derogatory names speak to the unlearned and uneducated. Name-calling limits our growth and potential and keeps us locked in a system of separation. Unfortunately, in some nations outside of the United States, we have become known as the nation where the use of these terms is commonplace. I experienced this when I was traveling abroad to Poland in early 2014 and had an encounter with two men from Sweden. We started talking about American culture, and it was amazing that these men clued in on the negative terminology found in our movies, music, and culture in general. One of them started imitating a movie and called me the N-word with a Texas accent (it was only indirectly toward me). I was caught off guard but not shocked. They thought it was perfectly normal to call me that name (they truly meant no harm, in my opinion) or use it in conversation with me because I was brown, yet it only highlights what I think is the problem. People see movies and hear music using the derogatory terms and believe these words are acceptable. Others may not have reacted as calmly as I did and might have become very angry. In fact, my friends of European descent interjected and led them to change the conversation. I was grateful to my friends for coming to my rescue. I have been told by my friends around the world that our own media, rappers, and music influence those around the world and convince them it is acceptable to say the N-word.

Let me share another example of how we as Americans can set bad examples for the world at large with our divisive language. A friend of my son who was of African descent was telling me about his experience in high school befriending a Russian student. As they grew closer, the Russian student began to use derogatory terms and called my son's friend the N-word. My son's friend had to explain that this was not acceptable. The Russian student was caught off guard; he meant no harm. The Russian student said he did not mean it as racism but explained that he thought he was simply calling the student from African descent "what he was." My son's friend had to politely explain that he is not an *N-word*; he is a human who happens to be of a different color or hue. These stories happen every day in our younger generation. Change is needed now. We must change every media outlet that continues to spew words of hate and discord. I see people joke about language and name-calling all the time, but when you dig deeper, you find that it is truly hurtful, even among the same ethnicities.

I submit to America that the problem is not just the N-word but any derogatory word or slur that hurts any ethnicity, such as the h-word or the c-word for Europeans or the s-word for Latinos. What about the derogatory names used against women? As I was researching material for this book, I found that there are two hundred or so derogatory and racist names for all people groups. Of course, I will not list them here. I was amazed at the list, but it also confirms human nature and what we can do or say about one another when there is hatred instead of love for our fellow humans. How did these slurs come about? I believe they came about through a misunderstanding of who we are as humans. In other words, if I see people of different complexions or physiological features as inferior, then I am more apt to deem a person who is different on the outside as different on the inside. As I have demonstrated in this book, nothing could be further from the truth. We are all humans, and once we honor that, we will begin to see the harm in racial slurs and disparaging terms. The point is that we must recognize that no people group should be called out of their name. It does not matter if one has origins from Asia, the Pacific region, or the Middle East, derogatory phrases said openly or in private are not helpful to building a society in America where all people come together. Let me emphasize that my experiences have shown that most racial slurs about other ethnicities are not used in public but in private, often with others who have a similar view or who look the same. Some of the videos that have gone viral on the Internet have been indicative of the bandwagon effect, in which once one person begins the racial slurs, and others feel compelled to jump in with similar slurs. Unfortunately, this is where we also begin to shape the future to repeat the past, as our children hear the racial slurs and begin to also identify with racial bias. Thus, racial prejudice and discrimination are passed on from generation to generation. I am convinced by the empirical evidence I have seen that if racial differences are not emphasized in young children, they will grow up with an open love for one another and without prejudice. Consider adopted children who are different ethnicities from their parents. In fact, we have all seen children of different ethnicities loved by parents of a different color. Try to tell those children that their father or mother is negative due to skin color, or tell the parents their children are animals or inferior because their kids have a different texture of hair or a different skin tone. It won't happen, and I believe genuine outrage will take place. This is the type of America we are pushing for, one where all people are respected and have the opportunity to excel.

I know I lean heavily on the military for my lessons of social life and my quest for acceptance of all and equality, but it is for good reason. I know I have spoken about the leadership of the military in confronting ethnic divisions, but it is not always perfect. For example, in early 2015, according to the *Army Times*, an army unit at Fort Wainwright, Second Platoon, C Company, Third Battalion, Twenty-First Infantry Regiment, had allegedly created Racist Thursday in their unit to "build camaraderie."[303] Every member of the unit was allowed to use racial slurs and call any other person a degrading name without the fear of facing punishment for violating the Uniform Code of Military Justice and various regulations and DOD policies that explicitly prohibit such language. Evidently, the outcome of this incoherent policy led to the suicide of a soldier, Pvt. Danny Chen, who was of Chinese descent and who allegedly shot himself as a result of the taunting.[304] Of course, army command and leadership have been investigating the situation. Unfortunately, these behaviors are covert and still happen today, even in the military—this is just one example. This is why these types of events have to be shared. What the military has taught me is that even though we are not perfect, there is a quest for rightness. The military leads the way in equality for people of all hues and all genders. Over the years, some have challenged the fairness of the officer and senior enlisted promotion systems in the military because there is some subjectivity in selection of promotees. Today the military services are pushing for inclusiveness and diversity throughout the forces. When derogatory phrases are used among the same ethnicity, and that ethnicity says it is okay to call itself the name, it is incongruent. This is nonsensical to me. Why would I permit the use of a negative word among those who look like me and then get angry when someone who looks different from me uses the same word? The excuse I have heard is that it carries a different meaning when coming from someone other than a person of your same ethnicity. Again, this is simply a justification, a thought that has been accepted to justify calling oneself negative names. Some even go as far to say they use racial slurs as a term of endearment because they really care for the person. So the spelling or enunciation is modified and that makes it different. Really? If I am to understand this correctly, I must accept that when I am called the N-word or h-word or whatever negative slang I am called, it's because you love me? It goes against common sense and does not compute for me. In fact, it is a lie of self-hatred and low self-worth. I will discuss this in more detail later in the book.

I was in graduate school at Columbus State University working on my master's in community counseling when I encountered this subject in relation to counseling people of different cultures. I recall a heated discussion that arose concerning the use of the N-word. The young lady in my class felt the N-word should be able to be used if you are of African descent; however, if you were of European descent or any other ethnicity, you could not use the N-word. She was African American and on her way to having a great career, but her viewpoint was very much skewed, like many in our generation today. She thought that the N-word was harmless and did not mean the same thing that it meant in the old days. Of course, she had no real experience with the word when it was used at the height of slavery or in the Jim Crow era. I relayed to her that she was missing key concepts with the use of this word in history. In fact, I went on to inform her that it is that type of thinking that perpetuates hatred and ignorance. I realize that an entire generation, including celebrities, has been pushing for a change and use of the N-word, but it is not right. I had to constantly remind her of the origin of the word and meaning.

The N-word is a negative term for a dark-skinned person. It was a derivative of the word *negro,* meaning *black* in Spanish. It has become one of the most divisive terms in the history of America and perhaps the world. Why? It is divisive because it speaks to the vile treatment of African Americans and serves as a humiliating term for all people of brown skin. By the way, the N-word was linked to other derogatory names for other ethnicities as well. If the word were acceptable, we would not have the reaction we have to it when it is used by leading authorities and public figures. Imagine a congressman or senator of today using that word as he or she speaks about a person of African descent. His or her career would be destroyed within hours as social media and the news outlets spread the news. Paula Dean, who built a multimillion dollar empire as a Southern chef, suffered greatly with her use of the N-word, calling for waitresses and waiters to dress as slaves at a dinner party, and using anti-Semitic language.[305] How could we forget Dr. Laura Schlesinger, the talk show host who was fired for repeatedly saying the N-word on air after a caller who was black asked for help to deal with her white husband's family and friends who use racial terms, including the N-word.[306] She was actually making the same point I am trying to make—that it is hypocritical for people of brown skin to use the word as if it is acceptable, but to express outrage if someone else utters the same word. She was actually quoting some of the HBO comics and others who make millions of dollars using the word freely because they are black, yet criticize anyone who is different for using the word and getting very sensitive about it. I don't think she was wise at all in the way she went about getting her point across, but her intent makes sense. Schlesinger actually apologized, to no avail in saving her talk show, and wrote in her blog, "I didn't intend to hurt people, but I did. And that makes it the wrong thing to have done. I was attempting to make a philosophical point, and I articulated the N-word all the way out—more than one time. And that was wrong. I'll say it again—that was wrong."[307]

Let's take it further. As I have stated, I cannot go on air as a newscaster or politician and use such phrases without grave consequences to my business or profession. What is even more confusing is that the same people who would protest Paula Dean for calling her employees the N-word will turn around and call themselves the same N-word and think they are justified in doing so. This is faulty reasoning. It is baffling to me. Why could sportscasters and public figures be removed almost instantly for using the N-word or other slang against women or other ethnicities and those of African descent can use it constantly against one another and say nothing is meant by it? It makes no sense! I believe I have said this several times—it makes no sense! On the football field or basketball court, you can sometimes hear professional players using the N-word. In 2014, the National Football League stated they wanted to fine or discipline those who used the N-word while playing the game, but they could only penalize them in the game. NFL rules committee member Jeff Fisher stated, "It [Rule 12, Unsportsmanlike Conduct] states that, 'Using abusive, threatening or insulting language, or gestures to opponents, teammates, officials, or representatives of the league is unsportsmanlike conduct.' The N-word would fall under that category. The officials will be empowered to call a foul if there are racial slurs or statements regarding another player's sexual orientation, or even bating and insulting with verbal abuse. It falls under that. It is going to be a very significant point of emphasis."[308]

It is a nice attempt, but equivalent to an average person being sued for 0.5 cents every time they use the word. I want to emphasize how this speaks to America's hypocrisy. How can we remove a sportscaster for saying the N-word, yet only give a minimal fine to the NFL player? This is an outrage. In the military, I could face disciplinary action for using that derogatory term and face charges under the Uniform Code of Military Justice. Further, why is the NFL trying to do this? It is obviously because many of the players of African descent are calling themselves derogatory names. Do you see how outrageous this is? The NFL has to regulate what people of African descent call each other! If this does not convince you of the need to change, nothing will. I will also state the obvious. If a football player of European descent were to openly make the same derogatory statement toward those of African descent in the NFL, you would have broadcasters, news media, and the Internet deploring these statements and calling for the player to be removed, suspended, or heavily fined. This is an amazing hypocrisy. Again, those who use the negative words justify it by saying the intent or meaning is different when I use it! When the word is used regularly and portrayed as normal, it will then begin to become a part of the apparatus that divides the nation. Note the OU case in the previous chapter with racist language being used. How did it make those entertainers, movie stars, and rappers feel when they heard about the story? Did they get angry and retort with their own racial slurs? Why should they get offended when they are perpetuating this hateful and disgraceful term? That is the hypocrisy I am writing about. Negative racial terms cannot be selectively used by some ethnicities and forbidden to others. The words must be ended, period!

Despite my outcry, as I have stated, there is an entire culture that believes it is okay to use the N-word. These people use the term like candy, not knowing or caring what it meant or means. Music moguls are using it more and more in their lyrics, and that is very disappointing and offensive. I get offended if I am at a movie and a song comes on from the hip-hop genre that uses the N-word, or if I am getting gas and someone pulls up at the station with rap lyrics spouting out the N-word like it is nothing, not caring about the origins of a word that was meant to represent hatred, denigration, and humiliation. How could we let our children (of any ethnicity) listen to music that is filled with hatred and derogatory lyrics? Don't we know the struggle and the battles that were fought over that word? Not only do top music artists push the use of the N-word in their songs, but they also spout out hatred and belittling of women or police officers. The problem is further exacerbated in our society when some parents use a slang word that is acceptable to them and they call their children derogatory words. Many try to use a derivative of the N-word by adding an *a* on the end of the word, versus *er*. This does not change anything. No matter how one tries to spin it, the use of the word, even a derivative of the word, is wrong, and it is not a term of endearment. It still represents the past hurts of millions, lynchings, beatings, and vile treatment. This word meant you were less than human, and others could do what they wanted to you—yes, even murder you for looking the wrong way. As I write this book, the hit TV show *Empire* is having great success in the ratings with rave reviews for its raw look at life and the music world. It is produced and directed by those of African descent and stars largely those of African descent. This is unique for TV in some respects. However, at the peak of its ratings, the producers went to the ultimate offensive level for me and used the N-word in primetime on national TV. Again, how can we allow this to happen in our society? There were no articles written the next day to blast this type of language on national TV. This is unfortunate, but yet accepted by American society. Producers justify it to show realism of what is being listened to and what happens in the inner cities of America every day. I do not support or understand their position, and we must take a stand. I am for freedom of speech, but there are limits. I cannot go into the movies and yell, "Fire, fire, fire!" if there is no fire. That is a crime, and it will get me arrested. I can't make threats against the president or Congress and not be arrested. Nor can I go on a plane and yell, "I have a bomb!" While society can easily understand that the above examples trump freedom of speech under the First Amendment, they cannot understand how using certain slang and derogatory words should also be banned. Again, I point to the military as a great example. I cannot use derogatory phrases in the military without punishment. I am calling for the N-word to be banned in society. According to some news reports, *Webster's Dictionary* has finally realized that the N-word should not be linked to those of African descent. Perhaps it will be changed in the next edition, although I could not find a definitive source for this claim. We do know, however, that many have pushed year after year, calling for Webster's publishers to remove the disparaging definition of the N-word. A recent article called for the removal again as *Webster's Dictionary* and at least thirty other available sources cite the N-word as "a black person," followed by definitions of a member of any dark-skinned race and a member of a socially disadvantaged class of persons.[309] I recall trying to teach my children that the use of this word, like foul language, was strictly forbidden. They accepted it and understood why it was negative to use the N-word or any other racial slang against any ethnicity. They understood early on, but as they grew older, they challenged me about my concept of forbidding the word. The reason was because they were beginning to experience the culture of America through school, music, media, and their friends, which allowed them to question the values my wife and I were trying to instill within them. I specifically recall one of them telling me, "Dad, one person cannot change the world!"

"Of course one person can," I replied. "Have you not heard of George Washington, Abraham Lincoln, Mahatma Gandhi, Rosa Parks, George Washington Carver, Frederick Douglass, Franklin Roosevelt, Nelson Mandela, Mother Teresa, or Martin Luther King Jr.?"

I realize none of the above changed the world by themselves, nor were they perfect, but they were a part of a moment or movement in history when they were elevated to lead and change a generation. The above are just a sample of the hall of fame that I could list to fill the pages of this book. I tried to emphasize to my children that, no matter what, you must stand for what is right, even if you stand by yourself. My kids were emphasizing that if the rest of society is doing it, then we might as well accept it. By the way, many of the same people who lobby for the Confederate flag to be removed because it represents past racial hatred are the same ones who would decry that somehow that using the N-word is not representative of the past, claiming they can change the meaning of the word today. Well, that would be hypocritical, because those who support the Confederate flag on state buildings hold to the same principle, saying that the meaning for them is not hatred. The fact is that both cases, the N-word and the Confederate flag, represent an era of hatred and disdain, and neither should be acceptable in our society.

As I have stated, the music world is known for using words that cut down women and belittle their self-worth, yet sales continue at record pace.

Rappers have made millions of dollars with raw language and the N-word. Thus, the revenue says my argument against the use of racial epithets is futile. Additionally, young Americans are bombarded with lyrics that talk about inappropriate acts of sex (much too early for most of the listeners), such as placing sperm on one's clothing like Monica Lewinsky or "sexing" a person out. This is what sells in America. Sex sells. However, I think we can all agree that a child at eight or ten years of age knows far too much about sexuality, and it is not age appropriate. I am not saying we need to go to the media days when saying the word *pregnant* was forbidden on television, but our standards have been consistently lowered. What would have been deemed only allowable in an R-rated (restricted) movie is now commonplace on television, on the Internet, and in the movies. I recall as parents of younger children often trying to figure out which movie to take them to, based on the ratings. Over time, the ratings became more difficult to use as a barometer of what would be shown. Now, we have a larger issue; the younger generation (the millennials and beyond) have a different world view, and they are soon to be the exclusive ratings determinants. That will change and is changing our society as we know it. Given the above, we still complain about the denigration of morals in our young Americans when the changes to what is morally acceptable have actually been like the frog in the slow boiling water. Perhaps artists hide behind music to spout lyrics because of the taboo on words that are not generally acceptable in our society. Why would I pump these negative lyrics in my heart and consciousness daily? Does it have to do with being accepted or believing that one is less than the other?

Perhaps those are not all the reasons for the projection of denigrating terms or low self-esteem, but I submit that a large part of subjecting oneself to those types of lyrics has to do with how a person sees himself. My hypothesis is as follows. If a people group has been berated for decades and even centuries and subjected to poverty, lack of education, societal disdain, lack of knowledge, emotional and physical abuse, and murder, there is a high probability that the person will not see him- or herself in a positive light. Thus, if I see myself as nothing or as an N-word, then I don't mind the lyrics. It is almost as if I accept what society has labeled me from the slavery or Jim Crow eras. The problem is that society as a whole is no longer labeling me with these terms—it is actually forbidden in mainline society, for the most part, with the exceptions previously mentioned. Imagine going on a job interview, walking into your potential employer's office, and saying, "What's up, my N-word?" as you extend your hand? Or what if you go into a female executive's office and call her the b-word or the h-word because you are not getting paid enough or are unhappy with practices of the corporation? In both cases, you will either never get employed or will find yourself fired or relieved quickly and perhaps sued in court based on the circumstances. I think most reading this book understand that concept, yet we try to justify using derogatory terms in recreational activities based on who uses the terms. When will we stand up and say this is not acceptable anymore? All we have to do is stop supporting entertainers, movies, stand-up comics, and singers who choose to hurt American children with negative lyrics. America does not force anyone to idly support these types of lyrics or words—indeed, it is a choice by each individual to purchase these products and support such lyrics or entertainment.

Why are these words so offensive to me? It is because of the history of the words. It hurts the nation and destroys people. The use of the N-word means a person is nothing, the lowest human on earth, with no knowledge, education, or dignity. It is a pejorative word that represents one of the most vile times in the history of mankind. Likewise, the use of the h-word or WT against Europeans was developed as a way to counter the N-word. These words too are vicious and should not be used. However, there is one difference; you don't often hear those of European descent calling themselves racial slurs. The N-word and its history is rich with vileness. It is abusive and insulting. Articles, cartoons, and other media would use the N-word to depict blacks as ignorant, lazy, nonhuman, and unintelligent. Again, it is not just the N-word that offends me, but all negative words said about one ethnic group or the other. Further, I do not believe in or support the movement that tries to redefine derogatory words as words of affection. That is not my love language—we must stop this madness. I want to continue to explain why I am so offended. Let me give you more on the history of the use of slang against other ethnicities over the ages.

In the very beginning of America, there was the natural battle to assimilate all Americans into one people group. If you had a different culture, it needed to be subjugated to the "American" culture. We were called the "great melting pot," as people groups were expected to assimilate and become American once they arrived in our great land. The only question was whose America was it? As you know, I want us all to be assimilated into our America, but the key word is *our*. Did the melting pot mean that all people had to look alike, talk alike, dress alike, and so on, to be accepted? I submit that was part of the problem and the birth of racism, prejudice, and discrimination in America. We tried to place everyone in the same category, and when they were different and could not change (skin color, language, ethnicity, etc.,) they were ostracized and seen as a threat to what was the new normal. If you were a person of Irish or Spanish descent in America in the early 1900s, you would have found an America that did not accept you because you were different. Many cultures, such as the Jewish, Hispanic, Italian, and Irish, were subjected to humiliation and degrading terms that I refuse to name here. I went to another website that listed thousands of derogatory names. Some people were beaten, ostracized, and murdered for being different, basically disenfranchised in the land we call America. This is why it is so important for our new America to be an America that celebrates all people and all ethnicities. I am not calling for a society where we look like the robots from the movie *I Robot*. Nor am I looking for a society where we can't tell who is who, because we all dress the same, talk the same, act the same, and look the same, as in a futuristic movie. Again, this was tried in America to some extent, and it failed. I am calling for an America where diversity is celebrated and all people have the opportunity to reach their goals and excel. We will not look the same or even listen to the same music or have the same interests, but we will have general respect for one another, not just tolerance. Tolerance is when we put up with inconvenience, whereas respect recognizes the value in others and demonstrates a genuine appreciation for who they are.

Change in America will only truly begin when we change our mind-set concerning what is positive and what is negative. I met a young nurse, Jessica, on a flight to LA, and in the discussion about my book, she shared some very important insights on ethnicity. Jessica happens to be of European descent. As a pediatric nurse, she noticed that when interracial couples had a baby, one parent or both would ask, "Will the baby have good hair or bad hair?" This is an amazing view into the mind-set that the superiority of one ethnicity over the other is revealed by the hair texture. This perpetuates the thought that one ethnicity is less than the other due to the texture of the hair. I often remind my family that having fine hair does not mean better or worse. Somehow we believe that if I have coarse or thick hair, it is bad. How can this be? These are the continuing challenges we face in America every day.

These are simple concepts, but they have a strong impact on how we see each other. This was an innocent conversation with Jessica, but it brought to light the greater issue that perceptions of what is good and bad can have a huge impact on our language, thoughts, and judgments. Again, this goes into the psyche of who people think they are. If in 2015, they believe their skin color or hair texture makes them less desirable, less intelligent, or less likely to succeed in America, we have failed in society. Together, we must communicate that these outward appearances are only natural and beautiful; it is who you are inside that matters most. All too often, we have communicated that the lighter complexion you have, the better you are, and it has harmed society. I have to share that I experienced this repeatedly as a youth in New Orleans. I alluded to it earlier in the book. I was constantly told that I had "good hair" because it was fine and curly. So naturally, if I had believed what they were telling me, it meant I was better and given an advantage in society because my hair texture was different. Does that make sense? No, it does not, but it actually is what takes place in conversations every day. Youth are ridiculed for their hair texture, and they are made fun of as they try to make hair that was not designed to go a certain way become different. Hence, the permanent and a variety of other hair changes and techniques to ensure you had fine hair in America. Again, I am glad there is a shift in society to recognize the beauty of your hair no matter what the texture is. Again, you may be wondering, why I am spending time here. It is because these are the types of things that lower the self-esteem and positive image of a people group. The group can feel as if it is not good enough or it is less than in our society. A people group with low self-esteem is less likely to perform to its highest potential and more likely to continue the negative stereotypes in education, poverty, crime, and violence.

I remember a few years ago, famed comedian Chris Rock put out a documentary of sorts where he explored the booming hair industry in a movie called *Good Hair*. In the movie documentary, his daughter asks, "Daddy, how come I don't have good hair?"[310] He found that people of African descent would pay hundreds of dollars for weaves and hair extensions so they could be more acceptable in America. In the documentary, most of the hair came from India—which meant great growth for the hair industry in India. Much of the hair came from women who cut their hair in religious ceremonies or because they were poor and they needed the money. Somehow free-flowing, fine hair is more associated with beauty. However, today there is a movement afoot to go "natural." In other words, go with the original hair texture you were born with and don't try to conform to what is considered the acceptable standard for beauty. In certain cultures, women are not even allowed to show their hair because it may seduce a man. Showing hair is considered improper and immodest. The world is fascinating when we begin to look at it through the lens of others. Ironically, hair texture is not necessarily tied to skin color, as with the Indians and Indonesians, for instance, who are brown-skinned and will often have fine or straight hair. This does not make the Indians or Indonesians better than Africans who have the same pigmentation but different hair texture. The study on hair texture is not new; it has been debated for centuries in America. We must also keep in mind that blacks are not the only culture that uses weaves or hair products to change their hair. I always found it interesting that blacks would get a permanent to straighten their hair and whites would get a permanent to curl their hair. At any rate, the hair industry is a multimillion dollar industry in America because people of all ethnicities are trying to reach the epitome of beauty. It should also be noted that there were times in America in the early mid to late 1900s where all women, especially those who were of African descent, were forced to change their hair style in order to maintain a job, such as with American Airlines. In the lawsuit *Rogers v. American Airlines*, the court ruled in favor of American Airlines, which restricted the style of hair and prohibited braiding of the hair for its stewardesses.[311] Once again, society has changed and realized that we had it wrong; now a braided hairstyle is acceptable in business and professional settings.

Hair or skin color is something we see on the outside. It is physical. Our emotional well-being is also critical to how we see ourselves. Negative thoughts about oneself go a long way in contributing to a pattern of behavior. Think about the parent who uses inflammatory language with his or her kids. It is not uncommon to hear a mother or father cursing out their children publicly and calling them the worst of names. Years ago, a YouTube video went viral because some young parents of African descent were teaching a young toddler to use bad language and racial slurs. They were laughing at the kid. They thought it was funny to show their friends what they had taught the kid. I believe the parents were arrested for child neglect and endangerment of a child. But some of America loved it for entertainment purposes, and it was a hit. Others, like me, simply thought, "This is what's wrong with America!" We perpetuate the negative stereotype that is seen in movies and heard through lyrics. This atmosphere of noncaring and negligent treatment of one another is egregious, to say the least. Thank goodness the police rescued the toddler from the parents. I am not sure if they were able to make a case of abuse, but at least the effort was made not to sit by idly and watch this negative indoctrination into society continue. I know some will think this is a stretch, but think of the terrorist group Boko Haram of Nigeria, which routinely kidnaps young Africans and turns them into sex slaves, cooks, and human shields.[312] A couple of years ago, Boko Haram kidnapped almost three hundred girls and committed vile acts against them as a way of sending a message to the African nations that they will be respected and included in the power base. When they released the girls, the majority of them were pregnant and were dealing with medical and psychological issues.[313] With more than seven hundred victims kidnapped over the last several years, Boko Haram acculturates those they kidnap by taking away all natural caring and normalcy in life and thus creating their own subculture. I submit that this is akin to what we do with our American children through heinous words and assimilation into a world that knows limited morals or values. When our children are bombarded with negative thoughts, negative words, and negative actions, it creates a subculture of low self-esteem and self-hatred. Most potential is stifled at an early age because we actually create a perpetual cycle of low education, negative self-perception, and ostracism in society and, thus, a perpetuation-to a life of crime, abject poverty, and hopelessness. Some will criticize me and think that I am exaggerating the facts, but I believe the contrary. We are in denial when we believe that the negative bombardment has not created at least in some part what we are dealing with in certain cultures, whether black or white or any other ethnicity. We can teach low self-esteem just as we can teach positive belief in oneself. We can also teach racism and discrimination through words and actions of hatred and bigotry. We all know and believe that if a child was raised in situations where skin color did not matter and was not emphasized, the belief that one is less than or greater would not be as prevalent. Take the case of the couple in the news who recently had twins who were blood sisters, but each with a different look, ethnically speaking. Lauren and Hayleigh Durrant are a unique set of twins because, even though they are identical, their skin and hair colors are in fact different.[314] Lauren has characteristics of European descent like her mother, including fair skin, blue eyes, and blond hair; and Hayleigh has African descent characteristics like her father, with brown skin, brown eyes, and darker hair.[315] The biracial couple, Allison and Dean Durrant, and family made headlines because they just had another set of twins (two girls), and yes, you guessed it, they were identical, but their ethnicity is different. I guarantee that those sisters will not hate each other and will accept one another for who they are with little regard to skin color. It will be society that points out their differences. With equal love and care, these children will not let the standards in America cause them to hate one another. These stories fascinate me because they prove my point that we are the same human race with differing levels of melanin in our skin pigmentation. We know that these kids are essentially the same. One is not better or worse based on skin color, hair texture, or eye color.

America has to recognize that negative and harsh treatment of our children and toward one another should not be the norm. Unfortunately, in many families of all ethnicities, it is just the way it is. This causes the children to continue the cycle of negative thoughts in their adult lives. It is an insidiousness that cuts to the core of the human spirit. Emotional and physical abuse can determine one's destiny. When children are neglected, not attended to, told they are nothing, cursed at, beaten, emotionally and sexually abused, and treated as property, the negative cycle of disenfranchisement continues. I will be talking more about disenfranchisement through the justice system later in the book. In this context, disenfranchisement means that we take away the positive self-esteem and drive of our children when we use slander and curse words toward them. No one wants to live under that type of barrage. Nothing positive comes out of it. When we communicate to our children that they are nothing and not considered valuable in this life, we create a cycle of pain. Our negative words hurt their potential and crush their spirits. They begin to believe they can never amount to anything. They assimilate to a life full of crime, negative thinking, and antisocial behavior. It drives them to seek love and fulfillment in the wrong places, such as gangs, drugs, and prostitution. I will speak to the broken families in the coming chapters, but this type of pervasive thought pattern erodes the family system and thus creates a cyclical battle with one's self. Parents' constant quarreling and rudeness teaches a learned behavior to our children. They become the innocent victims in the environment where love is lacking. When children constantly see bickering, arguing, violence, and screaming, they believe that is the proper method of communication. This follows them in their environment as they grow, and later, it invariably leads them to repeat the destructive cycle in their own relationships and marriages.

We need to teach pride and positivity to all Americans. We must stop tearing ourselves down with negative words and actions. Recently, two professors made the headlines with negative words and stereotypes. One professor was of African descent and the other was of European descent. They both made inflammatory statements toward the ethnicities of each other. Dr. Saida Grundy, an incoming assistant professor of sociology and African American studies at Boston University, made a statement concerning the "white male college population" being a problem population in society.[316] She was referring to college campus crime and rape. She was espousing that it is okay to say we have an inner city crime problem with black males, while providing no coverage on the growing problem on college campuses by white males. Of course, both issues need to be addressed, but how you address them also matters. For instance, Dr. Grundy allegedly also stated or tweeted that on "MLK week, she will avoid white-owned businesses."[317] This does not do our nation any good. There is no justification for racism in America or the world. Imagine me telling my air force colleagues that I don't support them during certain periods of the year. Tying into earlier comments, what was quickly noticed was the claim that the person of African descent can say what she says due to being a member of a minority group that has suffered oppression in the past. That is akin to saying the reason persons of African descent can commit heinous crimes of murder at alarming rates, rape, and other violent crimes in their own community or against society is because they were once slaves. The other professor, Dr. Steven Segal of UC Berkley, was caught in a firestorm when he was teaching in his community mental health class that he believed that black-on-black crime was a problem in light of the recent confrontations in the media between law officials and blacks.[318] He espoused that black-on-black crime had to be addressed when the group Black Lives Matter were calling for justice from alleged police discrimination. Segal was in error when he basically wrote several rap songs that called the attacks on law officials "scapegoating the cops" and put the ownership for the problems on blacks.[319] The professor was scolded by the media for his position. The reality is that both areas require analysis and discussion. Thus, the professor, being a part of the majority (white) population in America, was held to higher standards and received much harsher treatment due to his remarks. Those from the conservative view were quick to point out the inequality in media scrutiny given to the two professors' remarks. What is most interesting is we have two professors with higher education, making allegedly disparaging remarks about each other's ethnicity. I find it interesting; I believe that actually neither of them, based on their original controversial remarks, made outlandish racial remarks. They were simply pointing out the facts. My agreement with their positions does not include Dr. Grundy's alleged second set of remarks or tweets that she does not shop at white-owned businesses during MLK celebrations, for I believe that would be a racist statement. Nor does my agreement include the rap song from Dr. Sega stating that the black community is "scapegoating the cops" for their behavior, for I believe that was an inaccurate assessment.

What we essentially have is a major problem with ethnic relations in America. It appears you have to be a certain skin color in order to point out the obvious. That is ridiculous. We are Americans. If one ethnicity is having difficulty in one area, then as Americans it is our duty to point it out. By the way, you are well versed on my positions by now and what Dr. Segal failed to note is that white-on-white killings are too high, just as Hispanic-on-Hispanic and black-on-black killings are too high. They are all too high—*all lives matter*! Further, Dr. Grundy could be accurate in her assertion that many rapes or sexual assaults on college campuses are committed by white males and this should be addressed, but she must also point out that all ethnicities are guilty of the heinous crime of rape on college campuses across America. For instance, in 2012, according to Bureau of Justice statistics, 280 Asian Pacific Islanders, 283 American Indian and Alaskan Native descendants, 5,876 blacks, and 11,659 whites were arrested for forcible rape.[320] These numbers appear to count Hispanic and Latino ethnicity as either black or white. With regard to raw numbers, the numbers support Grundy's claim, as whites commit more forcible rapes, yet percentage-wise, per one hundred thousand of the population, whites commit rape at a rate of 4.7, while blacks commit rape at 13.6 per one hundred thousand of the population.[321] It is clear that Grundy's comments should have been more detailed, because her position only told half of the story. My point is that while we should not hide the obvious facts, we must be open to sharing the whole truth versus trying to stereotype or paint a one-sided, inaccurate, racially charged picture—that has been a major problem in America for years. My second issue revolves around the amusing reaction in the media to similar events, but with only one person scrutinized for the offensive comments. Is this what we have become as Americans? Of course, both sides should be talked to about the presentation of their comments but, from my perspective, not fired, simply reminded of their higher calling in education, what their positions represent, and the need for fair and balanced approaches. Please see the chart below for what we are facing in America.

The University of California has instructed its professors that there are certain phrases they cannot use.[322] These phrases speak to what I have been talking about in this book. Some of the interpretations of the statements point to the misunderstanding following the typical thought patterns that have been established for years. For instance, the university wants to point out that blacks have color and whites do not, but that is not the case. Every American and every human has color! They are trying to correct things without realizing they are doing it with the same thought pattern and same rhetoric. There has to be a paradigm shift in order for change to happen. It is similar to the media and news stating that we have to solve the racial divide in America yet using the same nomenclatures of *black* and *white* and emphasizing any incidents between the two cultures for ratings. We can begin to change ethnic relations in America by changing how we address one another and recognizing that America is indeed the land of opportunity. The same people who say we are not the land of opportunity still reside here. Not to be harsh, but if America is not the land of opportunity, then find a better nation to live in. I don't think that is wise, for America is the land of opportunity, and yes, you can work your way to a productive life. This is not to say one is guaranteed riches if he or she works, but one can earn a decent living. I recognize this chart is coming from a liberal perspective of America, and I am a conservative, but it is a good teaching point to what the divide in America is really about.

Examples of phrases listed as microaggressions within the University of California system:

Color Blindness		
Statements that indicate that a white person does not want to or need to acknowledge race.	• "When I look at you, I don't see color." • "There is only one race, the human race." • "America is a melting pot." • "I don't believe in race." • Denying the experiences of students by questioning the credibility/ validity of their stories.	Assimilate to the dominant culture. Denying the significance of a person of color's racial/ ethnic experience and history. Denying the individual as a racial/ cultural being.

| Myth of Meritocracy

Statements that assert that race or gender does not play a role in life successes, for example in issues like faculty demographics. | • "I believe the most qualified person should get the job."
• "Of course he'll get tenure, even though
• hasn't published much—he's black."
• "Men and women have equal opportunities for achievement."
• "Gender plays no part in who we hire."
• "America is the land of opportunity."
• "Everyone can succeed in this society if they work hard enough."
• "Affirmative Action is racist." | People of color are given extra unfair benefits because of their race.
The playing field is even so if women cannot make it, the problem is with them.
People of color are lazy or incompetent and need to work harder. |

Adapted from Sue, Derald Wing, Microaggressions in Everyday Life: Race, Gender and Sexual Orientation (Wiley and Sons, 2010).[323]

I am recommending a new way forward in America. All divisive language, as the military requires, must be eliminated. I know that will be impossible to fully embrace, but let's work toward that end. I advocate for legislation in our nation that punishes racial slurs and terminology similar to the way hate crimes are prosecuted. I know you may be thinking this is impossible, but I say it is not. I have made the case that racial slurs are already banned from the military, corporations, and most professional institutions. Yet I realize this is radical and a higher calling—a new America. The courage to stand deals with a new way forward for America. We have to unite and protect all people as best we can from harmful and derogatory language. We must set a new standard so that people might reach their fullest potential without the threat of denigrating terms and disparaging remarks.

In 2015, Terry "Hulk" Hogan, the famed wrestler, had to apologize for racist remarks from eight years ago. His remarks confirm what I have been discussing throughout the book. He was immediately fired from World Wrestling Entertainment (WWE) upon the discovery of the remarks.[324] He is quoted as stating,

> I don't know if Brooke was FXXXX the black guy's son. I mean, I don't have double standards. I mean, I am racist, to a point. FXXXX Ns. But then when it comes to nice people and FXXXX, and whatever … I mean, if she was going to FXXXX some N, I'd rather have her marry an 8-foot-tall N worth a hundred million dollars! Like a basketball player! I guess we're all a little racist. FXXXX Ns.[325]

The iconic Hulk Hogan did apologize for the heinous language and released this quote:

> Eight years ago I used offensive language during a conversation. It was unacceptable for me to have used that offensive language; there is no excuse for it; and I apologize for having done it. This is not who I am. I believe very strongly that every person in the world is important and should not be treated differently based on

race, gender, orientation, religious beliefs or otherwise. I am disappointed with myself that I used language that is offensive and inconsistent with my own beliefs.[326]

Up to this point in the book, I have tried to set the stage of where America has come from with a brief review of history and why a continued transition is needed with regard to ethnic relations and attitudes. I believe I have made a strong case for change in America. In the coming chapters, I will no longer use the terms *black* or *white* in relation to distinguishing between ethnicities. I will begin to implement the new terminology that I believe can effect change in America. You will notice that blacks will be identified as those of African descent, whites will be identified as of European descent, and the other ethnicities identified as known (Hispanic descent, Asian descent, Pacific Islander descent, and indigenous descent). Further, I am going to point to other issues I believe America must address in her quest to be a great nation and a new way forward. Some of my ideas may appear radical and will not fit neatly into the Republican or Democratic platform. These are simply suggestions to what I believe can change the landscape of America with regard to poverty, education, justice, self-esteem, and religion.

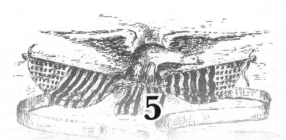

5

THE QUEST FOR RELIGIOUS FREEDOM

I've learned to never doubt in the darkness, what I believe in the light.

—Chaplain Major General Robert Taylor,
Chief of Chaplains, Air Force

Chaplain, Major General Robert Taylor

The opening quote of this chapter is from Chaplain Major General Robert Preston Taylor, who served as the third chief of chaplains for the US Air Force from 1962 to 1966. His courage to stand is recorded in his book, *Days of Anguish, Days of Hope*, when he was a prisoner of war (POW) in the Philippines during World War II.[327] He was on the infamous Bataan "Death March" through the streets of Manila to the prison camp approximately eight miles east of Cabanatuan, where he saw many men die during the war and their imprisonment.[328] Chaplain Taylor never gave up; he would keep fighting even though he was imprisoned for forty-two months. He ministered to more than ten thousand patients.[329] He was thrown into the hotbox at one point during his time as a POW for a fourteen-week period because he was smuggling food and medical aid to patients.[330] During his time in the hotbox, Chaplain Taylor encouraged another individual who was in the small, cramped box. Throughout it all, Chaplain Taylor kept his faith in God. At one point, they actually thought he would die when they finally removed him from the hotbox. He was placed in the infirmary with little hope for survival—it was an all-but-decided fate. But God intervened, and he slowly healed from his exhaustion and wounds. Of course, Chaplain Taylor credited God with giving him the strength and the courage to make it during those dark days in his life. According to historian Bill Keith, Taylor told his fellow soldiers in the midst of the harshest conditions, "Ask me about my condition. I'm dirty, nasty, and all I have on is my underwear. Can you smell the stench of my rotting teeth? Listen to me, listen without pity, I'm not going to die. I'm going to live and you are too, because God is going to give us strength."[331] Military men and women died for our freedom, and part of that freedom was the free exercise of religion. We live in a time when we are easily attacked for being spiritual or advocating for religious freedom. Chaplain Taylor was awarded the Silver Star for his gallantry in service during the war.[332] Chaplain Taylor's story is one of millions who have defended our nation and relied on their faith to sustain them. Yet I believe America is at a crossroads when it comes to ensuring religious freedom for all.

When President Barack Obama met with Pope Francis in 2014, they discussed significant issues in America, including the right to religious freedom, life, conscientious objection, and conflict resolution.[333] Further, when Pope Francis came to America in 2015, millions came out to see him. I had not seen anything like it in my lifetime. The media coverage was wall to wall, and I, like millions of other Americans, found myself gripped by the cable news broadcasts, following the pope's every move. Amazingly, the newscasts even covered the many masses that Pope Francis conducted. I had not seen religion and morality discussed so openly for hours upon hours in America during my adulthood. Needless to say, it reminded me of my book and what I had been espousing with regard to religious freedom and restoration of the family. Throughout his six-day tour, Pope Francis emphasized maintaining religious freedom, preserving the family, championing immigration reform, and providing assistance to the poor.[334] The Catholic church hoped to capitalize on the momentum built through the pope's visit. I lead off with these illustrations referencing the pope because I think what was discussed is critical in today's culture. This is not a religious book, but I would be remiss if I did not share that a strong America is an America that does not attack spirituality and religion. A strong America supports the rights of all who choose to worship a deity or power outside of themselves. One of the reasons our great nation was founded was to eliminate the oppressiveness of a state-run religion. In fact, the early settlers were fleeing the Act of Uniformity of 1558 set in place by Queen Elizabeth I.[335] The Act of Uniformity meant that there was only one official religion in England. Everyone had to attend church and practice this religion found in the Book of Common Prayer or face punishment and fines.[336] This meant the pursuit of religious freedom for all was not allowed in England at that time. It is a right of every American to pursue religion. The language in our historical documents clearly demonstrates that the architects of our great nation did not mean to suppress religion; on the contrary, they wanted to allow religious freedom for all. You often hear the phrase "separation of church and state" as a means to divorce religion from America at all costs, but what the phrase actually meant was that the church must be protected from the state, not the state protected from the church (i.e., not to create the same situation that was in England, where the state controlled religion). This is what the First Amendment and the Establishment Clause in our Constitution deal with. The First Amendment ensures religious freedom while ensuring that the government does not establish a religion. Today many have taken this out of context and want all religion removed from America. For example, you have heard of drives to get "In God we trust" removed from American currency or remove religious artifacts, such as the Ten Commandments or other sacred texts, from any government building. Of course, the infamous battle to remove prayer from public schools was actually won through the courts. I will address this later in the chapter. However, it does not stop there. Today teachers in America dare not even speak the word *God*, lest they face expulsion and firing. There was a time when those who worked in government positions thought they could not have a Bible or a religious article on their desks without facing ridicule and scorn. We have since corrected that misinterpretation of the separation of church and state. Government employees can discuss their faith when asked about their views but must always be respectful of others without using the government as a means to establish a particular religion. We often hear of schools prohibiting students from praying before a game or going to the center of the field to pray following a game. The most incredible movement has been to prohibit Christmas songs that reference Christ during Christmas or to stop people from saying "Merry Christmas" during the holiday season. I could go on and on, but rest assured, the quest to squelch religious freedom is a real movement.

From the birth of our nation, religion and spirituality have shaped our principles, values, ethics, and belief system. At the same time, America does not force religion on those who choose not to worship a deity or power outside of themselves. Some atheists would indeed argue that America penalizes those who do not worship God or a higher power. America must not become secularized or a nation that bans the right to worship or persecutes those who do. Some have thought America would move to the European model of widespread secularism. This has not been the case, and America had defied the odds through the years by continuing to be a largely religious nation. However, more and more, we are hearing stories and reading about events of the religious in America being forced to change their behavior. Some of the things we hear are not accurate, but others are factual and quite alarming. For instance, to deny that our nation was founded on spiritual principles from the Bible and other sacred texts is simply living in denial, yet this is stated by many. I have already shown that the early Pilgrims were religious and fleeing religious oppression. I also acknowledge that the Pilgrims were not perfect; they themselves would become a part of the system of oppression of those who were different from them.

The forefathers and mothers of our nation were in fact very spiritual. I have heard some argue that they were not spiritual, but deists only. In fact, out of the fifty-five delegates who participated in the 1787 Constitutional Convention to frame the US Constitution, forty-nine were Protestants, and two were Roman Catholics (D. Carroll and Thomas Fitzsimons).[337] That means fifty-one out of fifty-five were considered spiritual, while four could be described as atheists. The Protestant denominations represented included Presbyterian, Church of England (majority), Lutherans, Methodists, Dutch Reform, and Congregationalists.[338] Notably, Baptists were not represented at the Constitutional Convention. Baptists were considered radicals at the time, and were generally not allowed to practice in many states. Virginia, for example, actively tried to root out religions other than Church of England. The Baptist religion doesn't really take hold in the United States until after 1800. Given that the forty-nine were dominated by Protestant faith, one can see why almost a century later is was a big deal that a Roman Catholic, John F. Kennedy, would become the president of the United States. Some were worried that President Kennedy would be under the influence of the pope. There was a huge anti-Catholic strain in American religion until the 1960s. Of note, Benjamin Franklin and Thomas Jefferson were anticlerical. They felt that the institution of religion had tendencies to be corrupt and would rather emphasize faith in one God versus religion itself.[339] Thomas Paine was considered a deist because he thought the Bible was really not God's word, nor did he believe in institutionalized religion, yet he believed in one God.[340] My emphasis on religion in America's history does not mean that I am advocating that America should be one religion only or Christian only, but on the contrary, I want to remind the reader that America was founded by those who had faith. We want to support all who would pursue a spiritual walk with their God. This is what makes America strong: a respect for all religions and the allowance of those to pursue their religious rights. We must not become a godless America where faith is no longer acceptable in society.

I want to share some examples of oppression of free exercise of religion in America that have made headlines over the past few years. There was a recent story of an incident in a mall in America where a few women were prohibited from holding hands and praying before their power-walk through the mall.[341] According to the report, the security guard stopped the women from praying and informed them that these were the rules of the mall because it was private property. The security guard went so far as to say prayer before a meal was prohibited. There are many who are being forbidden to pray in a public space. As we all know, prayer cannot be an officially sanctioned part of public schools, and teachers are restricted from mentioning their faith. Thankfully, students are allowed to pray on school grounds each year during Prayer at the Pole and to create their own prayer groups, but the groups must be independent of the school administration. I believe this is in keeping with all of the previous court rulings.

In an August 2007, the Pew Research Center found that 69 percent of Americans believe that "liberals have gone too far in trying to keep religion out of the schools and the government."[342] That same poll also found that most Americans today (58 percent) still favor teaching biblical creationism or intelligent design along with evolution in the public school system.[343] We should note that prayers or religious activities in schools have been controversial in America since the 1800s. There were disputes between the Catholics and the Protestants on which version of the Bible to use in the classroom (this is when religion was taught subjectively in public schools) and some of the disputes turned violent.[344] It should be noted that the law allows religion to be taught as long as it is presented objectively as part of culture and history. In the early 1900s, the controversy shifted to a disagreement on whether or not Charles Darwin's Theory of Evolution should be taught in the classroom versus creationism (the dominant method used in teaching biology classes in that era). Of course, that has reversed today, with evolutionism dominating public schools even though most Americans still believe that creationism should be taught alongside evolutionism. The battle of religion in schools has been ongoing for the last century. According to the Pew Research Center, there were battles for religion in schools, such as the Scopes trial in the 1920s, the 1940 *Cantwell v. Connecticut*, and *Everson v. the Board of Ewing Township* in 1947. It was found that the First Amendment Free Exercise clause could be applied to the state level. By 1948, as a result of *McCollum v. the Board of Education*, the Supreme Court ruled that religious instructors from different dominations could no longer come into the classroom to offer religious instruction.[345] The Supreme Court did rule four years later (1952) in the *Zorach v. Clauson* case that students could leave school for religious training during the day.[346] Education in America was certainly different in the pre-1960s with regard to religion.

The two clauses in the First Amendment dealing with religion state, "Congress shall make no law respecting an establishment of religion, or prohibiting the free exercise thereof."[347] Thus, religion cannot be established by the government, but at the same time, Congress shall not prohibit the free exercise of religion. This is where the battle has been fought over the years. The First Amendment has been used by federal courts as a basis to forbid the school's involvement in prayer and other religious activities. This is interesting because the First Amendment guarantees the right to the free exercise of religion. However, most who oppose religions in state or federal entities use the Establishment Clause as their basis. School-sponsored prayer (even if nondenominational or nonsectarian) in the school was removed in America in 1962. In 1962, Steven Engel, a Jewish New Yorker, joined with other parents (*Engel v. Vitale*) and sued the New York State Board of Regents to remove prayer from the public school system, and the US Supreme Court agreed that the New York school board was establishing religion (the Establishment Clause).[348] The prayer was as follows: "Almighty God, we acknowledge our dependence upon Thee, and we beg Thy blessings upon us, our parents, our teachers and our Country."[349] What is most interesting is that Engel and the other parents originally lost their lawsuit because the prayer or invocation was in fact voluntary. Even though the Supreme Court eventually ruled six to one in favor to forbid school-sponsored prayer, one member, Potter Stewart, believed it was an error to end voluntary school-sponsored prayer in a public setting, because we were taking away the opportunity of sharing in the spiritual heritage of our nation.[350] It is important to note, as still current today, children can pray at school; prayer just cannot be school-sponsored. As I stated earlier, Prayer at the Pole happens annually at many public schools. Prayer at the Pole is a national event when mostly students of the Christian faith come together once a year at the school's flagpole to pray. The 1962 ruling was followed in 1963 by another ruling in which the Supreme Court ruled to take away school-sponsored Bible reading or citing of scriptures in public schools through the *Abington Township School District v. Schempp*.[351] This 1963 lawsuit was brought by a Unitarian family. Many in America still believe that prayer and biblical readings were forbidden in public schools. In 1990, the Supreme Court cleared up those misconceptions and ruled that students in public schools may form clubs for prayer and religious readings as long as they are conducted during noninstruction hours.[352] Not only are students allowed to form religious clubs in public schools, but

Justice Tom Clark of the Supreme Court wrote, "Nothing that we have said here indicates that such study of the Bible or of religion, when presented objectively as part of a secular program of education, may not be effected consistent with the First Amendment."[353] This means that religion can be discussed objectively in schools and used for educational projects. Yet many administrators and leaders in today's education system believe that religious study is prohibited in a public school setting. I believe the administrators have gone too far in most cases.

I propose that everyone should be afforded time to voluntarily pray or meditate at the start of each day, as it was when I was growing up in the public schools of New Orleans. I also believe that teachers should have the right to express their faith within limits. I don't believe a teacher should proselytize or push their faith or religious beliefs on students, but that does not mean that a teacher cannot wear a yarmulke or Kofi if they are Jewish or Muslim. Similarly, a Christian teacher should be allowed to wear a cross around his or her neck, and of course, they are allowed to do this. Displaying religious items does not mean that the school is "establishing religion." Take the case of the assistant high school coach, Joe Kennedy of Bremerton High School, Seattle, Washington, who has been suspended with pay for praying for the safety of his team after each game.[354] Coach Kennedy would pray by himself at midfield. He started his ritual in 2008. The coach has stated he does not invite students to pray, but acknowledges that some students have come out to join him. However, the school has stated that his prayers could have adverse effects on students and be perceived as establishment of religion. Coach Kennedy is fighting back, stating that he believes he should be accommodated because his actions are not egregious and he has a right to pray. I believe as long as the coach is not making students pray with him, and as long as he is not standing in the classroom and making the students listen to his prayer, he has the Constitutional right for prayer in accordance with the First Amendment.

A few years ago, a student was tasked to draw a picture of a famous historical figure or idol. The student was not allowed to turn in a picture of a historical God because of the religious connotations.[355] We all know that God is a historical figure, whether one chooses to believe in him as savior or not. God or Jesus, the man, can be examined from a historical concept and in light of his impact on society and the world from an educational standpoint. Why is the image or discussion of Jesus banned in some schools despite the Supreme Court's rulings? What about world religions and how they impact war, culture, and families? Can those topics no longer be discussed in American public schools? According to the court rulings, these discussions are legal. Yes, some educational systems are not in compliance and in fact are limiting religious expression. Here are a few others that have arisen in recent years: teen forbidden from singing a Christian song in a talent show, an eighth grader forbidden from putting a blessing or reference to God at the end of her graduation speech, and a student forbidden from bringing a Bible on school grounds.[356] These are just a few of the challenges spirituality faces in America. Again, an America that suppresses spiritual awareness and religious expression is not a strong America.

As a military chaplain serving our nation, I could not help but notice the frenzy concerning the state of religion in America. My views in this book, of course, are my own and do not represent the Department of Defense, the air force, the military Chaplain Corps, or the Church of God in Christ (my endorsing denomination). Many national events bring with them the risk of scrutiny. The headlines are filled with quotes during National Prayer Breakfasts and events from high-ranking officials, including the President of the United States. Nothing is done without close examination by those who oppose religion at the federal or state level. There are some who despise any reference to God by those of us in uniform, but we are indeed protected by the Constitution and the law to express ourselves, yet we must make sure we are respectful of those who do not believe as we do and that we support their rights. Military members must be respectful of each other and not try to force their religious or spiritual views on others. At the same time, we must respect the right of military members to exercise their religious rights according to the tenets of their faith as long as this exercise does not bring prejudice toward the military or interfere with good order and discipline. The key word is respect. I also add that we must respect those who do not subscribe to religion or spirituality. They should also be protected. Commanders must especially be sensitive to what they say to those under their command and ensure they are not using their position to compel others to espouse religion. I have shown that America was built on the principles of allowing the individual expression of sincerely held beliefs (conscience, moral principles, and religion). I am calling for

America to stand up and not give these types of attacks credibility. These attacks are used as a bully pulpit and actually generate revenue for the said organization.

The opposition to religious freedom is real and constant, and it damages America. Yet I must also acknowledge that our society continues to evolve with regard to individual religious expression. We are not the same nation religiously that we have always been. For example, General George Washington appointed chaplains to every regiment (which is why we have chaplains today in the armed forces) and required every commander at Valley Forge to be at Sunday worship or "divine service" at eleven in the morning to set an example for the troops.[357] We clearly recognize that requiring every commander to go to worship is not appropriate today. We have all seen the iconic image of General Washington praying during battle and asking God for strength, and we know from his many quotes and writings that he was a true man of faith. I believe prayer is still appropriate for commanders today, but they simply cannot require or mandate every person to pray or send out mandatory prayer cards to every soldier, as General George S. Patton did during World War II. His action took place at a critical juncture in the war in 1944 in the fight for democracy around the world. The Third Army chaplain, Monsignor James O'Neil, was given the mandate to get the word out, and it read like this, with 250,000 copies on three-by-five-inch cards:

> Almighty and most merciful Father, we humbly beseech Thee, of Thy great goodness, to restrain these immoderate rains with which we have had to contend. Grant us fair weather for Battle. Graciously hearken to us as soldiers who call upon Thee that, armed with Thy power, we may advance from victory to victory, and crush the oppression and wickedness of our enemies and establish Thy justice among men and nations. To each officer and soldier in the Third United States Army, I Wish a Merry Christmas. I have full confidence in your courage, devotion to duty, and skill in battle. We march in our might to complete victory. May God's blessings rest upon each of you on this Christmas Day.

—G. S. Patton Jr., Lieutenant General, Commanding,
Third United States Army[358]

This was certainly a powerful moment in history, and in fact, General Patton went on to urge every chaplain under his command with a detailed letter encouraging every soldier to pray. It goes without saying that it is a different era today, and this would not be appropriate for a commander to do. Conversely, it is indeed appropriate to allow for the opportunity for worship for our military under United States Code 8547 and others. I recognize that we needed to make a change, as our society has grown into a more pluralistic and versatile religious group allowing for the freedom to choose, but we should not eliminate one of the cornerstones of our nation, which is religion, in the process of growing.

A few years ago, the military started using the phrase "Happy holidays" in reference to the Christmas season so as not to leave anyone out or offend others by saying "Merry Christmas." This alarmed many of us, for it did not make logical sense regarding the holiday of Christmas. Stating "Merry Christmas" did not mean there was a disrespect of any other religion. In addition, the Christmas tree was called a "holiday tree" for the same sensitivity reasons. In recent years, stating "Merry Christmas" is no longer seen as offensive, and calling a Christmas tree by its name rather than calling it a holiday tree has become the norm again. These are important changes, as the pendulum has swung to both extremes in recent years. The key lies in a balanced and fair approach to religion and respect for all. As a chaplain and military member, I thought it was important to respect all religions without suppressing another. As a senior chaplain, I have supported all major religions celebrating their holy days. For instance, when I was senior chaplain, we ensured we had the Menorah lit for Hanukah as well as the manger scene outside of the chapel. The Muslim community worked with the Jewish and the Christian communities around the High Holy days. We believe in respect of all religions, and I have been personally thanked by many leaders from the Buddhist faith, the Muslim faith, Eckankar, Latter-Day Saints, Wiccan, Seventh-Day Adventist, Baha'i, and Jewish faiths. I met with these nonchaplain lay leaders monthly to ensure they were supported to meet their religious freedom. Further, the military would also ensure religious accommodation for all where they can, as long as it does not conflict with or impede the mission. I applaud the noble efforts of the Department of Defense to accommodate all religions where possible. We are getting smarter on how we do business in the military. In my opinion, religious freedom and religious accommodation is important to the Department of Defense as it strives for balance with all. As I have advocated earlier, I believe it is the military that leads the way on many social issues and has helped transform America with regard to equal rights for those considered in the minority, women, and all Americans regardless of their gender preferences. Yet the challenges continue from nonfederal entities and nongovernment organizations outside of the military to deny religious rights to all. Again, I could list a myriad of examples of religious challenges the military has dealt with recently. However, what is most important is that the military is trying to ensure the rights of all for religious expression and accommodation.

Some have complained that religion should not be a part of the government at all, and that chaplains should not be a part of the armed forces. Again, we have examined the two main clauses in the First Amendment regarding religion earlier: "Congress shall make no law respecting an establishment of religion, or prohibiting the free exercise thereof." First, let's be clear that the government, by law, cannot establish religion. Second, the First Amendment gives us the right to practice religion. Third, the government has gone to great lengths to accommodate the diverse religious makeup of America. Again, some want to rewrite history and change the laws to eliminate religion in the military and the chaplaincy. But remember, as I have stated and demonstrated earlier, it was our forefathers who thought to protect religion from the state, and not the other way around. In 1802, when President Thomas Jefferson wrote about the wall of separation between church and state, he was trying to ensure that the state would not interfere with the church.[359] Note that separation of church and state is not found in the Constitution. Here is what President Jefferson actually wrote: "I contemplate with sovereign reverence that act of the whole American people which declared that their legislature should 'make no law respecting an establishment of religion, prohibiting the free exercise thereof,' thus building a wall of separation between church and State."[360] It is critical that we understand the Establishment Clause and the Freedom of Religion Clause and that they are meant to preserve the right to worship without the government dictating how and when we worship. That is why recent language in the National Defense Authorization Act (NDAA) for fiscal year 2014, section 532, contains strong language protecting the rights of those who choose to worship or not and protecting the chaplains' consciousness of faith.[361] Chaplains cannot be forced to perform religious acts outside the tenets of their faith. This is very important, even as the government has changed its stance with regard to same sex couples serving openly in the military and receiving marriage benefits. As chaplains, we attempt to help all people regardless of their choice of marriage; however, each chaplain is protected to only perform religious rites in accordance with the tenets of his or her faith and personal conscience. The key is to continue to be respectful to all people regardless of their faith choice or lack thereof.

Some have advocated that prayer must not be allowed at military, congressional, or public events and that it is not appropriate to have the words or references to God in the pledge of allegiance. These are the antireligious movements I am speaking about. While we should not force people to worship God, we should also not restrict people from worshipping God. Our society must be a free and open society where all are allowed to worship as they choose without disrupting good order and discipline. For instance, while I support the freedom of religion and worship, I do not support setting up a religious meeting in the middle of a major highway, disrupting businesses and the work day. This would be an illegal assembly. The support for religious rights must continue, but we must be mindful of forcing our views on others.

Why am I advocating for religious freedoms? I have established that America is a nation founded on religious principles and religious plurality, not religious suppression. No matter how revisionists try to paint it, America was founded on the freedom *for* religion, not the freedom *from* religion. Our Constitution is replete with references that mirror religious texts. Yet there are many who will quickly point to our society today and state that we are no longer a religious society. A quick review of the religious makeup of our nation, according to the US Religious Landscape Survey of February 2008, revealed that 78 percent of the nation is Christian (either Protestant or Catholic), while the Jewish and Mormon populations are each 1.7 percent.[362] The rest of the religious affiliations are in the United States are comprised of Jehovah's Witnesses, Muslim, Hindu, Buddhists, and Orthodox. None of the smaller religious populations is greater than 1 percent in America. This survey was based on over thirty-five thousand people polled, and 16.1 percent said they have no religious affiliation. The 16.1 percent unaffiliated with religion is higher than the 1980s when the statistics showed between 5 percent and 8 percent as consistently religiously unaffiliated.[363] I must also point out that within the 16.1 percent, only 1.6 percent claim atheism and 2.4 percent claim agnosticism. Further, of the 16.1 percent religiously unaffiliated, 12.1 percent claim no particular religion with only 6.3 percent being secular and 5.8 percent being religious, but unaffiliated. These statistics clearly demonstrate that America is a spiritual nation, so we should not eliminate religion, but find ways to allow for its expression without forcing religion on others. Yet we face constant challenges across all facets in America with regard to our nation being supposedly too religious.

Religion and spirituality have positive impacts on the nation. Religion calls for peace and for treating each human being with dignity and respect. Religion and spirituality are not bad, but there are those who hide behind religion and use it as a shield to perpetrate heinous acts against us all through terrorism. For instance, the radical Muslim extremists do not follow the Quran, but they are an aberration of the Muslim religion. They are a hybrid that has used religion as a justification to perpetuate evil. They must not be lumped in with the majority of the world's Muslims who are peaceful and do not advocate or support the cowardly acts of terrorism.

Let's take this further: While some say America is not spiritual, the statistics show differently. Again, a Pew Research Center poll in 2007 showed that the American people want looser restrictions with regard to religion and that liberals have gone too far in trying to eliminate religion from the public sector, including schools. As I have shared earlier, we must remember 69 percent of Americans say we have gone too far to keep religion out of schools and the government. Further, I have shared that 58 percent of Americans believe we should teach creationism and evolution in the public school system. In some circles, if one were to bring up the thought that humanity actually began through God's creation, one would most likely be viewed as unlearned and ignorant. We need to ask ourselves how is it that we can talk about the possibility of life in space, but we can't talk about Jesus, the historical figure, in schools. This is a constant battleground in the schools of America. A recent review in the 2013 Pew Research Center on the restrictions of religion in the United

States as compared to other nations shows that in fact the United States ranks as moderate with regard to religious restrictions.[364] Of course, this is nothing close to nations such as India, Egypt, Uzbekistan, Iran, and China, where religious restrictions appear to be very strong. According to the Pew Research Center, there are cases in the United States that show suppression in terms of land development and building worship structures. The Pew Research also showed a more hostile treatment toward Jews and Muslims, with 76 percent and 71 percent of countries, respectively, displaying harassment and religious discrimination toward the groups. There has also been a rise of hostility toward Jews worldwide, according to the Pew Research Center in 2015, and it is at a seven-year high.[365]

When President Obama signed the new Executive Order 13672 (presidential directives) in 2014, dealing with sexual orientation and gender identity, it caused major shifts in policies in all federal contracts, including those who work in religious capacities within the government.[366] The executive order meant that even in religious situations within the government, with few exceptions (e.g., hiring based on specific religion; for example, a Catholic community cannot be forced to hire a Buddhist priest), there cannot be discrimination against those the government hires based on sexual orientation and gender identity. Musicians, youth workers, religious educators, and other government contracts must comply with the new executive order even in the chapel. As of early 2015, states sought to counter the executive order directives by reengaging the 1993 Religious Freedom Restoration Act (RFRA), which was signed into law by President Bill Clinton and basically protected a person's religious convictions and religious freedoms.[367] Approximately twenty states quickly adopted a version of RFRA, including Indiana and Arkansas.[368] There was a huge outcry from the same-sex community concerning these laws because of the potential for discrimination based on religious grounds. In other words, some businesses in the twenty states can choose not to serve same-sex couples based on their religious views. Of note, the courts found that the Establishment Clause of the First Amendment was not limited to federal laws, but also applies to state laws. I have stated earlier that, while I am a conservative with regard to my views on marriage, I do not believe all businesses should be able to discriminate based on sexual orientation. For instance, should I not rent one my houses to same-sex couples because their religious views vary from mine? The answer is clearly no, and we must not discriminate based on sexual orientation or status. Conversely, a pastor must not be forced to perform a wedding for a same-sex couple if the clergy is conservative in his or her views and same-sex marriage does not line up with the tenets of his or her faith. This is what America is about.

Within days of the protests about RFRA legislation in Indiana and Arkansas, both governors changed their language to try to be more open and supportive of all people regardless of sexual orientation. Many businesses and corporations also criticized the original bills in Indiana and Arkansas, and others, such as Connecticut, called for boycotts of several of the states which signed new RFRA legislation.[369] An incident that made headlines concerned a pizzeria that was basically shut down because the daughter of the Memories Pizza Business shared her conservative views supporting heterosexual marriage.[370] "If a gay couple was to come and they wanted us to bring pizzas to their wedding, we'd have to say no," said Crystal O'Connor, when asked by CNN affiliate WBND-TV South Bend, Indiana.[371] What is interesting is that the O'Connors said that they would not turn away gay people eating in their restaurants, but they would not cater a wedding for gay couples. The hate mail on social media was unbelievable. The store sign was also defaced, and the family received many threats. The daughter's statement was taken out of context, and many tried to use it as a means to display their own hostility. That is an odd response for those who said they feared discrimination. Those of the same-sex community, who were complaining about discrimination, demonstrated little tolerance for the pizzeria. In fact, the pizzeria owner thought he was going to lose his store, but the American people came together and raised $842,000 for him to continue his business amid the controversy.[372] Further, individuals and organizations from both sides of the issue spoke out against the dreadful behavior of ending a family's livelihood and threatening the owner and his family's life.

Again, I want to interject here that expressing one's personal views when asked should not be persecuted. This was essentially a setup from the media. This is what I am talking about. While all should remain free and all should be respected in the quest for religious freedom, we should not be made to change our religious views to comply with others in society. It is hypocritical for the group to claim they are being harassed by opposite sex couples and yet threaten the livelihood (no one's life was threatened) of those who speak out opposing same-sex marriage. While I support my relatives who have chosen to be in same-sex relationships and marriages, I do not approve of same-sex marriage. Like the average reader, I love my relatives with all my heart and would do anything to help them regardless of their sexual orientation or choices. It is only that my biblical worldview is different from theirs. It does not mean I should demean them or discriminate against them because of their choices. I should treat them as I would want to be treated. I love them, as they also love me. I am often asked if I would perform a marriage for same-sex couples. The answer for me is simple. No, I would not, because I believe we were not physically designed for that type of union. I stand on the tenets of my faith and what I believe the Bible teaches. Additionally, this is the position of my endorsing body, the Church of God in Christ Inc. Yet if one of my same-sex friends or relatives came to me for help, I would not hesitate to help. Further, if someone I do not know came to me as a chaplain in a crisis, I would not hesitate to help. We should respect all people, regardless of their beliefs. We must move beyond tolerance to embracing acceptance.

I do not believe same-sex couples should be discriminated against; they should be allowed full services at businesses. I don't believe a spiritual position should stop general business transactions. For instance, with regard to the pizza incident, all people should be served, no matter what their views are. I think most of America agrees with that statement. The rub is when we add spiritual rights into a religious activity. Let's continue with the pizza store. Is it okay for the pizza location to serve all who come into its doors but refuse to deliver pizza to a same-sex marriage ceremony? I would say as a business person that it is unrealistic when you try to delineate whom to serve and not serve with regard to moral or spiritual positions. If the choice of a business to not serve everyone is permissible based on religion, some might argue that their religion prohibits interracial marriages or people of different ethnicities, and thus, they cannot serve food or cater to them because of their intermarriage or ethnicity. What if the couple you want to serve doesn't believe in abstinence, and they lived together openly before marriage? Should the caterer ask if you had premarital sex before delivering food to a wedding event or prove that you have not sinned in any other way? It simply does not make sense to me. In my opinion, it will be very hard to justify serving some and not all. That is why I am always cautious about exclusive state laws that would counter federal laws, even though I am a conservative at heart. For I know that if you get the majority in any state to vote, almost anything could become law. I have demonstrated clearly in this book that America once used state laws to counter federal laws and the Constitution. Hence, we need greater oversight of the Constitution and the federal laws of the land to maintain balance in our nation and freedom for all.

The news has been flooded with the story of lead county clerk Kim Davis, a Democrat, in Grayson, Kentucky, who stood her ground and refused to issue marriage licenses to same-sex couples. She was put in jail because of her refusal.[373] Davis was incarnated for six days in a jail cell for her stance on religious freedom. The judge eventually released Davis, an Apostolic Christian, and allowed her to return to work as long as she did not interfere with the process of issuing marriage licenses as required by law. Clark has six deputy clerks who work for her, and all but one say they will issue licenses according to the new law recognizing same-sex couples.[374] Some say this case threatens the core of our nation's religious foundations. Davis did a heroic thing and stood up for her religious beliefs. I am not sure I can simply agree with this position. For instance, Davis understood the law, and no one forced her to agree with the law. Further, I don't believe same-sex marriage is God's will for mankind, yet I am not going to deny basic human rights to those who do support same-sex marriage. I am not suggesting Davis or I, or millions like us, give up our religious rights, but I don't believe issuing marriage licenses according to the law means you are condoning the activity or behavior. A clear example, as noted above, would be that when Davis issues a license to those who may have committed premarital sex or adultery, it does not mean she is condoning that behavior. The same could be said for a myriad of activities from the Christian worldview, such as stealing, lying, or cheating. Do you only issue licenses to those who meet the biblical standard of righteousness? Of course, that would be preposterous and unrealistic. Issuing a license does not condone any of those behaviors, including same-sex marriages. As a chaplain, I see many people of all different faith groups for varying counseling reasons, but that does not mean I agree with the tenets of their faith group, although I support the person who is in need. There were times in America when people were prohibited from voting or worshipping in certain buildings because their skin complexion was different—I don't believe we want to go back to that America. In fact, there was also a period in America when if one committed adultery, he or she could be tried before the local courts and prosecuted. Today approximately twenty-three states still have laws on their books stating that adultery is a criminal act.[375] No one is suggesting we continue to live by that standard, even though some states still have adultery on the books, including the military Uniform Code of Military Justice. Let me take it further. Not only do many states have adultery laws on the books, but some even have fornication laws (laws forbidding sex before marriage between two unmarried persons) on the books. That would be a hard law to enforce with as many as 80 percent of men and 75 percent of women reporting in a 1988 study that they had premarital sex by age nineteen.[376] America has come a long way with regard to prosecuting adultery. In fact, in early America, if one committed adultery, he or she could have an *A* branded on the forehead, be executed (we find at least three such executions in recorded American history), or be stripped from the waist down and publically whipped, to name a few of the punishments.[377] That is not the America I want. I believe we must respect the privacy laws of all Americans.

Having said the above, I still must emphasize that purely religious activities should be protected in America. The NDAA fiscal year 2014 section 532 protects me as a chaplain in that very issue—no chaplain is forced to perform duties contrary to his or her beliefs or tenets of his or her faith. Of course, this again is for strictly religious activities. Here is another example. If a same-sex couple came to me asking me to perform premarital or couple counseling after they were married, I can defer because the request is directly tied to my religious views on same-sex marriage. However, as I have stated, if the same-sex couple wanted to talk to me in a crisis (loss of a loved one or other emergency) or one of them was contemplating suicide, I would not hesitate to help them and in fact am obligated to do so. In these scenarios, I should not be criticized for not performing a same-sex marriage because it is my sincerely held belief in the direct performance of a religious rite or ceremony. I submit that the NDAA should be extended to every American citizen, as it is to every military member. America must protect her citizens.

I want to close this chapter with an appropriate quote from the first president of our great nation, General George Washington. On the same day, in a personal letter to Colonel Benedict Arnold, September 14, 1775, regarding the advance into Canada, General Washington noted,

> I also give it in charge to you to avoid all disrespect of the religion of the country, and its ceremonies. Prudence, policy, and a true Christian spirit will lead us to look with compassion upon their errors without insulting them. While we are contending for our own liberty, we should be very cautious not to violate the rights of conscience of others, ever considering that God alone is the Judge of the hearts of men, and to Him only in this case they are answerable.[378]

PURSUIT OF EQUALITY: LEVERAGING EDUCATION, POVERTY, AND JUSTICE

Education is the great engine of personal development. It is through education that the daughter of a peasant can become a doctor, that the son of a mine worker can become the head of the mine, that a child of farm workers can become the president of a great nation. [379]

—President Nelson Mandela, South Africa

I remember being invited as the guest speaker for a special worship service during African American Heritage Month. I had the opportunity to be the keynote speaker at many events, both secular and religious. I had clear expectations of the program format. I was surprised during the program when the children were called up to perform and cite key leaders of African American history in a segment called "Who am I?" I was astounded by what I witnessed. At least ten of the twelve children gave an illustration of someone who was either an athlete or entertainer of some type. Now, on the surface, this seems harmless, for after all, they were recognizing those of African descent who definitely made significant impacts on American society. As I pointed out in earlier chapters, some of these entertainers and athletes were the first in their professions to reach the milestone that they did. Again, remember when they broke the barriers, it was not because they could not do the things which they did all along, it was only that they were finally given a chance to break the barriers. Heroes such as Jackie Robinson, who broke the brown skin barrier in baseball, or Sydney Poitier, one of the first true movie stars of African descent who was able to play roles beyond the stereotypical slave, gangster, or poor person, were pivotal in demonstrating what African Americans could do if given an opportunity. They opened doors for others in the same field to do likewise. They not only opened doors in the field they were in, but it made America a little more accepting of each other in everyday life and removed real-life barriers and prejudice through entertainment. My issue was not with recognizing the legitimate legacy makers in their own right, but that the categories of these groundbreakers were curiously limited.

George Washington Carver, American Botanist and Inventor

For instance, there was no mention of key figures such as Dr. Charles Drew, W. E. B. Dubois, Shirley Chisholm, or George Washington Carver. These were pioneers in the fields of medicine, academics, politics, and science, respectively. It would appear to me that these were especially important to highlight in order to promote a balanced recall of those pioneers of African descent who made America stronger through their service. There is also a remarkable difference in the list of pioneers that I named in that they all excelled academically. This is where we must focus America to build equality. For too long, many in America have only seen those of African descent in limited roles and have built a separate society around those roles. America indeed has come a long way from the times when, if you were of African descent, you were not afforded an education (it was actually illegal to educate slaves in the early years of America), and once education was allowed in the late 1800s and early 1900s, the standards were dramatically inferior. Many were beaten to ensure they would not get an education. Others literally died fighting for the right to a fair and equitable education. Our American history is replete with African American pioneers in education, such as Booker T. Washington, who was born as a slave but eventually became the founder of the famous Tuskegee Institute with the help of other European-descent leaders; Mary McLeod Bethune, who rose from obscurity to become a world-famous educator, civil rights leader, and leader of women rights; or James Meredith, who became the first graduate of African descent from the University of Mississippi in 1963 after facing major obstacles, isolation, and discrimination with state laws.[380]

Booker T. Washington, American Educator, Author, Orator, and Advisor to presidents of the United States

Social separation also thrives on prejudice and discrimination. Limited interaction only builds on the stereotypes. Do you recall the movie *Remember the Titans*, which is set in the 1970s with an African-descent coach leading the team in a majority European-descent town? The team from T. C. Williams High School won the Virginia State football championship in 1971. The movie was based on the true story of Coach Herman Boone. It highlighted the racial tensions of the time and the courage of some to stand and move toward reconciliation.[381] The idea was to build a winning team despite the color of the players' skin. In the beginning, the discriminatory tensions are high and the ethnicities predictably refuse to integrate. They will only block for those who look like them. But the coach pushes them to grow and change what they have been taught their entire lives. Eventually, the team begins to come together and the cultures merge with one purpose—to win games as a team. It was truly a historic moment in America at a time where teens of both African and European descent broke down barriers through a game. That movie always inspires me. It is such a powerful depiction of what America can be. From my research, it appears that the racial tensions may not have been as high as depicted in the movie, but they were there, and many resisted integration. Coming together is only half of the battle. If we can get those of different ethnicities together with genuine care for one another, we will begin to see change in America. However, there are key areas that even unconditional love won't fix without a link to action. In this chapter, we examine the importance of education, defeating poverty, and correcting the justice system. I submit that it is through education that we can change the landscape of America; poverty and the justice system will follow. By the way, America is ranked number fourteen in education in the world according to Pearson's ranking in cognitive skills and educational attainment.[382] I believe we should strive to be number one in education because it relates directly to innovation and, ultimately, to national security.

First, I am happy to report that in 2011–12 the overall high school graduation rate in America was at an all-time high of 80 percent for all US graduates.[383] In the same period, from 2011 to 2012, the graduation rate for Americans of African descent was at 69 percent; Americans with Hispanic descent graduated at 73 percent; while Americans with European descent graduated at 86 percent.[384] How important are these statistics? I submit that these simple statistics are critical to what drives our nation. For without an education, one starts adult life at a great disadvantage in our society and in the world at large. Ultimately, a lack of education is one of the greatest determinants of poverty. This is a vicious cycle that we face in America as we attempt to turn the tide of disenfranchisement. In a 2013 study, with 10.9 million students aged seven to seventeen living in poverty in America, the data shows a direct correlation with lower academic performance and lower high school completion due to poverty.[385] We must do everything we can to combat dropout rates in America. America is doing well overall, with only a 7 percent dropout rate; yet Hispanics lead the way with dropout rates at 12 percent; while those of African descent have a 6 percent dropout rate; and those of European descent have a 7 percent dropout rate.[386] The dropout rate speaks volumes to those who simply decide that education is not for them. Interestingly, those of African descent drop out at a lower rate than any other group, yet they are the least likely to graduate high school. Some would point to the high incarceration rate of teens and those who are murdered as major determinants of low graduation rates. Of note, in 2011, the US Bureau of Labor Statistics reported that those Americans without a high school diploma earned a median annual salary of $451 per week or $21,648 annually, which is congruent with the statistics from the National Center for Education Statistics for the same period.[387] In 2011, according to the US Bureau of Labor Statistics, those who did complete their high school degree earned an average of $638 per week or $30,624 (just over the poverty level for a family of four).[388] Again, the National Center for Education Statistics for the same period is comparable. The trend is obvious; as one gains education, earning power increases. The US Bureau of Labor Statistics confirms this earning power. In 2011, those with an associate's degree earned $768 per week or $36,864, while those with a bachelor's degree earned $1,053 per week or $50,544, and those with a master's degree earned $1,263 per week or $60,624 annually.[389] These are critical statistics because they leave no doubt that education empowers a people. No matter what ethnicity one is, education can make a difference. It must be noted that there is still some disparity in the statistics when compared against different ethnic groups and genders. Yet even with the disparity, those pursuing education break the poverty cycle. But where does it begin? How can we get those who have more interest in being athletes or entertainers to recognize their opportunity? Thousands come to America annually to pursue higher education, while many Americans fail to take advantage of our incredible education system. I have met hundreds of transfer students personally who applauded the US educational system.

As evidence of the growing change and equality of opportunities in the education system, the Hispanic community has set a new high, with seven out of ten high school graduates entering college; Hispanic students lead the nation in this respect.[390] For the first time, Hispanics led the European-descent population in the rate of high school graduates entering college. It is through higher education that all Americans will grow. This is why it is extremely important that every person has an opportunity to excel in America. America is stronger through diversity, despite the majority in early America rejecting those who were different. because this is how it was founded. As I have stated, there was a time in America where those of brown hue and poor people did not have an opportunity to gain an education, and they were purposely not given the opportunities to grow intellectually. This included the poor from European descent, such as the Italians or Irish. Despite the oppression of the poor Europeans and those of brown skin, there were always some who found a way to learn to speak out against the tragedy of inadequate educational opportunities. Many have fought and died for the right to a fair education, and it should be a priority of every person. History is replete with the battles to integrate schools and education systems so that all will have the same opportunity for quality education. Of course, there are some who would argue that I am naive and that America's poor and inner city schools are still sorely lacking. I would agree with that assessment, and that is the purpose of this chapter. I am trying to stir the nation's conscience to provide the opportunity for education to all people, whether poor or rich. Separate but equal did not work in the past, and it will not work today. Today we need stronger and better education systems throughout America.

Many of my friends home-school simply because they are not satisfied with the status quo school system in America. The poorer neighborhoods receive inadequate education, and statistics bear this out. An article from 2011 confirms that low-income schools are more likely to receive inadequate funds for the education process. Specifically, the US Department of Education showed that in 2008–9, up to 40 percent of high-poverty schools received less than their fair share of state and local funding and thus have fewer resources than those who do not receive Federal Title I funds.[391] It is clear that poorer schools continue the vicious cycle of falling behind educationally. This is why former President George W. Bush implemented his No Child Left Behind program; he realized there was a great inequity in the US education program. US Secretary of Education Arne Duncan stated, "Educators across the country understand that low-income students need extra support and resources to succeed, but in far too many places policies for assigning teachers and allocating resources are perpetuating the problem rather than solving it."[392] Of course, this does not pass the common-sense test, but this seemingly vicious cycle of poverty and a lack of education will continue to haunt our nation unless we change.

The days of being denied an education are far behind us. Yet as I stated earlier, many inner city schools still do not have quality education programs for their youth. I attended several inner city public schools (not the top schools by any means) and successfully pursued higher education. Even though I was technically behind the proverbial academic power curve coming out of Joseph S. Clark High School, I was able to quickly make up ground through diligence and persistence. In fact, I had AP Honors classes throughout high school, and even though our school tested generally lower in the state and in the nation, there were those such as myself who benefited from honors courses. It would appear that early on, I did not quite leverage the honors courses because I quickly went on scholastic probation at the University of New Orleans. I was not focused and was downright overwhelmed. I graduated out of high school ranking thirteen out of approximately three hundred or more graduates, but I felt I should have been in the top ten, for some of those in the top ten did not take honors courses. However, the valedictorian and salutatorian both were in my honors courses and well deserving of their recognition. In those days, you had to work extra hard in the honors program because there were no programs to balance the GPA and give you extra points due to the intensity and level of the courses. Notwithstanding, the valedictorian and salutatorian went on to great success in their careers. In fact, the salutatorian and I are the only two of our class to pursue our doctorate to date.

Dr. Monique Cola (salutatorian) is a gifted research biologist who donates hundreds of hours to educating and mentoring youth. The valedictorian, Lester Blandin, is an engineer who graduated from Dillard University with a degree in preengineering (mathematics option) and has a very successful career. I could highlight many others in our class of '82 who are extremely successful in their careers. How did this happen from an inner city school? This has not only happened in my school, but in many schools around the world. I can tell you that each of those making the American median income or beyond in salary have garnered an educational degree of some type. I was in the math club in high school and thought I would have a career as an engineer. Although I did gain an industrial technology degree (School of Engineering) from Southern Illinois University, I never did make it to my dream. When perusing my yearbook, I found an interesting statement that I did not recall I had written. I wrote that one day I would own an engineering firm with Dr. Cola and Mr. Blandin. I believe that this is an indication that ambition, determination, and drive have to begin at a young age. Even though I did not reach my goal (it changed through the years), there was a drive to excel and not become the status quo. By the way, I did win at one point the Air Force Space Command Black Engineer of the Year Award when I served at Schriever Air Force Base, Colorado, in the Fourth Space Operations Squadron and the Fiftieth Space Wing's Mission Support Group. Of course, I was honored to win that award for a technical career field. Additionally, in 1999, I was recognized as the Company Grade Officer of the Year in the Fiftieth Space Wing, and given the Roy C. Wilkins NAACP Image Award for my community involvement. There was something deep down inside of me that told me that education would make the difference in my life. Even at a younger age, I knew education was the key to my place in the world. I was speaking to my good friend Kevin George in New Orleans not long ago, and we were discussing the impact of education in America. As we began to look closer at the twenty-five to thirty kids in our one-block radius who had grown up and gained an education, it became quite clear that education was the key to growing out of poverty and making a difference in society. In fact, we were on the phone with his sister, Dr. Janice George, an educator with an ED, discussing how to get minority youth to pursue education; we noted that the change has to begin at a very young age, meaning five to six years of age—this is where the major influence will happen.

Where did the drive begin? I submit that it began when I was a youth, because education was a priority in my family from the beginning. I started reviewing the over fifty academic awards or so from my formative years and realized that the drive and support was there from the beginning. But it was cultivated by those around me. Herein lies the key to the education thrust. If we know that education is the difference-maker in American society, it has become the equalizer for all people. Education is the bridge to success in economic terms. Education is what levels the playing field, generally speaking. Education gives one a chance to move from poverty to a median income. Are you thinking the same thing I am thinking? If the statistics clearly bear out that education is the equalizer for all Americans, regardless of ethnicity or creed, why are so many failing to pursue it? The answer lies within our mentality and attitude.

I was blessed to have family around me who told me I was destined to make an impact in the world by doing something special. I was told that I was unique, and I eventually believed it. Adults in my life, such as my parents, grandparents, aunts, and uncles, saw potential in me that I did not see early on. Even though I was told of my potential, it would be years before I truly self-actualized. Each of us has to make tough choices to either pursue education or not. Those in my family and in my neighborhood who pursued education are remarkably different, economically speaking. My parents were educated without having the same opportunities I had. My mother did not go higher than the sixth grade, and my dad made it to the tenth grade. This was very common for the poor in those days, in the 1930s. My mother relayed to me that she quit school to work and provide some form of sustenance, because they were extremely poor and literally living on bread crumbs. My mother would work at a laundry facility for most of her working years as a simple laborer sorting through linens for major hospitals. The family did not know where their meals would come from on any given day and would go by neighbors' to see if they could gain food. My only living aunt from my mother's family even relayed to me that there were periods where she and my mom would salvage food from the trash. It was tough in America because of the Great Depression, but even tougher for the poorest of the poor. My father was able to go higher in school and eventually did the same as his father, becoming a sharecropper in Mississippi. He took a job in the saw mill to help feed the family, and that built a strong work ethic in him that would stick with him for life. Neither ever graduated, but they understood that I would not make it in a world that was rapidly changing without a solid foundation of education. In other words, the opportunity for economic success is a viable option to all who would pursue it. Those who did not pursue higher education were more likely to suffer poverty, stress, and hardships. Education builds stability, while a lack of education builds chaos. I realize I sound dogmatic about this concept, but I believe it is extremely clear, with observed evidence, that those who suffer most in America are those with the least amount of education. There is empirical evidence to show the link between education and poverty, crime, and unacceptable behavior in society.

Education can also be linked to one's view of him- or herself. There are many who have low self-esteem and believe they will never do anything different from their current status or what they have been told they can accomplish. I call it self-hatred. In my opinion, it is why so many people can kill each other over the most ridiculous things, such as shoes, clothing, or wayward stares. It is as if life does not matter, and thus, murder seems to be fulfilling, because I am able to kill that which I despise—essentially myself or those who look like or remind me of me. This is a controversial position, but I believe through the years, many young people have developed a self-hatred syndrome, and thus, life itself is inconsequential. Many see themselves as worthless, nothing but animals. Of course, this is not true. But if my mentality is that way, it means I kill those who look like me for unjustified reasons, because in essence, I am killing myself. There may also be a hope that I am killed in the process of my crime. My hypothesis may not be too far off when juxtaposed against what we see happening often in the United States. Think about the headlines that often cover people (male or female) who kill everyone in the family and then themselves. We are always shocked when we read headlines of this type or when it strikes closer to home with one of our friends or family. Yet the theme is the same. Disgruntled individuals hate life so much that they kill all those who are close to them, because those they are killing are extensions of themselves; when they kill coworkers or family members, they kill themselves. Thus, if this is my attitude, I am able to engage in self-destructive behaviors and take risks that I know will most likely end my life or place me in prison in the worst case, or in the best case, I might get away with my deed and get money. I submit to the reader that education has to become the goal. America needs role models who will lead the way to push our youth of all ethnicities to excel and achieve more. As our three-hundred-million-plus society ages and changes demographically, we must leverage education to stay the world's leader and to remain strong. I will talk in detail about helping our youth through mentorship later in the book, but it is the thrust of investing our lives into the lives of our youth that will make the difference in America. I will say again that I believe a lack of education and low self-esteem can lead to a sense of self-depreciation and, ultimately, to self-hate. This self-hate ultimately leads to senseless murders and killings, as shown in the earlier chapters. Remember that most killings are committed by members of the same ethnicity as the victim. Again, my hypothesis is that these killings take place in the midst of hopelessness, poverty, and possible self-hatred. This does not imply, by any means, that the rich don't commit crime or murders, for the statistics clearly don't support that idea.

You may be wondering what I believe can be done to encourage postsecondary education for everyone in America. A new America is an America that can provide a new way ahead educationally. I have a proposal that may be considered radical, and in fact, it may not flow well with my conservative or liberal friends. In fact, I am sure others have proposed similar ideas over the years, and there may be some forms of this plan already in existence. Specifically, I believe in our great nation and that all should have the privilege of serving in the military if they are physically, legally, and mentally able. Thus, I submit that every American who is physically, legally, and mentally able shall, before age twenty-four, be required to serve a minimum of two years of military service in the Reserves or Guard with all benefits and pay. This does not prohibit, change, or eliminate the opportunity for those who volunteer to serve on active duty, or in the Reserves or Guard. However, if one does not volunteer, one would, as an American citizen, be required to serve in the Reserves or Guard. One exception to military service might be those who are religious pacifists; this would mean honoring the freedom of religion. This military service would earn those who serve the two years educational benefits and provide them with a skillset that could be transferred into the civilian workforce. Thus, all educational benefits are not given but earned. Those who earn the credit would be allowed to pursue technical and vocational school educations as well as general education classes that would push them toward a four-year degree. Technical and vocational schools would be highly encouraged, because their programs transfer more readily into an actual vocation (e.g., computer science, nursing, information technology, car mechanics, air conditioner repair, radiology, and dental assistance) and thus provide a major stimulus to the economy while breaking the cycle of poverty. Participants in the program would be required to maintain a 2.0 GPA throughout the school term. The difference in this program from the existing educational program through the military is that I am calling for a radical shift in which serving in the military is mandatory rather than optional. I believe this plan could spur major changes to our economy. It does not hinder those who can afford college or those who are academically gifted from attending the college of their choice. Even they could benefit from Reserve or Guard service and learning what it means to serve our nation as a military citizen-soldier. It does not delay their entry into college or prohibit them from waiting until age twenty-four to sign up for the Reserves or Guard.

There are many in the African, European, and Hispanic communities who believe that we are doomed, and there is nothing we can do about it. Some in America believe that their situation is hopeless, which I believe is a part of the reason for the violence in many communities. America needs to hope again. When you notice those who live in poverty, you will notice dilapidated buildings (meaning the cities and towns let the infrastructure go), poor educational systems, stymied health care, trash dominating certain areas laced with graffiti, and crime ravaging the communities. In other words, the situation is perpetuated generation after generation in a vicious cycle, with few breaking free from it. The only way to build America into an even greater nation is to realize that when one group of Americans is hurting economically, then we all are hurting. While welfare and other government programs have their place in some instances, they should be limited at best. I believe that free money for extended periods creates a culture of dependency. There needs to be enforceable end dates for every program that the government sponsors. These are intended to be temporary programs, but far too many people attempt to make these programs a way of life. Having more children should not gain greater benefits and should not restart the clock. I know my liberal friends may think that I am too harsh, but if America is to break the ties of poverty, we must teach responsibility and accountability while emphasizing education. Each of us will face difficult times in our lives, but those times should not be what defines us. We cannot become dependent on the government for all economic aid.

Overcoming Poverty

There are several areas that are not balanced in our American culture, and it is not all ethnicity related—much of it deals with poverty in our nation. America must deal with its poverty levels as a whole. This has to be addressed. I am not calling for more government assistance programs to end poverty, but I am advocating that we leverage education, skills, and jobs to break the poverty cycle. We cannot turn our heads to the fact that, while when we have the richest nation on earth, there are still many who do not break the cycle of poverty and thus are hindered in their development and progression. I believe we are smart enough to develop a path to middle-class status. Let's go further by looking at the rates of poverty across the ethnicities in America along with household income. According to the US Census Bureau, the nation's poverty rate in 2011 was 15 percent, meaning 46 million Americans living in poverty, with the threshold for poverty set at $23,021 for a family of four.[393] The overall median household income in America in 2011 was $50,054 and the median household income for families was $62,273.[394] When we look closer at the poverty by ethnicity, 30.849 million Americans of European descent were in poverty, or 12.8 percent; 10.929 million Americans of African descent were in poverty, or 27.6 percent; 13.244 million Americans of Hispanic descent were in poverty, or 25.3 percent; and 1.973 million Americans of Asian descent, or 12.3 percent, lived under the poverty line.[395] What does this mean? This means that poverty affects all Americans, but when you look proportionally, it is still clear that the African- and Hispanic-descent populations are still struggling at a greater rate than others. Again, I submit that it is education that will break the poverty cycle. Education produces income, and income breaks the vicious cycle of poverty.

When a family is in poverty, it is the children who usually suffer the most and who experience the greatest hindrance in development. A closer examination of children living in poverty across ethnicities reveals poverty for children under age seventeen continues to decimate the family structure. Those children of African ancestry suffer the most, with 39 percent of children living in poverty, while children of Native American descent live with a 36 percent poverty rate, and those children of Hispanic descent have a 32 percent poverty rate, Pacific Islander children live in poverty with a rate of 27 percent, and those of European and Asian descent make up 13 percent each of children living in poverty. These are amazing statistics when you peel them back. These statistics are telling us that those of African, Hispanic, Native American, and Pacific Islander descent have approximately one-third or more of their children living in poverty. The only unscathed groups, relatively speaking, are the Asians and Europeans. That is incredibly high, in my opinion, and we must unite together to beat the system. Not only do these numbers reveal the devastating effect of poverty on our nation, poverty impacts negatively the psyche of the child growing up. As I have stated earlier, the ramifications of poverty are enormous. The makeup of the family unit is greatly challenged by poverty. Statistics confirm that most of those who live in poverty are from single parent households. This means that the child is not getting the attention he or she needs. They may not have food or basic sustenance to survive. This state of poverty also affects the level of educational development and the safety of the child. Generally, children in poverty are more susceptible to being lured into a life of crime because they need money and are vulnerable to the criminal elements that prey upon them. This leads to a greater chance for incarceration and a lifelong battle with crime. If the child grows up and does not get a full education, the cycle of poverty has a greater chance to continue in that family, because they, still living in poverty, begin to have children of their own.

Since we know that poverty affects every ethnicity in America to one degree or another, let's juxtapose that fact with the unemployment rate by ethnicity in America along with the graduation rates for higher education by ethnicity. I believe we will see a connection and a pattern that needs to be analyzed. According to the US Department of Labor, Bureau of Labor Statistics, of 2015, America is currently at one of its lowest overall unemployment rates in ten years, at 5.3 percent.[396] Please note that in our current US labor tracking system, persons who identify with an ethnicity of Hispanic or Latino can also identify with any race as well. A deeper review of unemployment across ethnicities in 2015 reveals that those of Asian descent have the lowest unemployment rate in the nation, with 4.0 percent (employment-population ratio 60.2 percent), followed by those of European descent, with 4.6 percent (employment-population ratio 59.9 percent); while those of Hispanic descent are at 6.8 percent (employment-population ratio 61.5 percent); and those of African descent are at 9.1 percent (employment-population ratio 55.8 percent).[397] These numbers are magnified in comparison since the minority groups make up a much smaller part of the population. We can note that those of African descent have an employment-population ratio at the lowest rate (worst employment) in America. Once again, I believe education is the primary means to close the unemployment gap among ethnicities. It should be America's endeavor to see all people of all ethnicities working at productive jobs—this is what will make America stronger. Since much of this book has been about closing the social and economic gaps between ethnicities, I found the following statistics of particular interest. Specifically, unemployment rates for both sexes between the ages of sixteen to nineteen years of age are broken down as follows: European descent youth have an unemployment rate of 14.8 percent, while Hispanic descent youth have unemployment rate of 16.9 percent, and those youth of African descent have an astounding unemployment rate of 28.7 percent.[398] Those of African descent are employed at a rate of almost 50 percent less than those of Hispanic and European descent. On the surface, this looks nonthreatening, for they are youth, after all, but I submit it is in the youth that we can make the biggest impact for the future of our nation in bridging the gap for ethnic relations. If we can get our youth employed on an equal footing, it will take them off of the streets where they look for income through criminal activities. Further, equal status will cause them to feel accepted in American society, a part of innovation and growth. This is why I advocate for three major areas that can turn around our youth and, by extension, the future state of America: First, a strong education which leads to employment; second, mentorship (discussed in a later chapter); and third, reform of the criminal justice system.

New Orleans street corner with barroom in residential neighborhood

I want to share with you an anecdote about how poverty affects a neighborhood. When I was growing up in New Orleans, I clearly recall seeing alcohol establishments, or barrooms, on many corners of the neighborhood. It was not uncommon to have these bars in the residential neighborhoods, all competing against one another for business. Can you imagine growing up with a bar three doors from your house? That was my situation. I could literally walk one city block and find another bar room on the corner. Furthermore, if I did a quick estimation without actually mapping it out, I would venture to say there were over ten alcohol establishments within about a six-block radius. How did these businesses get permits to operate in these neighborhoods? This will always be a question that lingers. I believe that while these types of permits were given readily, many other types of business loans and permits were regularly denied. I do not have any empirical data to support my claim, but I do recall news reports pointing out lack of creditworthiness of those in poor communities. Perhaps covert racism played a part in permitting certain types of loans and denying others. I don't think I will fully understand why that happened. I do know for a fact that when some of my friends began to move into more upscale neighborhoods and suburbs, there were no bars on the corners. I remember we even commented on one community my friends moved to, pointing out that it was the new way forward with no bars. One caveat to all of this is that I lived near the French Quarter of New Orleans, and as the major tourist hub of the city, there were indeed bars in and around the area. Perhaps this is the rationale for my neighborhood because it was modeled after the quarter. Again, I am not sure how or why those establishments were placed there, but I am sure they were detrimental to the well-being of the community. I saw firsthand alcoholism, drug transfers, open sexual solicitations, violent events (arguing and fighting), and countless shootings, all centered on bars in our neighborhood. While we cannot undo the past or truly determine how some of these situations came about, we need to look for ways to improve communities and neighborhoods. I submit that we must change neighborhoods across America that are dominated by alcoholic establishments. I am not against these businesses, but let's move these establishments to the city areas or zones that allow for those types of businesses.

Another area that is shrouded in mystery in America is the Planned Parenthood Federation of America (PPFA) and its dominance in communities with those of African descent and other poor communities with differing ethnicities. Why are these establishments in predominantly minority neighborhoods? One could surmise that it is because the residents are poor, and thus, this federally funded, nonprofit organization is there to help. This is similar to the many bars placed in neighborhoods for those of African descent. Was this a systematic approach to slow down the reproduction of those of African descent? Some would hold to this view, but there is no definitive evidence to emphatically reach this conclusion. Others will point out that Planned Parenthood is located in poorer neighborhoods because it is the primary provider of female reproductive healthcare in the nation among poorer populations. While there is no empirical evidence to show that this is a systematic approach to slow down African American reproduction, the facts do support the proportionally large number of PPFA clinics in poorer neighborhoods. PPFA focuses on sex education, family planning, and pro-choice, and it is the largest US provider of reproductive health services including cervical cancer screening, abortion, breast cancer screening, and HIV screening.[399] There has been much controversy with one of the largest abortion providers in the United States. For starters, the founder of PPFA, Margaret Sanger, has been associated with eugenics, including the American Eugenics Society, which intimated that some ethnicities were inferior and that, through sterilization or other methods, they could help ethnicities eliminate the unfit.[400] Further, Sanger has been accused throughout the decades of purposely placing many of the more than seven hundred PPFA clinics in neighborhoods of those from African descent to commit genocide. She has also been accused of taking donations allegedly earmarked for controlling the population of those from African descent.[401] To say the least, this is a very controversial organization, and it is clear that the late Margaret Sanger associated with those who believed in race superiority and controlling race production as noted above. According to the Centers for Disease Control and Prevention, although only 13 percent of the population, or forty-two million, those of African descent accounted for 36 percent of all abortions in the United States between 2007 and 2010, while those of Hispanic descent account for 21 percent of abortions even though they only made up 15 percent of the US population at that time.[402] The CDC also found that 64 percent of all abortions in the United States during that same time were from minorities, while those of European descent (62 percent of the nation) accounted for the remaining 36 percent of abortions. Even though those of African and European descent each account for approximately 36 percent of all abortions, the proportion of African descent abortions is equal to almost five times that of any other ethnic group.[403] In 2015, the PPFA was wrapped in a major controversy concerning the selling of fetal tissues and body parts of the aborted babies for profit and was recorded by undercover associates of the Center for Medical Progress pretending to be interested buyers.[404] The tapes were debunked and proven to be fake and edited to make the PPFA seem as if they were trying to make a profit, but it is clear that selling/donating of fetal tissue was the intent even if not for a profit, which is not against the law as long as cost is reasonable. The Senate tried to pass legislation to defund the PPFA in August 2015 as a result of the videos, but it did not pass.[405]

Justice System

One of the most challenging areas in which to help bring healing to racial tensions is the criminal justice system. As I have stated, if we make education available for all, reduce poverty, and correct the illegal and unconstitutional practices that are sometimes found in our criminal justice system, including wrongful incarceration, positive changes can be made in America for all ethnic relations. The protests we see today are mainly about the criminal justice system and believing that minorities are discriminated against by law officials. As I have described previously, there has been certainly a period in American history where people who were not of European descent were treated with great disdain and prejudice. Yes, there are corrupt judges, government officials, district attorneys, prosecutors, and police officers, as there are corrupt people in every profession. The news recently highlighted the number of high-ranking law enforcement officials who had been arrested or imprisoned in 2015. This is evident in the data I have previously presented on law officials facing criminal charges. We also have established that the vast majority of America's law enforcement officials are positive and upright and, indeed, serve and protect our communities. Some of my relatives and friends are law officials, and I have the utmost respect for them and those with whom they serve. Today we live in a new era in America, where all people expect fairness and justice. Gone are the eras of slavery and Jim Crow laws, yet there are some who feel there are still remnants in our society. In this section, we will look at the criminal justice system and perhaps expose some misinterpretations and stereotypes. There are widely differing opinions in America on whether or not the criminal justice system is fair to all citizens. Further, just as strong are varying opinions about who commits the most crimes in America and who the most violent offenders are. The problem with all of these thoughts and arguments is that they can all be skewed based on how one spins the data. It is my endeavor to share statistics to clarify the thoughts that shape ethnic relations.

In 2012, according to the Bureau of Justice Statistics, those of

European descent committed 8,418,616 offenses, while 3,421,356 offenses were committed by those of African descent.[406] As with other statistics throughout the book, I try to ensure that we translate the raw numbers into the true impact per population. When you also include populations for those ethnicities in these overall statistics, you can approximate that .43 or 4 percent of the population of those of European descent are involved in crime and .79 or almost 8 percent of the population of those of African descent are involved in crime. This is a far cry from what you will hear others or the media randomly spout—that those of African or Hispanic descent account for 50 percent of all crime in America. That actually is a myth. However, we tend to believe what we hear over and over again, and what we must acknowledge is that this type of rhetoric is a part of the history of oppression. The reality is that in 2012, the total offenses committed in America were 12,198,491, and those of African descent committed 3,421,456, which means they accounted for 28 percent of all crime in America.[407] Conversely, using the same numbers with those of European descent committing 8,418,616 criminal offenses, it translates to 69 percent of all offenses in America. The following is where the numbers cause concern. Put another way, although those of African descent account for 13 percent of the population, they account for 28 percent of the crimes in America annually, while those of European descent account for 62 percent of the population and commit 69 percent of the crime in America annually. Both ethnicities' crime rates exceed their population sizes. However, the African descent population must face the fact that the number of crimes committed annually for the size of the population should bring great concern.

These statistics included Hispanic or Latino as part of either European descent or African descent; thus, they do not have a separate category for race, which again supports my position that there is only one human race. Further, the crime rates of 177,117 for American Indian and Alaskan Native and 181,401 for Asian Pacific Islanders are almost inconsequential to our discussion because the crime rate is so low for those groups.[408] But what does all of this mean for America? First, I believe it sheds light on the misinformation concerning crime in America and who commits the crime. Americans of European descent commit the most crimes in America by a wide margin. Secondly, it does confirm what I have been espousing throughout this book—per population size, those of African and Hispanic descent still commit too many crimes. Third, these basic statistics might inform why there are arguments from both sides who claim racism and discrimination when it comes to law enforcement officials. For instance, some will say that the media does not want to highlight that those of European descent commit almost 69 percent of all crimes in America, but wants the greater American public to believe that those of African descent commit the most crimes. Even though only 4 percent of people of European descent committed the crimes in 2012, those of African descent who claim that the police are too aggressive often deny that police are on high alert because, per capita, their chances of being confronted are higher when dealing with those of African descent. Yet we must point out again that the crime rate only represents 8 percent of the African descent population, and yet many are placed in the aggressive category based on the color of their skin. Thus, I am hoping for a wakeup call to America to end the erroneous thought that individuals of African descent are responsible for most crime in America. But individuals of African descent must acknowledge that too much crime is committed for its population size. Let me be clear, however, that this does not justify discrimination and unlawful arrest by law officials for those of African or Hispanic descent or other ethnicities. Before I move on to the next section in this chapter that highlights the justice system and incarceration rates, I want to share additional statistics from Bureau of Justice Statistics, 2012:

Offense	Total	European Descent	African Descent	American Indian and Alaskan Native	Asian Pacific Islander
Murder/ Manslaughter	11,075	5,288	5,515	136	135
Forcible Rape	18,098	11,659	5,876	283	280
Aggravated Assault	388,362	243,386	132,473	5,738	6,765
Other Assaults	1,199,476	783,315	381,220	18,087	16,854
Weapons Carrying	149,286	86,236	59,907	1,048	2,095
Sex Offense	68,355	49,353	16,867	837	1,299
Drug Abuse Violations	1,552,432	1,040,991	482,400	11,104	17,937

Gambling Offenses against the Family and Children	107,018	70,096	33,940	2,202	780
Driving Under the Influence	1,282,957	1,081,954	154,619	17,528	28,857
Violent Crime Index	521,196	304,600	201,116	6,965	8,515

Data source: Bureau of Justice Statistics, FBI, Uniform
Crime Reporting Program, 2012[409]

Criminal incarceration data shows the pattern with which we have now become all too familiar. In 2013, the US prison population was comprised of approximately 1,574,700 persons in state and federal prisons, which represented an increase of approximately 4,300 prisoners (0.3 percent) from 2012.[410] As a side note, the prison population increased in 2013 for the first time since the high of 1,615,500 prisoners in 2009.[411] When we look deeper into those who are incarcerated, those of African descent continue to make up the largest percentage of male inmates, with 37 percent under state or federal jurisdiction in 2013, while those of European descent make up 32 percent, and those of Hispanic descent make up 22 percent of the prison population.[412] These numbers are incredible when you think of the population size of America and speak to the mistrust of those of Hispanic and African descent with the current justice system. Specifically, one out of every fifteen males of African descent are in prison, while one out of every thirty-six males of Hispanic descent are in prison, and one out of 106 males of European descent are in prison.[413] The incarceration rates show a great disparity in justice, with the smaller populations having committed fewer offenses, yet having disproportionate numbers of prisoners. Females of European descent comprised 49 percent of the US prison population, while those of African descent made up 22 percent of the population. However, when we look at the numbers through the lens of population size, the imprisonment rate for those of African descent is an incredible 113 per one hundred thousand, which is twice the rate of those from European descent at 51 per one hundred thousand.[414]

Why should this be alarming to each of us as Americans? If America is to change, the problems with the criminal justice system must be corrected. According to the Bureau of Justice Statistics, an astonishing 3 percent of males of African descent of all ages were imprisoned on December 31, 2013, while only 0.5 percent of males with European descent of all ages were imprisoned.[415] Change will start when judges and prosecutors treat the accused fairly no matter what their skin tone. Somehow, those of brown skin are not afforded the best of the justice system and evidently receive harsher punishment and sentencing. This is evidenced again with the disparity of the number offenses committed annually, including the type of offenses juxtaposed against the annual incarceration rate. The incarceration rate of those of African descent is incongruent with the number of offenses committed in 2012. In other words, it appears to be a broken system that incarcerates males of African descent at an alarmingly high rate, even though they commit 50 percent fewer criminal offenses than those of European descent annually. Plainly spoken, our justice system is broken and clearly discriminates against those with brown skin. What has been reported constantly is that those of European descent tend to get lighter sentences, if they are imprisoned at all, than do their counterparts with brown skin for the same offense. Let's look deeper at the clearly discriminatory practices which must be addressed in every law enforcement jurisdiction.

According to author Jerome Miller, discriminatory practices in the law and justice departments today have been used to essentially continue where Jim Crow practices left off in the 1960s by establishing a hierarchy of superiority in America.[416] Under the leadership of President Reagan (1980–88), the War on Drugs initiative was instituted, which meant massive funding for the penal system and funding to fight crimes that eventually grew by 1992 into $32 billion annually to fight the drug war.[417] This was a great concept to clean up the streets of America, in my opinion, and get drugs off the streets, thereby protecting our vulnerable youth, but the problem was that somehow the War on Drugs began targeting those of African and Hispanic descent, even though they were not the primary users of drugs. For instance, in 1996, the Mental Health Services Institution reported that 76 percent of all illicit drug users were of European descent, 14 percent were African descent, and 15.9 percent were of Hispanic descent, yet arrests and incarcerations were disproportionately of people of African and Hispanic descent.[418] The Drug Abuse Act of 1986 had harsher punishments for distribution of crack cocaine versus powder cocaine, and it led to mass incarceration of those of African descent. Professor Michelle

Alexander went so far as to state that the War on Drugs was directly geared to incarcerating those of African descent.[419]

The criminal justice system has been challenged when it comes to arrest rates, police stoppages, police brutality, and, ultimately, discriminatory sentencing. Again, I will refer back to my earlier statistics to show that the number of arrests by ethnicity is incongruent with the rate of incarceration in the penal system. This can be as a result of the lack of funds by the poor (mostly those of African and Hispanic descent) to get the appropriate lawyer to defend them. It can also be the harsher penalties that will be levied upon those of African or Hispanic descent for the same crime as their European-descent counterparts. Many believe that targeting and racial profiling has become the accepted weapon of choice for police, allowing for those of African and Hispanic descent to be targeted by police and investigators.[420] Professor Michelle Alexander made this case by showing how racial profiling plays out in America. She showed video footage confirming that in Volusia County, Florida, police stopped one thousand individuals for traffic violations with 80 percent being African or Hispanic descent, yet that population group (African or Hispanic descent) only makes up 5 percent of the population in Volusia County.[421] This has been the claim throughout the years from those of African or Hispanic descent who report being stopped unnecessarily. They also report that drugs have been placed in the vehicles during searches to ensure quotas are met. Case after case shows that police are more aggressive toward those who have a brown complexion and that it is almost expected that there will be a confrontation.

I must admit, these practices cause me great concern, yet I trust my fellow defenders of our nation, the police force. I can remember defending them to many colleagues, but as I began to do the research, I must say that this type of behavior by law enforcement is unacceptable, and yet it happens too often. Again, I don't believe this is the entire law enforcement system, but there is a percentage who would revert to these types of practices. Let's take it further. Even if you had corrupt police practices, shouldn't prosecutors and judges be able to correct the injustices? That would be my hope, but unfortunately, my research shows that at times the entire criminal justice system is acting in concert to perpetrate discriminatory practices, from arrest to sentencing. Once the system is corrupt, it is very difficult to stop the cycle of harassment, arrests, sentencing, and incarceration. One researcher found that those of African descent are more likely to be subjected to pretext traffic stops, meaning that if you are brown-skinned and you have a vehicle violation, you are more likely to be pulled over and searched for illegal drugs.[422]

This system seems also to follow the same pattern with sentencing. Author Jerome Miller found that those of African descent receive sentences that are 49 percent longer than those of European descent for similar offenses.[423] Further, the "three strikes and you're out" law, life sentencing for serious criminal offenses, has made a huge impact on those of African descent, who receive life sentences at a far greater rate than those of European descent, mainly for drug offenses, even though those of African descent use drugs at a lower rate than those of European descent.[424]

Digging deeper statistically, Professor Miller reported that the Baldus Study on criminal offenses showed that defendants who murdered those of European descent were eleven times more likely to receive the death penalty than those who murdered individuals of African descent.[425] Professor Alexander went on to report that prosecutors in Georgia pursued the death penalty in 70 percent of cases where a person of African descent murdered a person of European descent, versus prosecutors only pursuing the death penalty in 19 percent of cases where a person of European descent murdered a person of African descent.[426] This is accentuated across America, with those of African descent in 2012 receiving 42 percent of all death penalties, a rate of five times more than those of European descent despite murders being committed at similar rates as far as volume.[427] Again, I want the reader to be constantly reminded of my earlier statistics in the beginning of this section on the criminal justice system. These numbers should convince any reasonable person that the system is skewed toward harsher punishments for those of brown skin and that we certainly have a discrimination issue with our criminal justice system, which has in some cases led to the ultimate price of death.

The news often reports on crime between ethnicities. I saw many interesting articles dealing with violent crimes between the ethnicities. One that stood out in particular is the rate of crimes between ethnicities, according to the Department of Justice. According to the Department of

Justice, those of European descent commit 82.4 percent of violent crimes against those from their own ethnicity, 7.8 percent against those of Hispanic descent, and 3.6 percent against those of African descent.[428] Conversely, those of African descent commit violent crimes in an almost equal rate against those of European descent (38.6 percent) and those of African descent (40.9 percent), while committing less violent crime against those of Hispanic descent with a percentage of 14.5 percent.[429] Finally, those of Hispanic descent commit most of their crimes against those of European descent (50.7 percent), 40.1 percent against those of their own ethnicity, and only 4.7 percent of crimes against those of African descent.[430] These statistics clearly show that those of European descent are not aggressive against those outside of their own ethnicity, generally speaking, while those of African descent are equally aggressive against themselves and those of European descent, but less against those of Hispanic descent. Finally, those of Hispanic descent are mostly aggressive toward those of European descent and themselves, but not against those of African descent. When these numbers are juxtaposed against population size, the overall violent crime rates show those of African descent commit violent crime at two and a half times the rate of those of European descent, while those of Hispanic descent are 26 percent more likely than those of European descent to commit violent crimes.[431]

Don't lose hope. We can reform our criminal justice system as Americans, but as I have said throughout this book, it will take all Americans to stand up, just as it took all Americans to end slavery and the Jim Crow era. Federal and state leaders have to get involved and begin changing the laws. We need to acknowledge the disparity in police stops, arrests, trials, sentencing, and death penalties for those of African or Hispanic descent even though they don't commit most of the crimes in terms of raw numbers. The reason that 98.4 percent of all repeat drug offenders sentenced to life imprisonment are of African descent is because there is a systematic approach to using the law to incarcerate those of African descent.[432] However, it does not end there. The recidivism rate of 66 to 70 percent within three years of release is horrendous for criminals and only exacerbates an already broken system.[433] Inmates lose most of their citizenship rights, such as voting, and are labeled, if and when they do get out. They are more susceptible to getting back into the criminal system because they do not receive the aid, treatment, or care that they need to actually get back into society. In some cases, those who are released from prison will find it difficult to earn a decent wage or an honest living. Unemployment rates are just as egregious, and the released prisoners cannot function in society. They are basically left behind. Low esteem and low self-worth often dominate those coming out of prison, because they are seen as social pariahs and are generally shunned. The cycle continues, with those of African and Hispanic descent dominating the penal system per capita and seen as the "thugs or criminals" of American society. This vicious cycle breathes racism and discriminatory practices throughout America. The main way to change discriminatory practices is to acknowledge the injustices and fix the entire system.

Finally, I would challenge the reader with another way to improve illicit criminal discriminatory practices. This applies to all ethnicities, but those of Hispanic and African descent must stop committing crime at such high rates in view of smaller population sizes. Stop doing illegal activity, and the justice system immediately changes. I don't fear the criminal justice system because I don't plan to commit crimes. I don't have to worry about being a repeat offender because it is my quest not to commit the first offense. I am not naive; I realize that the problem is that even if I don't commit a crime, I may still face unwarranted arrests and discriminatory treatment in the criminal justice system because I have African ethnicity, at least in part. I am not trying to be the moral police, but now is the time to determine a new way forward and live a life of love and peace. No, I am not dismissing the illegal and unconstitutional violations of our criminal justice system today, but I know that the best solution, along with an overhaul of the criminal justice system to expunge the illegal discriminatory practices, is for all Americans to determine to live with a sense of honor, love, and respect one for the other and stop committing the crimes.

RESTORING THE AMERICAN FAMILY

We think sometimes that poverty is only being hungry, naked and homeless. The poverty of being unwanted, unloved and uncared for is the greatest poverty. We must start in our own homes to remedy this kind of poverty.[434]
— Saint Mother Teresa,
Albanian leader and humanitarian

Saint Mother Teresa, Albanian Leader

As I have shown in the previous chapters, America can be stronger if we continue to root out the remnants of discriminatory practices and make every American feel valued. This change requires respect for all Americans. America, more than ever before, is facing the challenge of what we call the breakup of the American family. No matter what background or ethnicity, our children are bombarded with a culture that is degrading and full of violence that erodes the family structure. The American family is vulnerable because of the changing culture and values in America. From bullying, hitting, robbery, and emotional and physical assault, our youth are out of control. Violence is out of control in the United States, and in 2012, according to the Centers for Disease and Control (CDC), it was the third leading cause of death for youth ages fifteen to twenty-four.[435] Specifically, in 2012, 4,787 young people aged ten to twenty-four were victims of homicide for an astounding average of thirteen each day, and 599,000 young people aged ten to twenty-four years had physical assault injuries treated in US emergency rooms, with an incredible average of 1,642 assaults each day, costing more than $16 billion each year, counting medical costs and work lost.[436] In 2013, the CDC reported that 17.9 percent of high school students brought weapons to school, and 19.6 percent said they were bullied in school.[437] These numbers paint an austere picture of the mind-set of our youth and the cultural conditions youth face in America. As they mature unchecked, the youth become the perpetrators of crime as young adults. This does not take into account the number of youth who are simply attacked for being a different skin tone.

Not only is violence prevalent in America, but America's families have also become dysfunctional. Unfortunately, many of our youth are growing up today in broken homes and with broken families, and this is tied directly to violence, crime, poverty, and despair. I have talked about the vicious cycle in the previous chapter where those who are in desperate situations find it difficult to break the cycle without any direct change in their lifestyles. In fact, those who are most susceptible to violence come from poverty or live in an impoverished community; they have a prior history of violence; they tend to use drugs, alcohol, or tobacco; and they are influenced by an association with delinquent peers, poor family functioning, and poor academic performance.[438] Recent videos have surfaced in early 2015 depicting despicable behavior, with teens beating teens with apparently no regard for life.[439] When showing the videos of the vicious beatings and violence, the headline on Fox News read, "American Culture in Decline."[440] It is vividly clear that ethics, morals, and values are degrading across America. I believe the sense of rightness is lacking in America. The commentators were asked why this type of behavior is becoming more prevalent. One theory was that the American family is broken, and thus, single parents, both male and female, cannot administer the discipline, time, and care needed to raise their children. The unsupervised children then have limited boundaries, mentorship, and leadership and are able to act out as they choose. The commentators on the news show went on to report that teachers across the nation are complaining that they are facing greater and greater difficulties with disciplining the students, and that behavior is rapidly deteriorating. Please note that this is not limited to a particular ethnicity. It is an American problem. The news broadcast went on to show the actions of kids at spring break in 2015. In particular, there were college students literally fighting with police officers on the beaches in Florida, and the Mississippi State starting quarterback and then-rising star, Dak Prescott (now a member of the National Football League Dallas Cowboys), was shown being attacked and beaten.[441] Luckily, there were no major injuries sustained. These incidents could seem simple on the surface, but I see a growing trend with the lack of love and respect for one another. Some will make the argument that this is nothing new; it has been going on for years. The difference is now we have media to show what is happening. There is some truth to that sentiment, but let's look deeper at the structure of the American family.

Broken Families

America must overcome major hurdles with regard to the family if America is to be strong. One of the most devastating issues America faces is broken homes or single-parent homes. According to the US Census Bureau, America's demographics are continually shifting with regard to family and marriage. In 1970, 17 percent of US households were considered single parent, and 71 percent of parents were married; conversely in 2012, 28 percent were considered single-parent households and only 49 percent of America's households included married partners.[442] This means that over one-third of all children born in America are living in single-parent households. The Pew Research Center found that in 2014, 34 percent of all children were living with an unmarried parent as compared to 19 percent in 1980 and 9 percent in 1960.[443] These changes in demographics can seem harmless at first glance, but there are great consequences to the changes in the second- and third-order effects on our society. When the husband or wife is not present in the home, it makes a difference. Most commonly, it is the mother who ends up raising the family alone due to the natural maternal instincts that mean the female is less likely to abandon the family. In some cases, the maternal grandmother raises the children while the parents check in on them, causing much confusion and instability for the child. According to the Pew Research Center, there is a shift in never-married adults, with 8 percent of women and 9 percent of men never having been married in 1960 compared to 23 percent of men and 17 percent of women who have never been married in 2012.[444] These statistics deal with young adults from the ages of twenty-five to thirty-four. If you break it down by the different ethnicities, in 2012 you will find that the number of people of African descent who have never been married by age twenty-five and older was 36 percent, those of Hispanic descent were at 26 percent, while those of Asian descent were at 19 percent and those of European descent were at 16 percent.[445] The transition in the American family structure cannot be denied.

But why is this transition happening? I submit that there is a cultural shift in attitudes toward the importance of the family. For instance, the Pew Research Center also found that America is virtually split (46 percent versus 50 percent) today on whether marriage and family makes one better off, with 46 percent believing it makes a difference and 50 percent believing that it does not; however, most Americans (68 percent) believe that it is important for couples to still get married if they are to live together for the long term.[446] The problem with that mind-set is that most couples who live together for long periods of time have greater chances of divorce, and thus, the family is even more vulnerable to pain and suffering. Specifically, the divorce rate in America constantly hovers around 50 percent for those who are first-time married, 65 percent for second marriages, and 60 percent for those who cohabitate before marriage.[447] For every hundred cohabitating couples, only forty end up getting married, and close to 60 percent will divorce out of that forty. This means that out of the forty couples getting married, slightly more than twenty-three to twenty-five couples divorce in early years. In the end, that means that out of one hundred couples cohabitating, fifteen to seventeen couples would be married after three years, leaving eighty couples either never married, split, or divorced. Does that sound like a winning plan? I submit it is a risk you don't need to take if you intend to be with the other person for life. In fact, many of the sixty couples who never marry or split up end up with children out of wedlock, and those children generally enter life at a disadvantage socially and economically. Yet the cultural shift and wisdom in America is to live together before pursuing marriage in order to test the waters. Thus, single-parent households are birthed out of an erroneous concept that living together before marriage is a benefit, when in fact the children are left to suffer.

Unfortunately, all of America faces the devastating effects of single-parent households or broken families. No ethnicity is exempt from the impact of the broken family and need for restoration. Without a doubt, poverty increases with single-parent households. For instance, according to the US Census Bureau from 2007 to 2009, 37.1percent of the children in single-parent households live in poverty, while only 6.8 percent of children in married households live in poverty.[448] This was confirmed when the US Census Bureau reported in 2011 that 6.2 percent of married couples, 16.1 percent of families with male-only households, and 31.2 percent of families with female-only households lived in poverty.[449] These are clear statistics that point out the great value of dual parent households. The results are extreme, with major negative implications with regard to poverty for the single-parent household. First, let me make sure that no one will mistake that these statistics mean that single parent households are negative; that is not the case. There are children who grew up to make major impacts in America who were raised in single-parent households. Likewise, many single parents were found in their circumstance through no fault of their own and are doing their best to raise their families. I have many family and friends who were single parents, and they did a great job. I am simply pointing out there is an important aspect of families that we cannot ignore with regard to the impact of single-parent households. It is unambiguous, whether females or males are leading single households, poverty increases from three to five times versus those families where the parents remain married. Further, the US Census Bureau reports that marriage decreases the likelihood of child poverty by an incredible 82 percent.[450] How can anyone argue against the value of the family with those powerful statistics?

America needs strong families to turn the tide against poverty, which will, in turn, make us a healthier nation. Remember, poverty directly impacts education standards as demonstrated in the previous chapter. It is not a toss-up; marriage and the family structure make a difference for the life of the child. There is no doubt that, if the family unit is broken, there is a higher chance for instability in society, including economic impact. A study at Princeton University found that there is an elevated risk of children in single-parent households experiencing cognitive, social, and emotional problems.[451] This means that not only are the children affected economically, but even learning ability, stress, and emotional distress results from being raised in a single-parent household. These are things that are sometimes hard to quantify and measure. As I continually say, this does not mean that a child in a single-parent household cannot be successful; it just means that the odds are far greater that he or she will face challenges on the road to success. The vicious cycle continues in single-parent households when children are unsupervised and find it difficult to complete their education. The lack of education then leads to economic distress. Economic distress feeds into cognitive, social, and emotional issues. One can clearly see the cycle is difficult to break.

The research is equally striking when comparing the effects on children from single-parent households to children from married households. In the Princeton University study with seventeen thousand adolescents aged twelve to eighteen, it was revealed that 30 percent of children from single households repeated a school grade versus 19 percent from married couples, while 40 percent of children in single households were suspended as compared to 21 percent of children suspended from school for married couples being suspended, and children living in single households were 23 percent more likely to be in a violent altercation and 127 percent more likely to need emotional therapy.[452] The Princeton research went on to reveal that children of married couples are less likely to attempt suicide, smoke, or use drugs, experience emotional problems that require a therapist, or to have been in trouble for delinquency (stealing, breaking into a house, damaging property) or violence.[453] The data is consistent in that those children living with married parents are less likely to experience emotional trauma or violence. The studies show that these numbers are even more dramatic when the home is happy with two parents, as compared to a home with two parents who may not be as engaged in the life of the child. Thus, if a child grows up with both parents who are engaged in his or her life, it is much more likely that the child will have less chance of experiencing a traumatic life in childhood or adulthood. This is important, because the more traumatic a life one leads (criminal history, educational disadvantage, poverty, and social inequities), the more likely one will continue the same patterns in adult life. I can essentially sum it up in a simple statement: Single parenthood has a negative impact on society as a whole and hurts the well-being of children. Again, please do not take this to mean that single parents are bad and that no good can come out of that situation. I know many courageous single parents and their children who defy the odds and refuse to become negative statistics. I am simply showing the direct, empirical evidence of the benefits of a two-parent household and its impact on society.

When we juxtapose this data to ethnicities, it further highlights the devastating effects on society. Specifically, in 2013, while making up only 13 percent of the population, those of African descent have a devastating 67 percent rate (6.4 million) of single-parent households, while those of Hispanic descent have a debilitating 42 percent rate (seven million), even as those of European descent have a 25 percent rate (9.2 million) of single-parent households, and those of Asian or Pacific Islander descent have a 16 percent rate (550,000) as compared to those of Native American descent, with a 52 percent rate (three hundred thousand) of single-parent households.[454] Interestingly, those with two or more ethnicities have a 42 percent rate (1.7 million) of single-parent households.[455] The obvious stands out once again. While those of European descent have the highest number of single-parent households in America at 9.2 million, those of African descent have the highest rate per population size, with 6.4 million, or 67 percent. According to Dr. Patrick Fagan, the sociological research is plentiful that shows a stable family is built when a family follows the traditional route of completing school, getting a job, getting married, and then having children, in that order.[456] I am not saying everyone will be married or must be married, but I am saying that marriage is natural, and the results are positive for our society. When we build a society or nation that shuns marriage or downplays its importance, and the marriage rate goes below 50 percent of the population, there are clear negative effects on society as a whole, as depicted earlier in the chapter. One of the greatest hurdles to overcome is having children out of wedlock. When one has children out of wedlock, that person immediately puts him- or herself at a great disadvantage and can often be locked into the vicious cycle of poverty as described above. Having children before graduating high school is a devastating blow, but it can be overcome. Thus, I am calling for men in all of our communities and of all ethnicities to step up and take responsibility for raising their children. As demonstrated above, those of African descent and Hispanic descent are particularly susceptible to a trend of females raising children alone, and thus, the vicious cycle of poverty, despair, and crime continues in those communities at a higher rate due to lack of supervision, economic disenfranchisement, and lack of educational growth. Men, I challenge you to take the courage to stand and help begin a new America. We need specifically to take responsibility and return to the family.

The Battle over Abortion

Another sign that the family is broken is the high rate of abortion. I know some may be wondering how this affects the courage to stand in America. I see it as a moral imperative for America in the battle for life and human rights, such as ending slavery or segregation. Some may challenge me on that point and believe I am overstating my position. I link this subject to a new America because I believe it is an issue of respect for all lives, even those who cannot speak on their own. Personally, I believe in the right to life and not the right to arbitrarily take life due to how one might feel about getting pregnant, the mother's economic status, or if the pregnancy was intentional. I do understand traumatic instances, such as rape and incest, where one might feel more inclined to have an abortion or cases in which the mother's life is at risk. I could support abortion under those circumstances. However, I have seen enough reports of those persons who were born as a result of the unfortunate crime of rape who somehow were not aborted to know they sometimes turn out to be the best thing for the parent or make a major impact in America. I do not mean to minimize the heinous crime or the emotional, physical, and psychological pain that rape or incest brings, but I only submit that the child in the womb is innocent and has not asked to be created. Again, if a woman cannot bear the pain of carrying a child under those egregious circumstances or rape or incest, I can support her right not to complete the pregnancy. I know many of my conservative friends will not agree with my position, but some will. Thus, my greatest objection is for abortion at will for no apparent reason.

In 1973, the US Supreme Court, after thirteen months of deliberations in the landmark case of Roe v. Wade (named after Dallas County District Attorney Henry Wade), 410 US C. 113, forever shaped the discussion on abortion in America. The courts ruled 7:2 that a woman can legally make decision to have an abortion before the first trimester (twelve weeks) without question, but there must be a balance between the "woman's right" and the "potential of life" during the second trimester.[457] Essentially, the courts basically ruled that states would have a compelling interest after the first semester, in which fetal viability becomes apparent. The third trimester is definitely not feasible for an abortion, and the courts considered a compelling interest for the potential of life. The argument was basically the same that I made earlier in the chapter. When does life begin during the gestation period? Looking back at American history, abortion was first rendered illegal in Connecticut in 1800s and then deemed illegal in all states by 1900 due to the argument of the potentiality of life at all stages.[458]

In June of 1969, the case of Roe v. Wade, involved Norma L. McCorvey (the name Roe is a pseudonym), who was seeking an abortion during the pregnancy of her third child, S tried to claim she had been raped so she could have the abortion, but the clinic she went to had already been shut down.[459] Two lawyers, Linda Coffee and Sarah Weddington, were referred to McCorvey, and the case was filed in the North District of Texas in June 1970, even though by then she had her baby. The judges ruled in her favor on the grounds of legal merit for an abortion, but did not go so far as to grant an injunction against the enforcement of laws barring abortion.[460] Therefore, after the victory in the Dallas courts, an appeal was made to the US Supreme Court. This was certainly a volatile time in America, and abortion laws were being challenged constantly. In fact, before Roe v. Wade and Doe v. Bolton (which was a similar court case that the Supreme Court began working simultaneously with Roe v. Wade), the Supreme Court had just ruled (narrowly) that abortion was still illegal in the United States v. Vuitch except in the cases where the mother's life or health (physical or mental) was in danger.[461] Of course, all that changed a few months later when the verdict was rendered in Roe v. Wade. Interestingly, Norma L. McCorvey went on record and changed her position in 1995. She now espouses the right to life, rather than abortion. She has stated to congress in 1998, "It was my pseudonym, Jane Roe, which had been used to create the 'right' to abortion out of legal thin air. But Sarah Weddington and Linda Coffee never told me that what I was signing would allow women to come up to me fifteen, twenty years later and say, 'Thank you for allowing me to have my five or six abortions.' Without you, it wouldn't have been possible."[2] Weddington never mentioned women using abortions as a form of birth control. We have talked about truly desperate and needy women, not women already wearing maternity clothes.[462] Many states have enacted varying laws since the landmark case in an attempt to restrict the impact of abortion in America; thus, access to legal abortions is not the same in every state. The question really comes down to personhood and when that person (the child) is protected by the US Constitution. Many states have enacted laws as prescribed by the Supreme Court with varying restrictions and bans on abortions, such as partial birth abortions (a technique used in second-trimester abortions) ban of 2003, 18 US C. 1531, that was upheld by the Supreme Court as constitutional in 2007.[463] It was comforting to see that a partial birth abortion was seen as the clearly inhumane and cruel practice that it is, as it would be performed at five months and later, with a living baby literally being torn apart for no medical reason.

Let's look more closely at the number of abortions committed in America. In 2011, 730,322 legal abortions were captured by the Centers for Disease Control (CDC), with 13.9 abortions per one thousand women aged fifteen to forty-four years.[464] This amounts to an abortion ratio of 219 abortions per one thousand live births and marks a 4 percent decrease in the abortion ratio and a 5 percent decrease in abortions overall from 2010.[465] In fact, abortions have decreased dramatically from 2002 to 2011, to historic lows, with 19.1 percent of all abortions performed for medical purposes in 2011.[466] In fact, in 2011, the vast majority of abortions (91.4 percent) took place in the first trimester, while 7.3 percent abortions were performed between fourteen to twenty weeks (second trimester) gestation, and 1.4 percent were performed at twenty-one weeks or more of gestation.[467] This data speaks to my greatest concern and what we know; most abortions happen early on, and if we can get the mother to see that there is a child in her womb who is at a different stage of development in human life, it might reduce the number of abortions dramatically. With almost 20 percent (146,000) of all abortions in 2011 performed for medical reasons,

80 percent (584,000) of abortions were performed voluntarily, with most (531,000) performed in the first trimester. As we analyze abortion by ethnicity, the most recent data from the Centers for Disease Control indicates that in 2008, 37.5 percent of all abortions were obtained by those of European descent, while those of African descent accounted for 35.5 percent of all abortions, and those of Hispanic descent accounted 21.1 percent of all abortions. As usual, the raw numbers look very similar across racial and ethnic lines, but once we add in the population size and ratio per group, we see an astounding disparity, with those of European descent accounting for 8.7 abortions per one thousand women and 140 abortions per one thousand live births; while those of African descent account for 33.5 abortions per one thousand women and 472 abortions per one thousand live births; and those of Hispanic descent account for 20.4 abortions per one thousand women and 196 abortions per one thousand live births.[458] This clearly shows that those of African descent abort babies at almost five times the rate of those of European descent, and those of Hispanic descent around two and a half times the rate of those of European descent. What does this data mean for America? From our earlier chapter dealing with poverty, we know that those of African and Hispanic heritage have a higher rate of poverty in America proportionately. We can then draw a correlation between those who are in poverty and those who are more likely to abort babies.

Thus, one way to counter abortion in America is to break the extreme poverty cycle, as discussed above. I have already reported that the organization Planned Parenthood may have been strategically placed in poor and underprivileged neighborhoods, thus giving the opportunity for abortion to those of African and Hispanic descent literally in the neighborhood. In my opinion, as I stated earlier, abortion is a form of genocide. It does not take a degree in statistics to see that these high abortion numbers decimate the growth of these heritage groups over time. It is also no surprise that the large majority of those who have abortions are not married, with up to 65 percent to 90 percent of those obtaining abortions being single as reported by the CDC.[469]

My idea about life is simple: that it begins at conception in the womb—in what many call a personhood perspective. I believe there is a baby, and at conception this human life is protected by the Fourteenth Amendment (equal protection under the law to all citizens; the amendment also addresses what is called "due process," which prevents citizens from being illegally deprived of life, liberty, or property) of the US Constitution. The baby is a person from conception, not at only a certain number of weeks. I understand medically that we call the baby a fetus and not a human, but the fact is that new studies in 2003 and 2005 showed that 20 to 35 percent of babies born at twenty-three weeks (five and three-fourths months) of gestation survive, while an astounding 50 to 70 percent of babies born at twenty-four and twenty-five weeks (six months and one week) survive outside the womb, and an amazing 90 percent of babies born at twenty-six to twenty-seven weeks (six and three-fourths months) survive.[470] Should survivability outside the womb be the litmus test on whether or not there is fetus viability? I don't think this litmus test passes the common sense test. Stages of growth are all a part of life. Further, the argument is that the baby doesn't know what is happening to it, thus ending its life is not the same as killing a person. The courts have made it clear that purposely harming an unborn child after twelve weeks is a crime. If the mother is murdered with the baby in the womb, the perpetrator could be charged with double homicide. Why is this? Because we know there is a human in the womb. There are some who think that if they end the embryo's life at four weeks or even twelve weeks, the embryo will not miss anything, since it may or may not experience pain. Moreover, I have heard the argument that because the embryo can't fend for itself or survive on its own without the mother, taking its life is not the same as if it could survive. Imagine if I simply killed a newborn infant because of that same reasoning. This argument is not logical. If I leave an infant or newborn on its own, it will most likely die within days of hunger and thirst. Unfortunately, we have read those stories in the news over the last several years. Not convinced? What if I decided to rationalize that if I killed a toddler, it won't miss anything because it doesn't know what it will become as a young child or teenager? None of that makes sense, nor is it logical; thus, I only ask that the same common-sense test is applied to the unborn child in the womb. We know there are illegal establishments that still commit late term abortions. That being said, I know I have many detractors in the world, yet an equal number who would side with my point of view.

The nation is split concerning the morality of abortion. In fact, according to the Pew Research Center in 2013, slightly last than half (49 percent) of all Americans believe that abortion is morally wrong. According to researchers at Pew, this figure has been consistent over the last several years.[471] Yet, when the morality of abortion question is posed to religious groups, the numbers take a dramatic turn. Evangelicals of European descent are far more vocal about abortion than other religious groups, with 75 percent saying abortion is morally wrong, while 64 percent of Catholics who are of Hispanic descent reject abortion, and 58 percent of African-descent Protestants see abortion as morally wrong.[472] European descent mainline (traditional worship services) Protestants are far less likely to see abortion as immoral, with only 38 percent saying it is wrong as compared with 58 percent of European descent Catholics who perceive abortion to morally wrong.[473] When these numbers are juxtaposed across the dominant political lines in America, the Pew Center found that slightly more than two-thirds (64 percent) of Republicans believe abortion is morally wrong, while only 38 percent of Democrats believe abortion is morally wrong. This data tells us that abortion is far from a closed case in America. The debate, which literally divides the nation, will continue. It is an interesting debate from my perspective, because I can clearly see life that is developing at varying stages in the womb from the early stages of conception.

Substance Abuse

Another issue that breaks the American family is substance abuse. Who among us does not have an immediate family member or extended family member who has lost virtually everything due to substance abuse? We must find a way to fight against the substances that dominate the lives of many Americans of all ethnicities. The National Drug Intelligence Center (NDIC) reports annually a "state of illicit drug use in America" to senior and federal officials to make them aware of the potential threat to national security resulting from drug use.[474] This is a real American problem that affects the family and society as a whole. The end result of the NDIC report is an annual National Drug Threat Assessment (NDTA), which contains a comprehensive appraisal of the danger of trafficking and illicit drug use.[475] The costs and effects of substance abuse cannot be denied; they are real and tangible. Additionally, according to the Substance Abuse and Mental Health Services Administration (SAMHSA), substance abuse use is believed to cost America more than $700 billion annually in costs related to crime, lost work productivity, and health care.[476] This means that an already taxed criminal justice system is strained even more with substance abuse, and, likewise, the health care system is further challenged. The largest impact is tobacco use, costing $130 billion annually in health care and $295 billion overall, while alcohol costs $25 billion for health care and $224 billion overall, and illicit drugs are estimated to cost nearly $11 billion for health care and $193 billion overall.[477] It is clear that thousands of Americans are suffering from substance abuse. A National Survey of Drug Use and Health Institute (NSDUH) survey shows that alcohol is by far the most abused substance of choice. The survey revealed the following substance use in the past year: Specifically, alcohol was used by 70.1 percent surveyed in the past year; cigarettes were used by 24.6 percent; illicit drugs were used by 13.1 percent; cocaine was used by 1.40 percent of those surveyed; crack cocaine and heroin were each used by 0.30 percent of those surveyed; and marijuana was used by 10.10 percent of those surveyed.[478] The survey actually had many other categories, but I chose to highlight only some of the major substances to illustrate the prevalence of substance use in America. I have already shown that these are far more than simply harmless recreational drugs that do not affect productivity and life functioning. On the contrary, substance abuse should be a concern for all of America due to the costs shown above and the effect on American lives. The ultimate consequences are essentially an estimate, but we know they include such areas as physical and emotional damage, destroying families (including children), and negatively impacting friends and coworkers.[479] This does not include the increased sickness and disease and overall decrease in health, including possible death from overdose. In 2008, the NSDUH estimated that seven million individuals (twelve and older) were actually addicted to or had abused illicit drugs, and the Federal Bureau of Investigations found that 12.2 percent of more than fourteen million arrests in 2008 were connected to drug violations, which is the most common arrest crime category.[480] Finally, the NSDUH estimated that in 2008, 19.6 percent of unemployed adults (1.8 million) were current users of illicit drugs (and most likely connected to the criminal justice system).[481] This clearly shows the long-reaching effects of substance abuse on our society.

Essentially, substance abuse causes a lack of productivity and negative impact on society and comes with a large bill. Substance ab use impacts every aspect of life across all ethnicities and cannot be ignored. In fact, in

2013 the NSDUH showed that those of African descent used illicit drugs at a rate of 10.5 percent, or 4.4 million users; while those of European descent used illicit drugs at 9.5 percent, or 18.7 million users; and those of Hispanic descent accounted for 8.8 percent users of illicit drugs in America, or 4.7 million users.[482]

Further, the NSDUH reported that among the smaller populations in America, those of Asian descent used illicit drugs at 3.1 percent, while American Indians or Alaska Natives used illicit drugs at 12.3 percent, and Native Hawaiians or Pacific Islanders used illicit drugs at 14.0 percent.[483] Illicit drug use is a real and growing problem in America. According to the NSDUH in 2013, while all ethnicities have problems with substance abuse, those of European descent account for the largest use in terms of raw numbers for both illicit drug use and alcohol abuse (heavy drinking and binge drinking).[484] To no one's surprise, the NSDUH revealed that in 2013, the more educated people are, the less likely they are to use illicit drugs. College graduates are also less likely to be binge drinkers or heavy drinkers.[485] Of note, college educated people do tend to use alcohol casually more than the uneducated, but again, not in an abusive manner.[486] The lucrative money that is made through substance abuse will continue to make this one of the leading areas to challenge the American family. Through rehabilitation programs, education, and increased criminal tracking of illicit drugs trafficking in America, we can begin to make a slight impact on the effects of substance abuse on society. In 2016 and 2017, there is the growing awareness of the increase in illicit drug use and devastation to communities and families. For instance in 2017, emergency responders in Louisville, Kentucky, were called out fifty-two times in a thirty-two-hour period for overdoses; however, with only one death.[487] The Centers for Disease Control and Prevention reported that Kentucky is one of the five states with the highest rates of death linked to drug overdose, starting with West Virginia (41.5 per one hundred thousand), then New Hampshire (34.3 per one hundred thousand), followed by Kentucky (29.9 per one hundred thousand), and rounding up with Ohio (29.9 per one hundred thousand) and Rhode Island (28.2 per one hundred thousand).[488] In fact, the Drug Enforcement Administration's National Drug Threat Assessment survey of 2016 has reported that this is a growing epidemic, with the abuse of controlled prescription drugs, opioid (morphine-like pain reliever), fentanyl and heroin on the rise and resulting in ninety-one deaths per day from opioid abuse alone in America.[489] The issue of substance abuse will always plague the United States, but we can seek to mitigate the impact on the family and society. Simply put, prescription and illicit drugs destroy and devastate individuals and families and ultimately erode the foundation of a strong America. They now cause more deaths per year in the United States than firearms, vehicle crashes, suicide, and homicide. [490]

The HIV Crisis

Yet another health crisis looms large in decimating the American family. According to the CDC, there were approximately 47,500 individuals newly infected with HIV in 2010 in the United States.[491] This number is consistent over the past several years, with the United States gaining 50,000 new cases annually. The hardest hit class remains those men who have sex with men. Approximately 12,200 new cases were added last year for those men of European descent who engage in same-sex relations, while there were 10,600 new cases for those men of African descent who engage in same-sex relations, and 6,600 new cases were added for those men of Hispanic descent who engage in same-sex relations.[492] In fact, the numbers are overwhelming, with unprotected male-to-male sex accounting for more than three-fourths (78 percent) of new HIV infections among men in the United States and nearly two-thirds (63 percent) of all new infections in the United States in 2010 (29,800).[493] Once again, even though the raw data appears comparable across the ethnicities, the rate of infection for those of African and Hispanic descent is out of proportion for the population size. The rates of infection for women are also out of proportion for the population size of the different ethnic group. Approximately 5,300 new HIV cases were added for heterosexual women of African descent, while heterosexual women of European descent accounted for 1,300 new cases, and heterosexual women of Hispanic descent accounted for 1,200 new cases.[494] Of note, heterosexual men of African descent accounted for 2,700 new HIV cases in 2010, while heterosexual men of European and Hispanic descent were not even listed for new cases due to the negligible numbers.

To demonstrate how badly those of African descent are being devastated by HIV, I share the following data. While those of African descent represent approximately 13 percent of the total US population, they accounted for 44 percent (20,900) of all new HIV infections in 2010, which is eight times the incidence of HIV infection in those of European descent (68.9 versus 8.7 per 100,000 of the population).[495] This is literally nearing epidemic proportions, in my opinion. When one group is affected like this, it affects all of America. Looking at ethnicity further, those men of African descent represent 31 percent (14,700) of all new HIV infections in the United States in 2010 and an astounding 70 percent of new HIV infections among those of African descent, which is the highest rate of new infections among any ethnicity or gender and more than six times that of those men of European descent (103.6 versus 15.8 per 100,000).[496] Remember—this includes a majority of those men who practice same-sex or who are bisexual, but also some who are heterosexual. Similarly, women of African descent accounted for 13 percent of all new HIV infections in the United States in 2010 and 64 percent of all new infections among women of all ethnicities.[497] Additionally, while those of Hispanic descent represent approximately 16 percent of the total US population, they accounted for 21 percent (9,800) of all new HIV infections in 2010, while those men of Hispanic descent accounted for 87 percent (8,500) of all new HIV infections among all individuals of Hispanic descent in 2010.[498] Similarly to those of African descent, the vast majority of men of Hispanic descent who are infected with the HIV virus acquire it from same-sex relationships. Comparing the infection rate with other ethnicities, those men of Hispanic descent are three times more likely than those men of European descent (45.5 versus 15.8 per 100,000) to be infected with the HIV virus, while women of Hispanic descent are four times more likely than those women of European descent (8.0 versus 1.9 per 100,000) to be infected with the HIV virus.[499] Finally, those of European descent accounted for 31 percent (14,900) of all new HIV infections in the United States in 2010, but because those of European descent make up almost 63 percent of the US population, their HIV infection rate is substantially lower (8.7 per 100,000) than those of African and Hispanic descent.[500] Of note, just as in the other ethnic group, the vast majority of the infections rest with European men who participate in same-sex relationships.

Much more research and funding should be directed toward fighting HIV infections. It is clear that these infections have a higher prevalence in those communities that are poorer with limited medical access for HIV testing and education. Of course, the more prevalence in a given community, the more likely that community is to spread the disease among itself, as demonstrated with those of African and Hispanic descent. Again, the children are affected greatly, and families are destroyed by this disease. Greater awareness is needed in America, because this disease decimates communities. When one group is decimated in such dramatic fashion, America's strength suffers. Whether it is heroin that is beginning to grow into an epidemic in our northeastern states and greatly affecting our European descent population, HIV destroying those particularly of African descent, or growing illicit drug use in our high schools and college campuses across the nation, America is weakened, divided, and vulnerable.

We need strong families in order to turn the tide of poverty, drugs, crime, disease, and unwanted pregnancies. It is the family unit with strong parents that can counter the results of a broken family. My wife and I were committed to raising our kids in a strong and responsible environment. We set guidelines and rules that our kids had to abide by. There were very few instances where they were unsupervised. There were curfews, punishments for disobedience, and rewards for obedience. We set high standards and expectations. We poured our lives into their lives through time for reading, family, dinner, spiritual lessons or devotions, and fun time. We set a foundation for the kids that made them feel safe. This foundation led to accountability and responsibility for us as parents and for the children. We all knew what was expected of us. I believe these are some of the keys to changing our society and emphasizing the strong family unit.

The American family can be restored through hard work and facing challenges head-on. We cannot simply continue to ignore the overwhelming statistics that show that our family structure is broken. Our society is hurting when there are so many families missing fathers and mothers. The children are the ones who ultimately suffer, often through a life in poverty, lack of parental care and supervision, and educational disadvantages. Further, crime and emotional instability become more defined in those broken families. America must also deal with moral issues of the day, such as abortion and illicit drug use.

DEVELOPING THE FUTURE: MENTORSHIP

One person can make a difference and every person should try.[501]

—President John F. Kennedy

President John F. Kennedy

In the summer of 2005, I was home on vacation shortly before Hurricane Katrina would devastate New Orleans. As I pulled up to visit my old neighborhood and my aunt, I could not help but marvel at the kids playing ball in the middle of the streets. The scene brought back great memories of my early days playing football with my buddies while having to cope with cars and electrical wires above, not to mention the wooden telephone poles. I couldn't help myself; I wandered over and started throwing the ball with the young guys. My guess is they were about ten years of age. After a few minutes of my setting up some plays and helping them with their football stance, we decided to take a break. As we went toward the houses, I noticed trash in the front yard and filling the streets. I told them, "Let's do something positive and pick up the trash in front of the houses." As we started picking up the trash, I began telling them that they had to make sure they got an education, set goals, and determined what they wanted to do in their lives. As I continued to encourage them to take positive steps in their lives, one of them looked at me curiously and asked, "Are you the Rock?"

I smiled and responded with my best Rock imitation, "If you smell what the Rock is cooking!"

Of course, they smiled and laughed. I was amazed at their comments, and I laughed with them and then told them that I was not actually the Rock, the former World Wrestling Entertainment superstar and movie star actually named Dwayne Johnson. Of course, I was flattered by the comparison. As we parted ways, I could not help but ponder their question. Why would these young men equate me to a superstar in entertainment? Well, besides my looking like the Rock (just kidding), my guess is that they were amazed that someone would take time to play with them and encourage them to take charge of their lives. They must have thought to themselves that I had to be a celebrity to take the time for them. It told me they didn't have many role models to encourage them, and that was a unique encounter with me. Further, I believe those young men were ready to be influenced by something positive. I don't know how my fifteen-minute encounter will affect them, but imagine if that became the norm, and I met with those guys weekly. It would make a huge difference.

This book has been about hope for America and making a change through shifting our collective mind-set. The process will take time, and it cannot happen overnight. It will happen with one youth at a time.

This change does not deal with only ethnicity but with caring for all youth, regardless of their backgrounds. Mentorship needs to begin within every aspect of life—community centers, churches, recreation centers and leagues, neighborhoods, and prisons. When I was growing up in New Orleans in the 1970s, we had recreation leagues in the neighborhood. The teams were coached by volunteers who wanted to make an impact on the youth. They were mentoring and did not even know it. I played every sport except baseball growing up, and at every level, the coaches impacted my life. I can still hear the pep talks that translated from field to life. They were talks about hope, positivity, and growing up to make a difference.

Perhaps the greatest mentorship I received growing up came from my grandfather, Dave Williams. He would take me on every daily trip he possibly could to spend time with me. He would continually explain the facts of life and let me know important principles I would live by. For instance, he told me I should never doubt my abilities and should always believe in myself. He emphasized that I was unique, and he saw great potential. I cannot say that I understood what he was saying at the time, but as an adult, I can reflect back and realize that I would indeed have a unique life compared to those of many of my friends and relatives. I credit my grandfather with putting the desire in me to serve in the military. He was a World War II veteran who served in the army, and he would tell me stories of being in battle at sea. I was intrigued by the stories of the military. Perhaps more interesting is the fact that my dad also served in World War II in the navy but never mentioned it to me one time. My dad worked most of the time to provide for the family and hardly had time for mentorship verbally, unfortunately. My dad was a good man who provided for us, but when it came to teaching the issues of life, he was not verbally assertive. However, even though my dad did not have many long talks with me, he mentored me through acts of love and by demonstrating how a man provides for his family. My dad would never let us go without. He helped me buy my first car at age fifteen, taught me how to save, and demonstrated a spiritual life. Unfortunately, none of the men in my life would come to my athletic or academic events. That was a different era, and I am sure that was part of the culture for men in the community. Men worked and left those other types of events to their spouses. Not only did my grandfather and my father pour into my life in their own ways, but my uncle Edgar Williams Sr. was pivotal in teaching me about caring for the family and recreational time. While my grandfather and my father taught me valuable lessons on the practical level in their own ways, Edgar Sr. taught me how to treat a wife and what it meant to spend quality time in a recreational way. He would also teach me valuable lessons on how to process life through logical thought. He is a practical man who always sought to influence me through discovering the processes. Subsequently, Edgar Williams Jr. also played a pivotal role in my life, always encouraging me to pursue academics and setting an example of a college-educated man when being college educated was not all that common in our neighborhood. He also hired me when I was seventeen to work at a restaurant, La Potato Gras, that he owned with business partners, teaching me leadership, management, and entrepreneurship.

I was a strong academic performer as a youngster and won many awards in school, including graduating from kindergarten as an honor student, graduating from the sixth grade as a close second for the top academic student in a school of hundreds (McDonald No. 42), and graduating in the top thirteen of a high school graduation class of more than three hundred students.

As I reflect back on the many awards and athletic events, I realize that hardly anyone from my family would attend, not even my mother. I remember joining the military and coming home from overseas (England) and reminiscing with my mom about how she used to remind me to take off my football cleats and not "track up" her floor with muddy cleats. My mom looked at me without cracking a smile and asked, "Did you play football?" I was shocked and hurt that my mom did not even remember I had played sports. By the way, my mom and dad worked full-time to ensure we were taken care of and did not have the same mind-set that many of us have today. My mom showed me unconditional love that was second to none. Even though she could not help me do my high school homework or attend any of my games, she was always there for me in the home and made me feel special and loved. Again, even though she did not come to my sporting or academic events, she was always pushing me to reach success in life. Not only did I have my mother in my life, but I had the influence of perhaps the greatest aunt anyone could ask for, Marguerite Williams. Aunt Marguerite was and still is like a second mother to me. She was very influential in my formative years. She, along with Edgar Williams Sr., took me to social and recreational events when my parents could or would not attend. She would spend hours teaching us healthy principles of life during the recreational trips and showing great love. Further, Aunt Marguerite kept all of my awards and original report cards and would constantly encourage me to keep going academically. I remember she would periodically pull out the folders of awards and remind me of how proud she was of me, encouraging me to keep me going forward in education. She demonstrated exceptional love, and to this day, we talk every week, and she still mentors me with words of encouragement and advice. I also had other influential family members, of course, but there is not enough room to list them all here.

The truth is that I grew up in an era when, even though I had both parents in the household, they could not give me the full mentorship I needed due to their long work hours. I am grateful for the interaction with my grandfather, aunt, and uncle and a host of other relatives, such as my aunts Joyce Saxton and Mary Scott. I know my mother and father loved me dearly, but they did not understand the need to pour into my life in those other areas of recreational and academic support. They ensured we had food, great living standards, a spiritual upbringing, and all basic life provisions. They were great parents, given their limitations. My mom and dad did not graduate from high school and grew up in a labor-intensive Jim Crow era, when children would often drop out of school to support the family due to disenfranchisement in society. As outlined in the previous chapters, a lack of a two-parent household devastates the child and critically devastates parental mentorship. Thus, mentorship must be given by the family and community to make a difference in the lives of the young men and women around us. Whether we reside in cities or rural areas, mentorship is vital to shaping the values and belief systems of our youth.

A lack of mentorship and care can be harsh for a child. I was blessed to have mentorship and love surrounding me at every level. I am truly bothered when I see children being abused by their parents through yelling, physical abuse, and emotional trauma. I have seen videos in which children are being taught to curse and use vile communication that adults don't use in everyday language. This creates a vicious cycle of abuse, because these abused children grow up to continue the cycle with their own children. Their development is hindered, and their growth is limited. Positive mentorship starts at home.

Multiplication

Amazingly, I began to apply what I learned as a child to my adult life. I wanted to transfer what I had learned as a youth to those who would follow me. I had a strong desire to give back to my children and others. I believe that mentorship starts at home. My wife, Madeline, and I would spend hours mentoring our children academically every week. I made video tapes teaching them math and how to read, and we would help them to read at a very early age. Madeline would read to them daily as infants, and that would carry over for most of their childhood. Interestingly, each of our children scored exceptionally high on reading comprehension examinations in their formative years with a large vocabulary. Mentorship makes a difference in every way possible. We met with them three times per week outside of their other activities—this could be seen as extreme, and I understand that. However, my emphasis is that families meet together and share precious time beyond simply talking about homework and tasks around the house. Each weekend included a family day that everyone had to participate in. We would go to the movies, parks, hiking, zoo, circus, and a host of other activities through the years. I recall that when the kids became older and started hanging out with their friends, they found it awkward not to be with the family on the weekend. To demonstrate how important family had become, I recall on one occasion my oldest daughter Ashley came at the age of sixteen and apologized profusely for wanting to miss a family weekend event to be with her friends. Furthermore, we got our kids involved in dance, gymnastics, karate, sports, and every imaginable activity. We ensured they had an opportunity to participate, and I even coached every sport I could. I was either lead coach or assistant coach in many of their athletic endeavors. On one occasion, I was the soccer coach even though I had no idea how to play the game, nor had I ever played a day of soccer in my life. I purchased a book on coaching soccer so I could understand the rules of the game. But it wasn't actually knowing how to play the game that allowed me to impact those young men I coached, it was that I took the time to learn something new and throw in life lessons of resilience and perseverance along the way. When I coached my kids' athletic events, a strange phenomenon was happening—I was also coaching all of the other children on that team. I was actually mentoring a community. It was about sacrifice, giving, and mentorship. These types of activities built up their social acumen. Not only did we mentor our kids academically and socially, but we led the way spiritually. We established a full regimen, including weekly Bible studies, prayer, and Sunday worship. We began a weekly Bible study to teach them the principles and values we wanted them to learn without relying on the church, their friends, the media, society, or the school system.

As I stated, my mentorship was not limited to my own children, but I knew it was important for me to mentor in the community as well. This is what I advocate for each person. For approximately fifteen years, I mentored our youth in prisons or churches in places such as Montgomery, Alabama; Colorado Springs, Colorado; and Custer, South Dakota, impacting the lives of thousands of all ethnicities. I also visited incarcerated adult members from the all four branches of the armed services in Hawaii and provided weekly teaching and mentorship. In Colorado, I fondly remember being called Chief Shon as I mentored my son and about twenty other kids every Sunday night for approximately two years in a Royal Rangers mentorship program. That era was amazing, as I taught the youth simple values and basics of life. They would run up to me every Sunday and call out my name. Of course, my son would look in amazement at how all of these kids wanted to be near me—it was indeed a fun time. I don't know what happened to the hundreds of children I was able to influence over the years, but I can guarantee the foundation was set on a positive course. This is all I am advocating. Statistics show that those who are mentored are more likely to stay in school without skipping classes. In fact, according to Big Brothers Big Sisters in a study, students who meet with mentors are 53 percent less likely than their peers to skip a day of school and 37 percent less likely to cut a class.[502] Further, Big Brothers Big Sisters reported that mentored youth are 46 percent less likely than their peers to start using illegal drugs and 27 percent less likely to start drinking.[503] In a 2013 study, "The Role of Risk: Mentoring Experiences and Outcomes for Youth with Varying Risk Profiles," mentoring was shown to have many positive impacts on a youth's life, including higher academic performance, college attendance, positive attitude, higher self-esteem, lower crime rate, and lower depression rate.[504] It is clear that mentorship positively affects lives. Imagine if every person, religious organization, and community decided to be intentional about mentorship in the community in which they reside. Millions of lives could be changed by giving time. All too often, families are closed and do not go outside of their four walls. At times, churches, synagogues, and mosques are too inwardly focused on the well-being of their constituents and not as committed to the communities in which they reside. It appears to me that this is not congruent with most major religions that focus on making a difference in the lives of those in their communities. There are approximately 350,000 religious institutions in America by most estimates, with the overwhelming majority (314,000) as Protestant churches, an estimated twenty-four thousand Catholic and Orthodox churches, and approximately twelve thousand other faith organizations.[505] If each religious organization would send fifty volunteers to mentor and tutor one hour per week, that would equal approximately 17.5 million volunteers and an estimated 980 million hours per year in mentorship—almost a billion hours of mentorship each year. These numbers are unfathomable, but they will most certainly have a positive impact on society.

Another area of mentorship is tutoring. Here is a simple example of how powerful this can be. Last year while attending National War College in Washington, DC, I was assigned as the lead for outreach to an inner city school. I organized thirty volunteers over the academic year, and we accumulated over eight hundred hours of tutoring math and reading. It was a great experience for the future senior leaders of the armed forces. Interestingly, Senators and Congressmen would come to the same school and also serve as mentors. Imagine if every church, synagogue, and mosque in America decided to choose a school and would get involved in neighboring schools. When we mentored in the national capital region, I soon realized that it was not just the basics that we were teaching, but we were imparting hope and inspiration for life. Thirty volunteers donated more than eight hundred hours, but imagine what seventeen million volunteers could do for our nation with regard to mentorship.

My particular denomination, the Church of God in Christ (COGIC), has a program led by Bishop Charles E. Blake Sr. (the presiding bishop), called the Urban Initiative. It is a noble effort to ask the twelve thousand COGIC churches in America to implement five key programs: education (access, excellence, and equity); economic development (job training and job creation); crime prevention (reduction, prevention, and rehabilitation); family life (developing healthy men, women, and children); and financial literacy (earning, saving, investing, and spending wisely).[506] The goal is to have each of the five programs implemented at every church, meaning ideally sixty thousand programs throughout America that would be designed to impact their communities with healthy individual and family concepts for living and thriving.

Similar to the COGIC Urban Initiatives, I believe that a major change can happen in America through mentorship if the three hundred fifty thousand to four hundred thousand religious institutions decide to impact not merely their city but simply their neighborhood or community with an intentional plan for canvassing the children in the neighborhood and inviting them for mentorship opportunities. A strategy to open the doors of the religious facilities with fifty trained volunteers from each institution targeting children from ages five to seventeen will make a dramatic impact on society. I call it Operation AIM, which stands for "a positive attitude, living with integrity, and demonstrating motivation." Specifically, my plan calls for a person, male to male or female to female, to be assigned to each child in the neighborhood for a minimum period of one year. During this year, the mentor and protégé will meet a minimum of once per week on the grounds of the religious institution, with appropriate safeguards, such as meetings only in the presence of a mentor program organizer or supervisor, background checks for every mentor, and mentorship in an open environment. Further, each parent or guardian will sign a consent form agreeing to the child's mentorship. Each mentor will be trained in mentorship after he or she is vetted and approved through a local law enforcement background-check process. The mentoring sessions will consist of age-appropriate subjects of reading, math, and science. While this type of mentorship program can vary at each location across America and may face challenges at the start, it can make a difference in the lives of children who have no alternatives. Perhaps a fitness or game aspect can be added to the mentorship program, but in the end, it is about making a positive impact on the lives of the youth.

On one particular trip, I met a young man who was intentional about mentorship and impacting a community. His name was Bryan. Bryan shared a story about making a difference in the community by simply building a playground for the kids. This was a huge success for the community because it got children together outside of the home, but Bryan noticed something was missing. He intimated that he believed the kids needed more than just an area to play, but also needed to learn practical ways to grow and develop. He began to raise money to buy supplies and to improve the area. Bryan and his fiancée, Jessica, participate yearly in these events. The goal was to get them outside of their homes. The project is called KaBOOM! The intent is to change one neighborhood at a time, and that's exactly what happened in DC. KaBOOM! is a place for young people to grow and develop needed life skills. In fact, Bryan noticed how the entire community was affected by this project, with people coming together and supporting one another. These are the types of inspiring stories that are happening all across America. From the Little League coach to the tutor who donates countless hours to help kids read, from the dance instructor to the church religious instructor, change happens when Americans come together to make a difference in the lives of our youth. Mentorship is not limited to any specific ethnicity; everyone will benefit from a positive role model.

Mentorship, coaching, and tutoring will not happen without a change in attitude. It will happen when America decides to come together and move from an inward focus to an outward community focus. When we see our fellow humans as important, we will be able to make a great impact on our nation. Positive mentorship will also begin to change the negative cycle of self-hatred that I believe plagues our youth of all ethnicities. As I have demonstrated in earlier chapters, self-hatred is demonstrated across all ethnicities with high rates of murder. As a reminder, 91 percent of those from African descent are murdered by others from African descent, while 84 percent of European descent murders are committed by those of European descent, and an estimated 90 percent of those of Hispanic descent are murdered by those of Hispanic descent. Of note, Hispanic descent data can be elusive, because it has only been over the last fifteen years that Hispanics have been no longer consolidated with European-descent data; there are great sources of the rate of violence of Latinos in America.[507] When one sees oneself as useless and an outsider in American society, it is easier to get locked into a pattern of self-destruction. Self-hatred is a vicious part of what plagues America, and mentorship is a vehicle to counter low self-esteem. Many of our youth don't see a way out of their circumstances; they believe their lives are meaningless. Thus, they take high risks and live volatile lives laced with crime, poverty, lack of education, lack of spiritual direction, and an aversion to community and social standards. This pattern can be broken with early intervention into the lives of our youth.

These are the types of programs I am hoping this book inspires in America. Many of the athletic programs that I experienced in the inner city growing up ceased over the years due to a lack of city funding. I am advocating that every major city and every rural area build youth programs throughout the states. I am not calling for larger government programs to fund these programs, but I am calling for business owners and volunteers to make it happen. Both small businesses and corporations could get together to pay the expenses needed for these programs in their cities. This is certainly one area that America should invest in. These businesses should subsequently get tax breaks for community projects and mentorship programs. Many of the major cities do have sponsorship programs, but it seems to be predominantly in the suburbs or areas of America with middle and upper classes. What would happen if these programs went to our rural and urban areas, especially to those who are underprivileged and who can't afford to pay for such programs?

We need more programs such as the National Mentoring Partnership to happen in many of our major cities. Their website, http://www.mentoring. org/about_mentor/faq3/, allows parents to sign their kids up for mentoring by zip code all across America. Mentorship is critical to our nation. It is what has inspired millions to do great things in our society. We must find a way to reach at-risk youth and close the mentorship gap. The pages of this book could be filled with story after story depicting the life-changing interactions with positive adults who shaped our youth throughout the United States. Most of these youth have grown up to develop into positive role models themselves. Young lives have been saved, and America is stronger because of mentorship.

9

UNLEASHING UNCONDITIONAL LOVE: BEYOND TOLERANCE

Darkness cannot drive out darkness; only light can do that. Hate cannot drive out hate; only love can do that.[508]
—Dr. Martin Luther King Jr., civil rights leader and president, Southern Christian Leadership Conference

Dr. Martin Luther King Jr.

In March of 2015, the news captured a heart-wrenching scene that quickly went viral. A slightly overweight woman of African descent who was fighting for her health and running her first 10K race could be seen struggling to make it to the finish line. A police officer of European descent from Louisville, Kentucky, noticed her struggles and decided to reach out to the woman. He literally put his arm under hers and simply walked briskly with her over the finish line so she could finish the race and reach her goal.[509] The woman, Asia Ford, was on a quest to drop two hundred pounds in two years and had been successful in doing so. She was exhausted, but she was quickly filled with joy, strength, and courage because of this act of kindness. The mayor of Louisville stated this is "what a compassionate city looks like."[510] This was not a small moment in her life. This message went viral across the Internet and the airwaves because America is ready for change. My wife showed me the post, and although it had only been posted for one day, there were well over 750,000 views. I must admit the video was very moving, because it showed that unconditional love is not limited to what someone looks like, but can be shown to all people. Of course, the police officer was humbled by the experience, and I can guarantee that when he helped her across the finish line, he did not think of ethnic differences. He was basically helping a fellow human, an American, to reach her goals. This scene meant a lot to America because, at the time of the video, America had faced several incidents with ethnic relations. Similarly, another video went viral as reported by CNN. In a life-threatening car crash, an army captain, Steve Voglezon, pulled his car over to help a distressed family in Chatham County, North Carolina.[511] According to witnesses, he literally reached into the crashed car and pulled the distressed man, William Thompson, and his wife out of one car while another car less than ten feet behind it was on fire and could have easily engulfed the lead car.[512] The army captain happened to be of African descent, and the family he rescued was of European descent. I submit to you that that army captain did not stop to think of the ethnicity of the perishing family when he rescued them, he only saw human life. Again, this type of event happens almost every day in America, but generally they go unnoticed. What comes to forefront are the opposite and polarizing events that somehow appeal to the human psyche.

What would happen if we all began to think like the police officer or the military captain? Americans would develop further, with every person helping the other and showing great love. I know many are saying

I am being too positive at this point, but a change of heart can make America even greater. We are indeed a great nation, but there is room to grow, just as we did during the Civil War and in the 1960s. As I have demonstrated throughout this book, we could not have gotten where we have as a nation without unconditional love. Yet another story was reported in the media where seventy-year-old Ken Wayne Broskey met twenty-two-year-old Roland Gainer during a trip where Broskey was driving for Uber to raise money to pay off his mortgage because his death was imminent.[513] Broskey was battling cancer and had just received a diagnosis of stage four oropharyngeal cancer with lung metastases. He was only given weeks to live. When Gainer, a college student, heard Broskey's story about just wanting to leave the house and earn some money for his daughter, a waitress, and his grandchildren, he decided to take action. Gainer began a GoFundMe campaign that raised over $22,000 in three days, well on the way to paying off the house for Broskey's daughter and grandchildren.[514] This is what friendship is truly about. This story it demonstrates how love can change the world. Incidentally, Gainer is of African descent and Broskey is of European descent. The ethnicity of the two men did not matter, but the act of kindness came at a time when the nation was used to seeing division of ethnicities rather than unity, friendship, and love. Unity can happen, and this story is proof. Gainer unleashed unconditional love in a most powerful way to fulfill a dying man's last wishes.

Civil Rights (Robert F. Kennedy)

Unconditional love will be a catalyst to change our society and birth a new America. Dr. Martin Luther King Jr. wrote a book in 1963 entitled *The Strength to Love*, which was a collection of his sermons dealing with racial segregation and reconciliation through harmony and brotherhood.[515] In that book, he calls for the country and for mankind to love one another unconditionally. It was actually one of the first books I read outside of required classroom reading as a youth. The Civil Rights movement, 1955–68, led by Dr. King, was based on nonviolence and love. It was one of the most courageous strategies known to the world. We recently saw the movie *Selma* and it highlighted the historic 1965 three-day march from Selma to Montgomery over the Edmund Pettis Bridge to highlight the heinous condition of voting rights in the South. It was one of the pivotal moments in American history that captivated a nation and led then President Lyndon Johnson to sign the Voting Rights Act of 1965, guaranteeing reformation in America and voting rights to all Americans regardless of skin color.[516] The nation and world witnessed what was called Bloody Sunday because of the vicious beating the six hundred demonstrators took on their first attempt to cross the Edmund Pettis Bridge out of Selma.[517] The nation was moved by these horrific acts of violence, and the National Guard had to be called upon for protection in order for the march to take place. Unfortunately, the struggle for freedom in the Civil Rights movement was highlighted by legislative change only after the loss of life and displays of brutality on innocent demonstrators. For instance, the significant Civil Rights Act of 1964 only came after the horror in Birmingham, Alabama. In Selma, a young deacon, Jimmy Lee Jackson, of African descent, was shot by a state trooper of European descent during the demonstrations.[518] Jackson died eight days later in the hospital, but his death was not forgotten. It sparked a movement in the South for voter rights by Dr. King and the Southern Christian Leadership Conference. Secondly, after the second attempt to march to Montgomery was blocked by Alabama State troopers, a young minister of European descent, James Reeb, was murdered by a European-descent segregationist in an altercation in Selma because he was supporting voting rights for all people.[519] It was then that people, especially clergy and religious organizations, of all ethnicities came together to say enough is enough. This is nonsensical; we are all Americans. In the end, the three-day march became a five-day, fifty-four-mile march from Selma to Montgomery, and it finally happened on March 21 to March 25, 1965, on the third attempt, with heavy protection. The significance was that the Civil

Rights movement was growing into a pluralistic religious and multicultural movement that was highlighted on that five-day journey where 33 percent of the eight thousand marchers were of European or other than African descent.[520] It was an American march for justice, change, and what was right. Let's stand up, America, and not go backward with regard to ethnic relations. It is time to move to a new level. When the marchers arrived in Montgomery, they were met by fifty thousand American supporters of both European and African descent who were tired of the same conditions in America and wanted to effect change.

As Dr. King would often remind the crowds, American destiny could not be separated by color lines, for all Americans had a role to play in justice for all. Remember, we are all people of color, and we are all human. If one people group is crushed down in America, all people groups are crushed down, for America cannot change without the movement of all people, all ethnicities, all religions, and all political preferences. The change I have been referring to is about all Americans coming together and ensuring justice and equality for all—this change is for Americans in the inner cities, outer suburbs, and rural countryside and hills. Thus, it is where we are today, fifty years removed from Bloody Sunday, where all Americans must come together in brotherly love for true change in America. The protests we saw in America in late 2014 and early 2015 in response to police shootings of those who are both of European descent and African descent may lead the nation to change and balance the laws for all people. The protests may help improve relationships with law enforcement in all communities and call attention to the disproportionate sentencing and incarceration of poor people who cannot afford private or personal representation in the court system. But perhaps they will also call for the nation to move to respect and love for all, where we honor our fellow person. We must move the nation to a new level of unconditional love for one another, and the violence and senseless murders must stop. I know I am calling for somewhat of a Utopia where we feel good about life and demonstrate love, but why shouldn't I call for it? We are America, and nothing is out of our grasp. We can rise up and live out the true meaning of democracy and freedom for all. In his special address to Congress on March 17, 1965, on the historic Voting Right Act, President Johnson stated,

In our time we have come to live with moments of great crisis. Our lives have been marked with debate about great issues; issues of war and peace, issues of prosperity and depression. But rarely in any time does an issue lay bare the secret heart of America itself. Rarely are we met with a challenge, not to our growth or abundance, our welfare or our security, but rather to the values and the purposes and the meaning of our beloved Nation. The issue of equal rights for American Negroes is such an issue. And should we defeat every enemy, should we double our wealth and conquer the stars, and still be unequal to this issue, then we will have failed as a people and as a nation. There is no Negro problem. There is no Southern problem. There is no Northern problem. *There is only an American problem.* And we are met here tonight as Americans—not as Democrats or Republicans—we are met here as Americans to solve that problem.[521]

The cry has always been the same from great Americans who realized the injustices to all people. President Johnson said it is not just Negroes, but it is about all of us. The president was referring to Americans—yes—all Americans had a part to play in overcoming the injustices to our fellow man. At the highest public office in the land, a cry for change was made and enacted. So it is today that we must overcome the crippling legacy of racial prejudice, poverty, inadequate education, hatred for others, prejudicial behavior, lack of moral values, and injustices in the criminal justice system. I realize it is a hopeful call, and that some would say I am dreaming, yet I make the call for Americans to treat each other as they would want to be treated. We need to dream again as Americans. At the end of the march from Selma to Montgomery in his address to the massive crowd on the steps of the state capitol, Dr. King stated,

On our part we must pay our profound respects to the white Americans who cherish their democratic traditions over the ugly customs and privileges of generations and come forth boldly to join hands with us. Today I want to tell the city of Selma, today I want to say to the state of Alabama, today I want to say to the people of America and the nations of the world, that we are not about to turn around. We are on the move now. Let us therefore continue our triumphant march to the realization of the American dream. The end we seek is a society at peace with itself, a society that can live with its conscience. And that will be a day not of the white man, not of the black man. That will be the day of man as man.[522]

This is essentially what I am calling for—a day when we are not known with hyphens in our names or by antiquated, disparate color terms, such as *black* or *white*, that do not really describe anyone but as Americans living the dream, respecting one another and living beyond tolerance.

When I published my book on unconditional love, *Loving When You Don't Feel Like It*, the first reaction I received was that it was a book that every relationship needed. The title represented what everyone thinks in a long-term relationship but is afraid to state or deal with. The book resonated with people because they immediately recognized that it takes work to love unconditionally. It takes strength to forgive and look beyond the faults of the other. To be devoted to one another in brotherly love is always a work in progress. We need to honor one another above ourselves. This means that we will no longer seek to harm the other but to build each other up and push for success for all Americans. This means that every American respects each other regardless of ethnicity. It is an America where we see ourselves in our fellow man. A few years back, I remember seeing a distressed elderly lady standing on the side of a main thoroughfare one evening as my family and I were driving home from the movies. I could see her standing on the side of the road, frantically attempting to wave the cars down, but no one would respond. I told Madeline I was going to stop but asked her to please stay in the van and watch the kids (all three of them). I quickly responded, and the elderly lady led me to her vehicle, where her husband was passed out at the wheel of the car and foaming at the mouth. I quickly pulled him out of the car, laid him on the ground, and began CPR on him. By then, Madeline had called 911, and the ambulance arrived within minutes. I continued to try to revive the man by pumping his heart until the emergency technicians arrived. Upon arrival, they instructed me to keep pumping his heart as they placed an oxygen mask on the fallen man. They finally told me to stop, and then they loaded him on a gurney and took him away. He was alive when he left in the ambulance—I did not know if he would survive. Later on, I would be called by the family members and thanked for stopping, aiding their mother, and giving their father a chance to live. Unfortunately, their father expired before he could get to the hospital. The family invited me to attend the funeral so they could thank me personally. I did attend, and it was my pleasure to pay homage to this man and provide what little comfort I could to the family. When I pulled over to assist, the ethnicity of the elderly woman did not matter, and frankly, it never crossed my mind. As I started CPR, it was my one goal to save a life. The elderly couple was of European descent, and I can tell you from firsthand experience, when life was on the line, my brown hue did not matter to the elderly woman or the man, just as their skin color did not matter to me. I saw a couple and a person, a fellow human, an American in distress. Their complexion did not make one bit of difference to me. This is what this book is about. If we can respond to one another with love and respect, it will make a major impact in the world. All lives matter!

Love must be demonstrated. Kindness toward one another is vital to develop and demonstrate unconditional love. Being kind is the right thing to do. Kindness means that we care for the others in our lives in such a way that we want the best for them. Furthermore, kindness has many synonyms: benevolence, generosity, mercy, charity, philanthropy, sympathy, compassion, tenderheartedness, friendliness, and the like. I see a continual link to each of these characteristics. There are many examples that can illustrate kindness, such as speaking with gentleness and not using harsh words toward one another. By kindness, I am referring to doing the best one can do given the circumstances. Kindness is not based on income, status, or power, but on character. Walking in kindness means demonstrating care and sensitivity for one another. Imagine, if you will, that all you lived for was to make your spouse happy through random acts of kindness. The world is not used to kindness; rather, we are used to everyone looking out for themselves. We give of ourselves and want the best for the other. Who will you lay down your life for? Is your kindness limited to those in your family or to those who are of the same ethnicity?

One of the best examples of kindness going beyond the ethnicity is the parable of the Good Samaritan (Luke 10:25 NIV), found in the Holy Bible. A man asked our Lord, "Who is my neighbor?" Our Lord responded by telling him a story about a man who was attacked by thieves and left for dead on the roadside. Jesus told this parable about a man who was traveling from Jerusalem to Jericho. It was a winding and meandering road. Robbers beat and stripped him, leaving him for dead. A priest passed by, a Levite passed by, but both crossed over to other side to avoid the incident. However, a Samaritan passed by and stopped when he came upon the man. He fixed the man up, took him to the nearest inn, and paid for him to rest. This was a selfless act, and as the Samaritan helped the man, a Jew, he knew he was putting his own life at risk by getting involved. Jews and Samaritans didn't get along, and they were divided because of their national heritage. Jesus contrasted mere religious beliefs with the true love, kindness, and goodness that goes beyond ethnicity, color of skin, and class or status. Christ then concluded, "Go and do likewise." Really, it comes down to doing the right thing for our neighbor without regard for ourselves and no matter what their ethnicity happens to be. The essence of kindness is to give oneself in love, even to the point of putting oneself at risk. It is the ability to love and move to a higher plane. This is what America needs today—the ability to move beyond its own self-perspective and to show love for one another. Through compassion for others and reasonableness in our interactions, we can change America. I am submitting that we wake up and rise to a new level of love and respect for all humankind.

10

A NEW AMERICAN SUCCESS IS IN OUR GRASP

The time is near at hand which must determine whether Americans are to be free men or slaves.[523]
— President George Washington

President George Washington

I cannot say it any differently than the title of this chapter. Success is in your grasp! If you have completed this book, it is my hope that it has motivated you to make a difference in the community where you reside or maybe in your life. President George Washington could see that being a slave to the nation of England was not appropriate for America; however, he could not fully see that free men included those of different complexions, or that all men were created equal. Nevertheless, I believe this quote is appropriate to what this book has been about. Perhaps you can take the lead to begin to change the tide for racial reconciliation. This book is a call to end the racial divide and move to a place of unity in the United States. I've tried to take us through a brief review of our history to show that we can move forward instead of remaining stagnant. I believe that each of us has the ability to change our destiny. Some of us have been limited because we don't have the confidence to believe that things can change in our lifetimes. Perhaps you were thinking about the racial divide in a way that was not productive, but have since changed your perspective after reading this book. I know I do not have all of the answers, but I do believe that the way forward begins with each person taking accountability for him- or herself, and all Americans taking a stand for justice and righteousness. I know that is my conservative view, but I think it is the right view. Change in America has to begin with us. It will not be the government that makes the changes; it will be we the people who can make the change. The government most definitely has a limited role and cannot solve all of the issues. In this chapter, I will share some key principles that I believe have made the difference in my life. Additionally, a couple of my colleagues have contributed to this chapter and will share their perspectives on success. I believe that success is indeed in our grasp. America is unique in that it is among the most diverse nations on the earth. That diversity, if accepted, means that we are stronger as a nation, and each person can be successful. There are many who state that I should not have to remind America of her past in order to move it forward, but I disagree. Our past informs our future. While some seem to lean on the past of slavery and make excuses to justify violent behavior today, others believe that the past has no effect on American society today or the behaviors we choose. I believe that neither extreme is true, but that the truth lies somewhere in between. We must recognize past atrocities in order to inform attitudes and behaviors today, yet we cannot use those atrocities to justify murder, violence, division, and hatred today.

Success is finding your passion in life without being limited to your environment. I want to share a brief excerpt from my life story and how I have gotten to this point. Somehow I have always had a drive to succeed, and I discovered I had leadership qualities. I grew up in the inner city of New Orleans in what is called the Seventh Ward. Louisiana continues to use wards instead of districts because of its ties to the Catholic church; it arranges counties on a parish model. The housing and neighborhood would definitely be considered lower class, without the amenities of a suburb. There was little park space, and the houses were built side by side with little space in between them. Further, as I pointed out earlier in the book, the neighborhood was full of bars on many of the corners, which made an easy environment for excessive drinking and chemical dependency. I was raised a Christian, although I wouldn't say I was a Christian early on. As I look back, it seems that I was always in a leadership position. I didn't ask to be in those positions, but that's eventually what happened in most instances. There are key things that happened in my life, and I alluded to some of them earlier in the book. I believe they were key to making the difference in my life and helping me to become a successful person in society. First, I had a two-parent household where my parents nurtured, mentored, and loved me. I wrote about this earlier in the book; even though they were not perfect, they were a large part of my life and invested in it as they could. They poured love into my life and helped me to believe in myself. Second, I had a positive environment with meaningful family members. Third, I believed in academics. I won at least fifty to seventy-five academic awards from elementary through high school. I was an honor graduate from kindergarten at Martinez Academy. I was the second-ranked student in elementary at a public school in New Orleans named McDonald No. 42, with a host of awards along the way. The trend continued in junior high and high school. The fourth element I believe that kept me grounded was my Christian background, even though I cannot say I fully embraced Christianity until I was nineteen years old and in the military. While I participated in a Christian upbringing, I don't think I fully understood what it meant to serve God. Needless to say, my Christian upbringing had a huge effect on my morals and sense of rightness. I believe those four elements are what drove me to have a vision and goals in life.

I did not know what I would become, but I knew I was destined to break out of the system I grew up in. I saw the crime, drugs, smoking, sexual promiscuity, and poverty. I knew education was the way out of the environment, and my family gave me an advantage economically because they made a sizeable income for the late sixties and seventies. We would have probably been classified as lower-middle class, with an income over $60,000 for the household. Although I had drive, I did not discover my destiny until much later. The drive was there, but not necessarily the direction. In fact, although I graduated in the National Honor Society and took honors courses in high school, my first year in college was not what we would classify as successful. I was on scholastic probation by the end of the second semester, and during the third semester, I did not do well enough to return for the fourth semester. It was then that I entered the air force. I knew I had the ability to be successful in college, but I was not focused as a seventeen-year-old. The air force provided me a fresh start and allowed me to restart my college career. Within one year of being in the air force, I moved to the dean's list. Not only that, but I was a leader in Basic Military Training and in Technical Training for Logistics Management. In fact, I was up for Distinguished Graduate in both programs, but I did not earn the award, falling a few points short in both cases. However, in Technical Training I earned Red Rope status and was student leader for up to five hundred students. I quickly moved from Green Rope to Yellow Rope as student leader. There was certainly something going on, and it felt like I was a fish in water. I excelled in the air force, and by a year's time on active duty, I won Airman of the Year for the installation and was nominated for the air force's Top Twelve Airmen of the Year. That was amazing for a kid who had moved from scholastic probation just two years earlier. However, I was not surprised, because, as I said earlier, I was an academic award winner throughout my formative years, and I knew I had the ability. For two consecutive years, I won Airman of the Year, including Transportation Airman of the Year, and was nominated for the Air Force's Top Twelve Airmen of the Year again. Although I was never selected for the Top Twelve Airmen award, the nominations demonstrate the kind of career I was having as a young airman. I went on to win the John Levitow Leadership Award in Airmen Leadership School and was promoted with my third stripe to Senior Airman, Below the Zone. That means I was promoted earlier because of my potential to serve at the next level. I share just some of my career to demonstrate that success can happen when there is determination and resiliency. I continued to do well in the military, and today I am still in serving at the highest levels in our government. I don't say this in a proud way, but as a statement to say that a kid from the inner city was not limited by my complexion in America. I was not perfect, nor am I perfect today, only driven to do my best.

My story is not yet finished and is ever-evolving, but along the way I know that I could not have achieved what I have achieved without the support of friends from all ethnicities. I have many more accomplishments that I will not attempt to list here, but my point is that, with determination and hard work, everyone can be successful. It is within our grasp. As I write this book, I have reached the rank of colonel in the air force, and I could not be more fulfilled in my military career serving as the Command Chaplain for the United States Air Force Materiel Command. Having been to the top military schools and served in the highest positions commensurate with my rank, I know that America is the land of opportunity and home of the brave. The military has afforded me opportunities beyond my greatest dreams, but I know that even if I had not joined the military, the opportunities exist in America to be successful. America can grow even stronger if we determine that we will accept all people and treat them with dignity and respect and end the racial divide. We need to refurbish the justice system and eliminate biases. America must move away from the antiquated terms of *black* and *white*, and change the environment. We must continue to preserve the right for the free exercise of religion, while increasing opportunities for all people to be empowered economically and socially. Too many are left behind in our society. We can help them find the way by stemming the tide of violence and increasing education.

I make no apologies for my love of this country and my more than thirty-one years of service to our great nation. I am grateful for the opportunity to serve. I end this book with two case studies from very close friends of mine, one of European descent and one of African descent. While they don't necessarily agree with all of my views presented in this book, they believe that change is needed in America. They both illustrate in their own words what success looks like and how they reached the highest level in America.

Case Studies

RICHARD L. KING JR.

Ethnicity is such a sensitive issue that we can't discuss it openly and honestly in the United States. That is one of the reasons I am writing this short personal note to be included in the book of my dear friend, Col. Shon Neyland. He and I don't agree 100 percent of the time—including on some conclusions in this book. However, we are in complete agreement that you can succeed in life no matter the color of your skin, your family, or economic status. Success is a choice, as I will try to show with a few insights into how I've become a "successful" person. You can be successful regardless of your ethnicity, gender, nationality, or any other label the world puts on you.

First and foremost, God doesn't see us by ethnicity or skin color. He only sees us as His children—those who belong to Him by having chosen Jesus as their Savior—and those who have rejected Christ. Our enemy knows this and uses every means possible—including ethnicity—to keep us from having a personal relationship with our Heavenly Father through His Son, Jesus. Whereas God seeks to bring all mankind to Him one individual at a time, our enemy uses every means possible—including ethnicity—to distract, divide, and destroy us. We should never allow our enemy to succeed! We should be wary of individuals and groups that call attention to our differences, that seek to define us and allow hate to divert us from God's purpose for our lives. All ethnicities have extremists and agitators who proclaim divisiveness instead of unity, loathing instead of love, and suspicion instead of trust. We should seek and strive for a color-blind society that judges a person based on character—not color—just as God does. As for me, I came from humble beginnings. My parents were very young when I was born. My dad was twenty and my mom was seventeen. They were married, and I was the firstborn child and grandchild, on both sides of the family. Though my parents divorced when I was in college, they did the best they could to provide a good environment for my two sisters and me to grow up. As the firstborn, I had the privilege of personally knowing and remembering the majority of my great-grandparents. Generally, the men worked and the women stayed home to take care of the children ... though many of the women in my family worked out of the home—including my mom. They were also almost all Christians who passed along their faith and personal relationship with God through His Son, Jesus Christ. It was the most important legacy they left me and that I can leave my children—which my wife and I have done. So trust God and choose to have a personal relationship with Him through His Son. It will change your life forever!

Another family legacy was hard work. My family was never wealthy. They were mostly blue-collar working class and provided for each other with hard work. We didn't have an abundance of material things, but we never lacked for anything, either— especially love. Some of the occupations of the men in my family included farmers, brick masons, railroaders, plumbers, electricians, and a pastor. My dad worked for the telephone company, and my mom became a realtor when I was in junior high. Both had high school educations and worked their way to successful careers. I was the first member of my family to earn a college degree, and it was paid for by the hard work of my parents ... and me.

My first paying job was working for a dog groomer on some Saturdays when I was five to six years old. I vacuumed hair and helped wash the smaller dogs. I also pulled my wagon up and down roads collecting empty glass soda bottles to return to grocery stores for money. The Social Security statement that I receive each year records income going back to when I was twelve years old, working for the YMCA as a day camp counselor, and later as their janitor and maintenance man. I also bagged groceries, mowed yards, and worked in a warehouse—all before beginning college.

As I grew older and gained more freedom, I tried to choose wisely and make good decisions. I watched peers make poor decisions and took note of the consequences. I kept my grades up in high school ... mostly Bs and As—though I could have done better, and many times since I have wished I had pushed myself harder to learn more. Though I experimented with alcohol during my senior year, I never tried drugs, tobacco, or premarital sex. I kept going to church and generally chose good friends who would be good influences on me.

My family also had a history of serving in the military. I had members on both sides of my family that fought in the Civil War. Two of my great-grandfathers fought in World War I in the army. My grandfather King and his two brothers fought in World War II in the navy. My father was a marine during the Vietnam War, though he never deployed to Southeast Asia. I am an airman serving during the Global War on Terror. Giving back to your nation is one of the most important choices you can make, and I am proud to have a family heritage that answered the bell when the nation called.

I have always been goal oriented, and one of my goals was to become a full-bird colonel. By working hard and doing well in my duties, I have been promoted several times and am now a colonel—a rank that is in the top 2 percent of all military personnel. I just went over twenty-five years of active-duty service, though I have actually been wearing an air force uniform since I was seventeen in AFROTC. Because of my military service, I have been blessed to have traveled to about thirty-five different countries, lived on three continents, helped people in need, learned skills that will last me a lifetime, and made dear, lifelong friends at every duty station (twelve so far). Another goal I had was to go to both Air Command and Staff College and Air War College in residence. God blessed me with all those goals, and I have now completed three master's degrees and am currently researching PhD programs—something I never dreamed of until just recently.

As a colonel, I am paid well, and my wife and I have tried to make good financial decisions. Except for mortgages, we don't borrow and pay others interest. We believe in giving back to God a portion of what He has blessed us with and have developed a good system for doing so. We have an automatic draft set up from my paycheck that sets aside a percentage of my income into a particular checking account that is used for only God's work. From that account, we can pay our tithe to our church, plus gifts and offerings for other endeavors. We sponsor three children through Compassion International, multiple missionaries serving all over the world and in the United States, and many other ministries and charitable foundations. It is the most gratifying and enjoyable use of our money that I can imagine. We don't drive fancy or new automobiles, take luxurious vacations, or have many expensive toys to play with. However, we have fun with family activities and don't have any unfilled material needs.

My life, as with all others, has had its fair share of challenges and obstacles. I was always a skinny kid. But I loved sports and was fairly good at most of them. I eventually had to give up playing football—a game I dearly loved—because of my size, and basketball because of my height. I eventually grew to become six feet and about 155 pounds. However, I was around 120 pounds from high school until after I got married at thirty years old. It negatively affected my psyche, and I felt, from a very young age, that I was different and that something was wrong with me. As a result, I had a deeper empathy for others and tended to treat people kindly. I wasn't a mean kid. As an adult, I have had to overcome numerous health issues—including double-digit surgeries and chronic back/neck pain. However, God got me through all of that, with my family's help, and I am still scoring "Excellent" on my annual Air Force Physical Fitness Tests.

I want to leave you with the fact that I am nobody special by the world's standards. Nevertheless, to God, who is all that really matters, I am special—just like you are! With His help, there is nothing for which you can't be forgiven, no obstacle you can't overcome, and no goal you can't achieve. I am living proof. Good luck, and may God bless and keep you on your journey through life!

The Measure of Success

FAMILY, EDUCATION, SPORTS, AND FAITH

(Excerpts from the book, Living Without Them, My Journey with Loss, *2012)*

Rev. Dr. Jose H. Tate

A couple of months ago, my good brother and longtime trusted friend, Rev. Dr. Shon Neyland, asked me to write down some thoughts regarding what has caused me to be successful in life. Since the term *successful* is a derivative of the word *success*, I searched for a definition of *success* that would capture thoughts about my life. Though I ran across some very viable definitions regarding success, the *New Oxford American Dictionary* seemed to say it best: "the accomplishment of an aim or purpose." To complete this definition, I would also add "in the face of obstacles and challenges." Since

I believe God has a purpose and plan for everyone's life, I've strived to align my goals and ambitions with God's direction for my life. And in doing so, there has always been a mountain to climb or a hurdle to overcome to achieve that goal. Nevertheless, upon reflection, there are four things that helped me to be successful in my life, military career, and ministry—family, education, sports, and faith.

From the very beginning, I came into this world with a certain set of unique challenges. I was born out of wedlock, and my conception was unplanned. I was born African American in the 1960s when blacks were fighting for human and civil rights. My biological father (may God rest his soul, whoever he was) did not want me; I was given up for adoption when I was a baby, and my adoptive parents (who were also foster parents) resided in a ghetto. Yet at an early age, God put a desire in my heart to succeed and move forward in my life.

Growing up in the ghetto was not easy. All the trappings of inner city life surrounded me—undesirable and poor living conditions, crime, drugs and alcohol, promiscuity, gangs, and negative attitudes. Though it would be inaccurate to say I didn't see people in my environment achieve some measure of success, the role models in my life were few and far between. Fortunately, I had two loving (adoptive) parents who were very supportive and stable. They gave me their name, a home, and a sense of belonging. I never really felt adopted. I felt part of the family. So my initial foundation for success began with my parents—my family. Now, I'm sure this acknowledgement might seem somewhat contradictory, because my parents did not get beyond the tenth grade or have high-paying jobs (sanitation worker and maid) or accomplish very much in our community or acquire great wealth or material things. However, their love and support affirmed my self-worth and gave me the confidence to pursue goals and risk falling short.

For some reason, I thrived in school. In the third grade, I was the leading writer of a book of poems written by my class—a project that allowed the class enough funds for an amusement park trip. From fourth to sixth grade, I was selected to attend enrichment classes and regularly got good grades. Though my classwork in junior high left much to be desired, I excelled in high school. In the tenth grade, I received the Martha Holden

Jennings Awards for academic improvement from my ninth grade year. In the eleventh and twelfth grade, I consistently made the merit and honor roll. Also in the twelfth grade, my cumulative grades for all subjects were all As.

Unfortunately, my mother died one month before I graduated from high school, and my first year of college was subpar. However, months after I finished my first year of college, I joined the United States Air Force at nineteen years old in the enlisted ranks and served in the medical administration career field. Through much prayer, hard work, and determination, I pursued and attained my education in the air force—most of it on active duty. Though I would lose my father to cancer in 1984 and one of my brothers was murdered less than two months after my father died, I would move on and receive my associate degree from the Community College of the Air Force in 1987. In 1988, I lost my grandmother. But I received another associate degree and my bachelor's degree at Park University in 1989 (while working full-time active duty). In 1990 and 1995, I lost two more brothers. But I started my master's degree program on active duty, left active duty, was selected in the Chaplain Candidate Program (a reserve type program for chaplain candidate students) as an officer, and finished my degree in the Air Force Reserves. In May 1996, I received my master's of divinity from United Theological Seminary, and five months later, I became a full-time chaplain officer in the air force. In 1998, my wife was diagnosed with leukemia and given three to five years to live, until God through medicine put her cancer in remission in 2001. In 2003, my last brother died of a heart attack. But in 2007, I received a doctor of ministry degree from Virginia Theological Seminary. In 2008, I retired from the United States Air Force as a chaplain in the rank of major with close to twenty-seven years of serving my country. With God's help, hard work, and perseverance, I became the first in my (adoptive) family to graduate from high school, finish college, and complete a military career. Along with the love I experienced from my family, education played a vital role in helping me to be successful in life.

Sports paved the way in helping me to be confident, competitive, and ready to achieve in life. Growing up, I was a very good football, basketball, and baseball player. I played basketball in grade school and went undefeated. I played Pop Warner–type football for the East Cleveland

Chiefs for four years and received several trophies, including the Most Outstanding Player of the Season trophy. I played high school football for two years and received a varsity letter. When I joined the air force, I played football overseas and stateside. In my first season at Wright- Patterson AFB in Ohio, I was the most productive player on my team and scored the most touchdowns in our league. In addition to playing football, I began lifting weights. Sports and weight training gave me confidence in pursuing attainable goals on and off the field. It helped me to believe if I put my mind to it and utilized my talents and abilities in the proper way, I could obtain positive results. Through these experiences, I learned it didn't matter where one came from or how much money or popularity one had. It only mattered how much you focused and applied yourself in order for good things to happen!

As much as family, education, and sports have provided a platform toward me succeeding in life, God and my faith in Him has been the single most influential factor in my military career, ministry, and life. Growing up, my mother and grandmother were the ones who introduced me to church. My mother took me to church at a very early age, and my grandmother was a very devout Christian. Though my mother probably wasn't as spiritually strong as my grandmother, she showed me the love of Christ through her care for me. As I got older, Mom didn't have to take me to church. I started going on my own. Then, in 1973, I had an encounter with God. I got lost after running away from my brother at a baseball game while visiting my grandmother in Knoxville, Tennessee. Trying to find my way back home, I asked God for His help and was reconnected with my family. Later that year, I accepted Christ in a Methodist church and began my lifelong journey as a Christian. Though I've hit many bumps in the road and would never claim to be a spiritual giant, God has guided my life, put goals in my heart, and given me the will and wherewithal to experience success in my life.

I began the air force as an airman and retired as a major. I began serving in the military as a medical administrative specialist and retired as a chaplain. When I joined the service, I had one year of college, but I retired with a doctorate degree. I faced rejection at birth, lived in a very challenging environment growing up, and experienced many losses throughout my life. By most people's assessment, the odds were stacked against me, and I wasn't supposed to make it. However, God had other plans. He empowered me to dream and achieve my dreams in life.

Family, education, sports, and faith in God all played a part in me succeeding in life. But none of it would have ever happened if God did not watch over me and give me the determination, energy, passion, and focus to stay the course. May my life be a testimony of what one can do if one puts his life in God's hands and takes advantage of the resources God makes available for them.

NOTES

1   Dave Huber, http://www.thecollegefix.com/post/21832/ 30 Mar 15.

2   Justin Worland, http://time.com/3694053/veteran-suicide/ 6 Feb 15.

3   http://www.aauw.org/research/the-simple-truth-about-the-gender-pay-gap/.

4   http://www.trumanlibrary.org/anniversaries/desegblurb.htm.

5   http://www.nps.gov/inde/learn/historyculture/stories-libertybell.htm.

6   Ibid.

7   http://www.history.com/this-day-in-history/mayflower- departs-england.

8   Ibid.

9   Ibid.

10   http://americanhistory.about.com/od/revolutionarywar/a/amer_revolution. htm.

11   Ibid.

12   Ibid.

13   Ibid.

14   Ibid.

15   Ibid.

16   http://www.revolutionary-war.net/slavery-and-the-founding- fathers.html.

17   Ibid.

18   http://www.ushistory.org/us/38c.asp.

19   Ibid.

20   Ibid.

21   http://www.crimeinamerica.net/crime-rates-united-states/.

22   Ibid.

23   Donna Leinwand Leger, "Violent crime rises for second consecutive year," *USA Today*, 10:56 p.m. EDT October 24, 2013.

24   Mariano Castillo, "Is a new crime wave on the horizon?" By CNN. Updated 2:58 p.m. ET, Thu, June 4, 2015.

25   https://rankingamerica.wordpress.com/category/education/ page/2/ 3 Nov 11.

26   https://rankingamerica.wordpress.com/category/education/ page/5/ 21 May 09.

27   http://knoema.com/nwnfkne/world-gdp-ranking-2015-data-and-charts.

28 Gross Domestic Product (GDP) Definition | Investopedia http://www. investopedia.com/terms/g/gdp.asp#ixzz3rVaDgiOq.

29 Ibid.

30 http://knoema.com/sijweyg/gdp-per-capita-ranking-2015- data-and-charts.

31 Ibid.

32 http://www.politifact.com/truth-o-meter/article/2014/feb/27/ debt-vs-deficit-whats-difference/.

33 http://useconomy.about.com/od/fiscalpolicy/p/US_Debt.htm.

34 Ibid.

35 Ibid.

36 Bullard, James (January 2010). "Quantitative Easing—Uncharted Waters for Monetary Policy." Federal Reserve Bank of St. Louis. Retrieved 26 July 2011.

37 http://taxfoundation.org/article/short-history-government- taxing-and-spending-united-states.

38 Jack Kenny and John Larabell, Monday, 04 February 2013, "100 Years Ago: Instituting the Income Tax" http://www.thenewamerican.com/culture/ history/item/14410-100-years-ago-instituting-the-income-tax.

39 Ibid.

40 Randall G. Holcombe, "Federal Government Growth Before the New Deal." Posted: Mon. September 1, 1997, http://www.independent.org/publications/ article.asp?id=360

41 http://useconomy.about.com/od/usfederalbudget/p/Discretionary.htm.

42 Ibid.

43 Ibid.

44 www.nsi-ins.ca/.../2013-Foreign-Aid-and-Crises-Examining-2012-Aid-Data.

45 https://freedomhouse.org/report/freedom-world/2015/united-states#. VdiUZBFRHVI.

46 http://www.wearethemighty.com/top-10-militaries-world-ranked-2015-05.

47 Ibid.

48 Ibid.

49 Pew Hispanic Center. Unauthorized Immigrants. December 6, 2012.

50 "Health Care for Illegal Immigrants Cost $1.1B in 2000, Study Finds."

51 Nico Gomez, spokesman for Oklahoma Health Care Authority, before the Oklahoma Senate Task Force on Immigration, September 18, 2006.

52 http://www.pewsocialtrends.org/2013/08/22/50-years-after-the-march-on-washington-many-racial-divides-remain/ st_13-08-21_ss_raceinamerica_01.

53 Ibid.

54 Ibid.

55 http://kxan.com/2015/06/09/mckinney-officer-resigns- after-incident-at-neighborhood-pool/.

56 http://www.nytimes.com/2015/06/11/us/texas-officer-was-under-stress-when-he-arrived-at-pool-party-lawyer-says. html?_r=0Texas Officer Was Under Stress When He Arrived at Pool Party, Lawyer Says By Manny Fernandez, June 10, 2015.

57 http://www.foxnews.com/us/2015/06/10/resigned-officer- actions-at-texas-pool-party-incident-indefensible-police-chief/.

58 http://www.aol.com/article/2015/08/04/bottle-in-car-of-ohio-man-shot-by-police-held-fragrance-coroner/21217999/?icid=maing-grid7%7Cmain5-news%7Cdl1%7Csec1_lnk3%26pLid%3D1120000905.

59 Ibid.

60 http://www.genome.gov/19016904#al-1.

61 Kate Smith, http://www.sensationalcolor.com/color-meaning/color-words-phrases/origin-black-940#.VSnTcuIFBjo.

62 Ibid.

63 Lerone Bennett Jr. http://www.virginia.edu/woodson/courses/aas102%20 (spring%2001)/articles/names/bennett.htm, *Ebony* 23 (November 1967): 46-48, 50-52, 54.

64 White Americans Admixture Serving History; "The Ancestry of Brazilian mtDNA Lineages." National Library of Medicine, NIH; "Y-STR diversity and ethnic admixture in White and Mulatto Brazilian population samples." Scielo.

65 Uniform Crime Reporting Handbook, US Department of Justice. Federal Bureau of Investigation. P. 97 (2004).

66 http://en.wikipedia.org/wiki/Caucasian_race.

67 http://www.understandingrace.org/history/science/early_class.htm.

68 "Through the Decades." United States Census Bureau. Retrieved 2012-01-18.

69 *A Brief History of the OMB Directive.* American Anthropological Association. 19 Retrieved 2007-05-18.

70 Race, the Power of an Illusion, http://www.pbs.org/race/000_About/002_02-godeeper.htm

71 Skin Whitening Big Business in Asia. Public Radio International. 30 March 2009.

72 Verma, Harsh (2011). Skin 'fairness'-Culturally Embedded Meaning and Branding Implications. *Global Business Review 12* (2): 193–211.

73 Hunter, Margaret (2007). "The Persistent Problem of Colorism: Skin Tone, Status, and Inequality." *Sociology Compass 1* (1): 237–54.

74 Kerr, A. E. (2006). *The Paper Bag Principle: Class, Colorism and Rumor in the Case of Black Washington, DC.* Knoxville: University of Tennessee Press.

75 Hill, Mark E. "Skin Color and the Perception of Attractiveness among African Americans: Does Gender Make a Difference?" *Social Psychology Quarterly* 65.1 (2002): 77–91.

76 Keith, V. M.; Herring, C. (1991). "Skin Tone and Stratification in the Black Community." *American Journal of Sociology* 97 (3): 760–78.

77 Roediger, "Wages of Whiteness," 186; Tony Horwitz, *Confederates in the Attic: Dispatches from the Unfinished Civil War* (New York, 1998).

78 Tehranian, John (2000). "Performing Whiteness: Naturalization Litigation and the Construction of Racial Identity in America." *The Yale Law Journal* 109 (4): 825–7.

79 John Martin, Global Research, March 17, 2015, Oped News and Global Research 14 April. 2008http://www.globalresearch.ca/the-irish-slave-trade-the-forgotten-white-slaves/31076.

80 Ibid.

81 US Department of Health and Human Services: US Department of Justice; Free the Slaves.

82 http://quickfacts.census.gov/qfd/states/00000.html.

83 Pew Research Center: Immigration to Play Lead Role in Future US Growth." Pew Research Center. 11 February 2008.

84 Table 1. United States—Race and Hispanic Origin: 1790 to 19 (PDF).

85 Dworkin, Shari L. The Society Pages. "Race, Sexuality, and the 'One Drop Rule': More Thoughts about Interracial Couples and Marriage." Accessed 27 February 2015.

86 Ibid.

87 Laws of the State of Florida, First Session of the Fourteenth General Assembly Under the Amended Constitution 1865–'6. Chapter 1, 468 Sec. (1)-(3).

88 For Drake, see Virginia R. Dominguez, *White by Definition: Social Classification in Creole Louisiana* (New Brunswick NJ: Rutgers University, 1986).

89 Ibid.

90 Pauli Murray, ed. *States' Laws on Race and Color* (Athens, 1997), 428.

91 Conrad P. Kottak, "What is hypodescent?" Human Diversity and "Race," *Cultural Anthropology, Online Learning*, McGraw Hill, accessed 21 April 2010.

92 John Hawks (2008). "How African Are You? What genealogical testing can't tell you." *Washington Post*. Retrieved 2010-06-26.

93 Joel Williamson, *New People: Miscegenation and Mulattoes in the United States* (New York, 1980), p. 93.

94 Steve Sailer, "Race Now": Part 2: "How White Are Blacks? How Black Are Whites?" UPI, Steve Sailer Website.

95 Ibid.

96 Henry Louis Gates Jr., *In Search of Our Roots: How 19 Extraordinary African Americans Reclaimed Their Past* (New York: Crown Publishing, 2009), 20–1.

97 http://www.pbs.org/wnet/slavery/timeline/.

98 Ibid.

99 *Afric's Muse: Black Literature in Early America.* by Cliff Odle. See more at: http://www.thefreedomtrail.org/educational-resources/article-africs-muse.shtml#sthash.MJtS3haG.dpuf.

100 http://www.pbs.org/wnet/slavery/timeline/.

101 Ibid.

102 Ibid.

103 Henry Louis Gates Jr., *In Search of Our Roots: How 19 Extraordinary African Americans Reclaimed Their Past* (New York: Crown Publishing, 2009), 20–1.

104 Ibid.

105 Ibid.

106 Groves, Harry E. (1951). "Separate but Equal—The Doctrine of *Plessy v. Ferguson.*" *Phylon 12* (1): 66–72.

107 Koffi N, Maglo. "Genomics and the Conundrum of Race: Some Epistemic and Ethical Considerations." Johns Hopkins University Press. Retrieved 4 October 2011.

108 Plessy v. Ferguson. (2010). *Encyclopedia of American Studies.* Retrieved 2012-12-22.

109 *Brown v. the Board of Education* Decision. Civil Rights Movement Veterans.

110 Territorial Kansas Online: John Brown (1800–59), territorialkansasonline.org; accessed August 29, 2015.

111 Freeman, Douglas S. (1934). *R. E. Lee, A Biography.* Charles Scribner's Sons.

112 Fellman, Michael (2000). *The Making of Robert E. Lee.* Random House.

113 Gerber, Richard; Friedlander, Alan (2008). "The Civil Rights Act of 1875 A Reexamination." Retrieved 2009-05-05.

114 Ibid.

115 http://www.civilwar.org/education/history/faq/.

116 Ibid.

117 Ibid.

118 http://www.archives.gov/exhibits/charters/constitution_amendments_11-27.html.

119 Ibid.

120 http://www.infoplease.com/encyclopedia/history/reconstruction. html.

121 Ibid.

122 *The Decline of Race in American Physical Anthropology* Leonard Lieberman, Rodney C. Kirk, Michael Corcoran. 2003. Department of Sociology and Anthropology, Central Michigan University, Mt. Pleasant, MI. 48859, USA.

123 http://humanorigins.si.edu/resources/intro-human-evolution

124 "American Anthropological Association Statement on "Race"." Aaanet.org. 1998-05-17.

125 Roberts, Dorothy (2011). *Fatal Invention*. London, New York: The New Press.

126 Thomas D. Rossing and Christopher J. Chiaverina (1999). *Light Science: Physics and the Visual Arts*. Birkhäuser. p. 178.

127 https://explorable.com/stereotypes.

128 Ibid.

129 Ibid.

130 Joanna Moorhead, http://www.theguardian.com/lifeandstyle/2011/sep/24/twins-black-white, Friday 23 September 201119.06 EDT.

131 "Votes for Women: Timeline." Memory.loc.gov. August 26, 1920. Retrieved June 29, 2011.

132 "Domestic Violence and the Rights of Women in Japan and the US." *Human Rights Magazine*, Spring 1998 | "Section of Individual Rights and Responsibilities." Americanbar.org. Retrieved June 29, 2011.

133 *Women in Early America: Struggle*. Google Books. Books.google. com. 2004. Retrieved June 29, 2011.

134 A. Elizabeth Taylor, "Revival and Development of the Woman Suffrage Movement in Georgia," *Georgia Historical Quarterly 42*, no. 4 (Winter 1958): 339–54.

135 David B. Parker, "Rebecca Latimer Felton (1835–1930)," New Georgia Encyclopedia (2010) online.

136 Edith Wharton." Womenwriters.net. July 14, 1998. Retrieved June 29, 2011.

137 "The Women's Army Corps." History.army.mil. Retrieved June 29, 2011.

138 "Women in Military Service for America Memorial." Womensmemorial.org. July 27, 1950. Retrieved June 29, 2011.

139 http://www.loc.gov/teachers/classroommaterials/presentationsandactivities/presentations/immigration/native_american2.html.

140 Ibid.

141 Ibid.

142 Ibid.

143 Armitage, David. *The Declaration of Independence: A Global History*. 76–7. Cambridge: Harvard University Press, 2007.

144 Ibid, 77.

145 Peter Kolchin, *American Slavery, 1619–1877* (1993), pp. 77–9, 81.

146 Day, Thomas. Fragment of an Original Letter on the Slavery of the Negroes, Written in the Year 1776. London: Printed for John Stockdale (1784). Boston: Reprinted by Garrison and Knapp, at the office of "The Liberator" (1831). p. 10. Retrieved February 26, 2014.

147 Gamboa, Suzanne (March 29, 2012). "Florida Shooter's Race a Complicated Matter." Associated Press. Archived from the original on April 6, 2012. Retrieved April 11, 2012.

148 Jon Greenberg Allen West. "More black-on-black murders in six months than by 'KKK' in 86 years." Wednesday, November 27, 2013 at 10:10 a.m.

149 http://www.latintimes.com/latino-murder-report-homicide-rate-hispanics-more-double-whites-169664.

150 Ibid.

151 http://www.nbcchicago.com/news/local/40-Shot-in-Spate-of- Chicago-Weekend-Violence-256887211.html.

152 http://www.killedbypolice.net/andDANIELBASES,12 Sep 2015, NY police release video of ex-tennis star James Blake's mistaken arrest. http://www.aol.com/article/2015/09/12/ny-police-release-video-of-ex-tennis-star-james-blakes-mistaken/21234989/?icid=maing-grid7percent7Cmain5percent7Cdl3percent7Csec1_lnk1percent26pLidpercent3D-1543792755.

153 Ibid.

154 Namomi Martin, http://www.nola.com/crime/index.ssf/2015/01/new_orleans_murders_fall_again.html, January 02, 2015.

155 324,000 US Blacks Killed by Blacks in Only 35 Years, December 21, 2014 http://americanfreepress.net/?p=21594#sthash.RJzQrWJ7.dpuf.

156 http://www.nola.com/crime/index.ssf/2015/03/suspect_named_in_eastern_new_o.html, "Boyfriend is suspect in eastern New Orleans triple shooting that killed girlfriend, her daughter, NOPD says."

157 http://www.scpr.org/news/2015/04/10/50930/san-bernardino-sheriff-s-deputies-must-justify-eve/ "San Bernardino sheriff beating update: FBI launches investigation; 10 deputies on paid leave," by Frank Stoltze and Sharon McNary, April 10, 2015.

158 http://www.legendsofamerica.com/20th-gangsters.html.

159 http://topdocumentaryfilms.com/hidden-secrets-gangsters-1920s-1930s/.

160 Ibid.

161 http://www.fbi.gov/about-us/history/a-centennial-history/fbi_and_the_american_gangster_1924-1938.

162 The Associated Press, 20 August 2013, http://www.nydailynews.com/sports/teenagers-allegedly-murder-college-baseball-player-boredom-article-1.1431445.

163 http://seattle.cbslocal.com/2013/08/23/daughter-in-law-world-war-ii-vet-beaten-to-death-with-big-heavy-flashlights/

164 Summer Ballentine and Jim Suhr, "University of Missouri president, chancellor leave over race tension," Nov 9, 2015 2:38 p.m., http://www.aol.com/article/2015/11/09/university-of-missouri-

president-says-he-will-resign/21261389?icid=maing-grid7%7 Cmain5%7Cdl1%7Csec1_lnk2%26pLid%3D102592924.

165 Ibid.

166 Ibid.

167 Ibid.

168 Anthony Romano Tue Nov 10, 2015 3:34 p.m. EST "University of Missouri president, chancellor out after race protest," Columbia, Mo. http://www.reuters. com/article/2015/11/10/us-missouri-boycott-idUSKCN0SY1M120151110.

169 Ralph Ellis, Faith Karimi, Ashley Fantz and Nic Robertson, "Train heroes 'gave us an example of what is possible,' says French President." August 24, 2015 | http://www.cnn.com/2015/08/24/europe/france-train-shooting/.

170 Ibid.

171 Ibid.

172 Ibid.

173 Jason Horowitz, Nick Corasanti, Richard Pérez Peña, "Church Shooting Suspect Dylann Roof Is Brought Back to Charleston," June 18, 2015.

174 Adam B. Lerner, "KKK chapter to hold rally on South Carolina Statehouse grounds," 6/29/15 2:29 p.m. EDT http://www.politico.com/story/2015/06/ kkk-chapter-north-carolina-rally-south-carolina-statehouse-confederate-flag-119548.html#ixzz3eVHlUWxF.

175 Ben Brumfield, "Confederate battle flag: Separating the myths from facts." By CNN, Updated 10:33 a.m. ET, Wed June 24, 2015.

176 Ibid.

177 Ibid.

178 Ibid.

179 http://www.nbcnews.com/politics/2016-election/jeb-bush-says-confederate-flag-racist-symbol-n383906 Jun 29 2015, 4:31 p.m. ET "Jeb Bush Says Confederate Flag a 'Racist' Symbol," by Andrew Rafferty.

180 http://www.huffingtonpost.com/entry/black-police-helps-white-sup remacist_55ac6160e4b0d2ded39f48c6

181 Eliott C. McLaughlin, "Why are black church fires associated with acts of hate?" CNN Updated 6:51 p.m. ET, Thu July 2, 2015.

182 German Lopez, "The latest fires at Southern black churches invoke memories of a long, terrible history." June 30, 2015, 11:25 p.m. ET.

183 Ibid.

184 Ibid.

185 Ray Sanchez, "Officer Michael Thomas Slager of South Carolina: What we know about him." CNN, Updated 7:22 p.m. ET, Thu April 9, 2015 http:// www.cnn.com/2015/04/08/us/south-carolina-michael-slager/index.html.

186 Ed Mazza, Sean Groubert, "South Carolina State Trooper, Fired and Arrested After Shooting Unarmed Man." *The Huffington Post*. By Posted: 09/25/2014 4:11 a.m. EDT Updated: 09/25/2014 8:59 a.m. EDT.

187 Ibid.

188 Anthony M. Destefano, Matthew Chayes, 2/11/15 anthony.destefano@newsday.com, matthew.chayes@ newsday.com http://www.newsday.com/news/new-york/peter-liang-rookie-nypd-officer-indicted-in-killing-of-akai-gurley-unarmed-man-in-nyc-stairwell-1.9924331.

189 Taylor Berman, Video: Black Man Fatally Shot by NJ Cops Apparently Had Hands Raised, 1/21/15 4:24 p.m. http://gawker.com/video-black-man-fatally-shot-by-nj-cops-apparently-had-1680911215.

190 Ibid.

191 Kim Bellware "Chicago Releases 'Chilling' Video Of Cop Shooting Teen 16 Times The Cook County state's attorney said the officer 'was on the scene less than 30 seconds' before opening fire on Laquan McDonald, 17." http://www.huffingtonpost.com/entry/laquan-mcdonald-video_5654e329e4b079b281897fc2.

192 Ibid.

193 Ibid.

194 Ibid.

195 http://www.policemisconduct.net/npmsrp-2009- preliminary-police-misconduct-statistical-report/.

196 Ibid.

197 Ibid.

198 Ibid.

199 Jia Tolentino, 3/18/15. http://jezebel.com/reports-black-uva- student-beaten-by-police-for-having-1692199936

200 David A. Graham (April 22, 2015). "The Mysterious Death of Freddie Gray". *The Atlantic*. Retrieved April 26, 2015.

201 Juliet Linderman; Curt Anderson (April 23, 2015). "Rough Ride? Lawyer Says Fatally Injured Arrestee Lacked Belt". Baltimore: ABC News. Associated Press. Archived from the original on May 6, 2015. Retrieved May 6, 2015.

202 http://www.breitbart.com/big-government/2015/05/12/50- teens-beat-white-man-to-a-pulp-for-asking-brawling-girls-to- get-off-his-car/.

203 Ibid.

204 Brian Anderson, March 14, 2015, Brian Anderson March 14, 2015 http://downtrend.com/71superb/hispanic-man-yells-im-going-to-kill-you-white-boy-before-slashing-victims-throat.

205 Snejana Farberov For Dailymail.com Published: 13:34 EST, 9 July 2015 Read more: http://www.dailymail.co.uk/news/article-3155248/

Cincinnati-police-chief-asks-hate-crime-charges-Fourth-July-beating-white-man-black-youths-lower-ranking-officer-denied-race-related. html#ixzz3fY7rGtfw. http://www.dailymail.co.uk/news/article-3155248/ Cincinnati-police-chief-asks-hate-crime-charges-Fourth-July-beating-white-man-black-youths-lower-ranking-officer-denied-race-related.html.

206 Ibid.

207 Dailymail.com Reporter 09:22 EST, 5 July 2015 http://www.dailymail. co.uk/news/article-3150082/White-family-black-friend-stay-wake-truck-covered-hateful-KKK-graffiti.html#ixzz3fae0G4q.

208 http://www.thenewamerican.com/usnews/crime/item/20320-hispanic-cop-kills-white-man-media-authorities-silent-18-months.

209 Ibid.

210 Chris Moody. "O'Malley apologizes for saying 'all lives matter' at liberal conference." CNN Senior Digital Correspondent; Video by Jeremy Moorhead Updated 10:11 a.m. ET, Sun July 19, 2015 | Video Source: CNN http://www. cnn.com/2015/07/18/politics/martin-omalley-all-lives-matter/.

211 Sarah Kaplan November 6, "Chicago police: Slain 9-year-old was targeted, lured into alley," https://www.washingtonpost.com/news/morning-mix/ wp/2015/11/06/chicago-police-slain-9-year-old-was-targeted-lured-into-alley/.

212 Ibid.

213 Susan Bahorich, Shawn Maclauchlan. "FBI: White supremacist suspects planned to bomb black churches." Posted: Nov 10, 2015 10:43 a.m. EST. Updated: Nov 10, 2015 4:08 p.m. EST. http://www.nbc12.com/stor y/30481405/ fbi-white-supremacist-suspects-planned-to-bomb-black-churches.

214 http://www.prisonplanet.com/kill-whites-and-cops-black-lives-matter-affiliated-radio-show-calls-for-race-war.html.

215 "Suspects in custody after 5 shot at Black Lives Matter rally." By Associated Press Bottom of Form Nov. 24, 2015 http://nypost.com/2015/11/24/ white-supremacists-shoot-black-lives-matter-protesters/.

216 Ibid.

217 Celona, Larry; Cohen, Shawn; Schram, Jamie; Jamieson, Amber; Italiano, Laura (December 20, 2014). "Gunman executes 2 NYPD cops in Garner 'revenge.'" *New York Post*. Retrieved April 11, 2015.

218 http://www.theblaze.com/stories/2015/05/04/25-year-old-nypd-officer-dies-after-getting-shot-in-the-head/.

219 http://www.theblaze.com/stories/2015/05/04/25-year-old-nypd-officer-dies-after-getting-shot-in-the-head/.

220 Ibid.

221 http://www.clarionledger.com/story/news/2015/05/09/ two-hattiesburg-police-officers-killed/27072893/.

222 Ibid.

223 http://abcnews.go.com/US/omaha-police-officer-killed-hours-maternity-leave/story?id=31215053.

224 Trymaine Lee, "FBI: Number of cops killed on duty has spiked." 05/11/15 03:50 p.m.—Updated 06/09/15 07:29 p.m. http://www.msnbc.com/msnbc/fbi-number-cops-killed-duty-has-spiked.

225 https://www.odmp.org/search/year.

226 http://ktla.com/2015/06/20/suspect-allegedly-shoots-kills-new-orleans-police-officer-transporting-him-to-prison-manhunt-underway/ Posted 3:31 p.m., June 20, 2015, by CNN Wire.

227 Holly Yan, Joe Sutton and Dana Ford, CNN Updated 4:08 a.m. ET, Mon August 3, 2015 http://www.cnn.com/2015/08/02/us/memphis-officer-killed-traffic-stop/.

228 Ibid.

229 Ibid.

230 https://www.youtube.com/watch?v=t8p_NGuQq6Q.

231 http://fox2now.com/2015/08/19/9-year-old-girl-shot-killed-in-ferguson/.

232 http://www.cnn.com/2015/08/24/us/louisiana-trooper-shot/.

233 Ibid.

234 Faith Karimi, CNN, Updated 9:06 a.m. ET, Sat August 29, 2015 http://www.cnn.com/2015/08/28/us/texas-sheriffs-deputy-shot-gas-station/.

235 http://www.nwherald.com/2015/09/01/fox-lake-police-officer-killed-in-shooting-is-veteran-lieutenant/a9c4ywa/.

236 Mariano Castillo, CNN, Wed November 4, 2015 http://www.cnn.com/2015/11/04/us/fox-lake-illinois-police-officer-joe-gliniewicz/index.html.

237 Ibid.

238 Jon Swaine, Oliver Laughland and Jamiles Lartey in New York Monday 1 June 2015 08.38 EDT http://www.theguardian.com/us-news/2015/jun/01/black-americans-killed-by-police-analysis.

239 http://mappingpoliceviolence.org/reports/.

240 Ibid.

241 Jareen Iman, CNN, 10 Aug 15, http://www.cnn.com/2015/08/06/us/seneca-teen-dead-police-shooting/index.html.

242 Khaleda Rahman For Dailymail.com, 5 October 2015 http://www.dailymail.co.uk/news/article-3260527/Shocking-video-shows-moment-mother-pinned-ground-police-officers-repeatedly-punched-face.html#ixzz3ntoLKWsw.

243 Ibid.

244 http://www.latimes.com/world/mexico-americas/la-fg-dead-mexicans-20150306-story.html.

245 Josh Sugarmann Executive Director, Violence Policy Center, "Murder Rate for Hispanics Is Twice the Murder Rate for Whites," 05/12/2014 11:32 a.m. EDT.

246 Ibid.

247 Ibid.

248 http://www.vpc.org/studyndx.htm., January 2014 Violence Policy Center.

249 Gauthreaux, Alan G., *An Extreme Prejudice: Anti-Italian Sentiment and Violence in Louisiana*, 1855–1924, History4All, Inc.

250 Moses, Norton H. (1997). *Lynching and Vigilantism in the United States: An Annotated Bibliography*. Greenwood Publishing Group.

251 Schoener, Allon (1987). *The Italian Americans*. Macmillan Publishing Company.

252 Ibid.

253 Campbell, R., *Media and Culture: An Introduction to Mass Communication*, St. Martin's Press, New York, 1998.

254 "Lynchings: By State and Race, 1882–1968." University of Missouri-Kansas City School of Law. Retrieved July 26, 2010. Statistics provided by the Archives at Tuskegee Institute.

255 Michael Quinion (December 20, 2008). "Lynch." World Wide Words. Retrieved August 13, 2014.

256 Mariano Castillo. "Is a new crime wave on the horizon?" By, CNN Updated 6:11 p.m. ET, Wed June 3, 2015| Video Source: CNN.

257 Ibid.

258 "Lynchings: By State and Race, 1882–1968." University of Missouri-Kansas City School of Law. Retrieved July 26, 2010. Statistics provided by the Archives at Tuskegee Institute.

259 Richard H. Pildes, "Democracy, Anti-Democracy, and the Canon," Constitutional Commentary, Vol. 17, 2000. Accessed March 10, 2008.

260 "The 15: Racial Barriers Broken In Sports." Posted on April 12, 2013, By Dave Lomonico.

261 Ibid.

262 Ibid.

263 Ibid.

264 Ibid.

265 Ibid.

266 http://abcnews.go.com/Sports/story?id=99759/ "Mr. Williams Alleges Racism at Tennis Tourney." Arlington, Va., March 26.

267 http://tuskegeeairmen.org/explore-tai/a-brief-history/.

268 Ibid.

269 Ibid.

270 "Freedom To Serve: Equality of Treatment and Opportunity in the Armed Services. A Report by The President's Committee." Washington, DC: US Government Printing Office. 1950.

271 "There is No New Black Panther Party," The Dr. Huey P. Newton Foundation. Gus Martin (15 June 2011). *The SAGE Encyclopedia of Terrorism*, Second Edition. *SAGE Publications*. 106.

272 10 Point Platform at official website.

273 "New Black Panther Party." Retrieved 23 May 2012.

274 "On Fox News, ex-Civil Rights Division Lawyer Blasts DOJ." July 2, 2010.

275 Huey P. Newton Foundation. "There Is No New Black Panther Party."

276 Morello, Carol and Mellnik, Ted. "Census: Minority Babies Are Now Majority in United States." *Washington Post*. May 17, 2012. Accessed 2012-05-17.

277 Ibid.

278 David Pilgrim, Professor of Sociology Ferris State University Sept., 2000, http://www.ferris.edu/jimcrow/who.htm.

279 http://www.ferris.edu/jimcrow/what.htm.

280 Strother, Z.S. (1999). "Display of the Body Hottentot," in Lindfors, B., (ed.), *Africans on Stage: Studies in Ethnological Show Business*. Bloomington, Ind., Indiana University Press: 1–55.

281 http://atlantablackstar.com/2014/09/09/13-shameful-pictures-europeans-placing-african-people-human-zoos/4/13 "Shameful Pictures of Europeans Placing African People in Human Zoos." September 9, 2014. Posted by ABS Staff.

282 http://www.ferris.edu/jimcrow/what.htm.

283 Ibid.

284 January 5, 1998. http//www.nps.gov/malu/documents/jimcrowlaws.htm.

285 http://en.wikipedia.org/wiki/Caucasian_race#cite_note-11.

286 http://blogs.channel4.com/factcheck/factcheck-black-americans-commit-crime/19439.

287 Ibid.

288 Ibid.

289 http://thinkprogress.org/justice/2013/05/22/2046451/white-people-stopped-by-new-york-police-are-more-likely-to-have-guns-or-drugs-than-minorities/.

290 Ibid.

291 Joe Martino, "Black Man vs. White Man Carrying AR-15 Legally. This Is Crazy." (Video) May 18, 2015 http://www.collective-evolution.com/2015/05/18/black-man-vs-white-man-carrying-ar-15-legally-this-is-crazy-video/

292 Michelle Ye Hee Lee. January 9 "Are black or white offenders more likely to kill police?" http://www.washingtonpost.com/blogs/fact-checker/wp/2015/01/09/are-black-or-white-offenders-more-likely-to-kill-police/.

293 Ibid.

294 "Professor and Native American scholar is slammed after researchers find no evidence to back her claims of Indian heritage."

295 "Sandra Bland's death ruled suicide by hanging." Greg Botelho and Dana Ford, CNN Updated 8:26 p.m. ET, Thu July 23, 2015. Video Source: CNN AP http://www.cnn.com/2015/07/23/us/sandra-bland-arrest-death-main/.

296 Ibid.

297 Ray Sanchez. "Who was Sandra Bland?" CNN Updated 9:17 p.m. ET, Thu July 23, 2015 http://www.cnn.com/2015/07/22/us/sandra-bland/

298 "Racial Divide Persists in Texas County Where Sandra Bland Died." By Sharon LaFraniere, Richard A. Oppel Jr., David Montgomery. JULY 26, 2015 http://www.nytimes.com/2015/07/27/us/racial-divide-persists-in-texas-county-where-sandra-bland-died.html

299 Daniel Bases, 12 Sep 2015, "NY police release video of ex-tennis star James Blake's mistaken arrest." http://www.aol.com/article/2015/09/12/ny-police-release-video-of-ex-tennis-star-james-blakes-mistaken/21234989/?icid=maing-grid7percent7Cmain5percent7Cdl3percent7Csec1_lnk1percent26pLidpercent3D-1543792755.

300 Ibid.

301 Ibid.

302 http://www.dailymail.co.uk/femail/article-1201841/I-turned-black-white-How-skin-disordered-changed-mans-identity-place-world.html.

303 http://www.military1.com/all/article/569802-army-investigates-racial-thursdays-at-military-base.

304 Ibid.

305 http://www.huffingtonpost.com/2013/06/19/paula-deen-racist-comments-n-word-caught-on-video_n_3467287.html.

306 http://jezebel.com/5612060/dr-laura-apologizes-for-n-word-but-shes-still-a-racist.

307 Ibid.

308 Chris Burke. "NFL Competition committee Passes on n-word rule, considers extra point changes." http://cdn-png.si.com/sites/default/files/styles/si_blogpost_author_image/public/writers/chris_burke_400x400.png?itok=lKmiIFcP" >http://www.si.com/nfl/audibles/2014/03/19/nfl-competition-committee-passes-on-n-word-rule-considers-extra-point-changes.

309 Tanya Young Williams, http://www.huffingtonpost.com/tanya-young-williams/a-nigger-is-a-black-perso_b_3786242.html, 8/28/13

310 *Chris Rock's 'Good Hair.'* HBO Films, LD Entertainment, Chris Rock Productions, Roadside Attractions, January 18, 2009.

311 Crawford, Bridget. "The Currency of White Women's Hair in a Down Economy," *Social Science Research Network* (2011): 1-17. Web. 05 Feb 2011. http://papers.ssrn.com/sol3/papers.cfm?abstract_id=1748103.

312 http://www.jpost.com/International/Boko-Haram-releases-275-kidnapped-women-and-children-400992.

313 Jill Filipovic, http://www.cosmopolitan.com/politics/news/a40182/nigerian-rape-victims-abortion/.

314 http://sfglobe.com/2015/03/09/family-gives-birth-to-two-sets-of-black-and-white-twins/.

315 Ibid.

316 Colleen Flaherty, 12 May 15 https://www.insidehighered.com/news/2015/05/12/boston-u-distances-itself-new-professors-comments-about-white-male-students.

317 Ibid.

318 http://www.thebolditalic.com/articles/6983-students-at-uc-berkeley-turn-the-tables-on-a-racist-professor.

319 Ibid.

320 http://www.bjs.gov/index.cfm?ty=datool&surl=/arrests/index.cfm#.

321 Ibid.

322 Josh Hedtke—UCLA •June 10, 2015. "California professors instructed not to say 'America is the land of opportunity.': http://www.thecollegefix.com/post/22839/.

323 Adapted from Sue, Derald Wing, *Microaggressions in Everyday Life: Race, Gender and Sexual Orientation.* Wiley and Sons, 2010.

324 Nick Venable, 24 Jul 15, "Hulk Hogan Fired From WWE Over Racists Comments, Read Them Here," http://www.cinemablend.com/television/Hulk-Hogan-Fired-From-WWE-Over-Racist-Comments-Read-Them-Here-73687.html.

325 Ibid.

326 Ibid.

327 Jason Nulton, April 9, 2015, "Unsung Heroes: The World War II Chaplain Who Survived The Bataan Death March." http://taskandpurpose.com/unsung-heroes-the-world-war-ii-chaplain-who-survived-the-bataan-death-march/.

328 http://www.af.mil/AboutUs/Biographies/Display/tabid/225/Article/105393/chaplain-major-general-robert-p-taylor.aspx.

329 Ibid.

330 Ibid.

331 Jason Nulton, April 9, 2015 "Unsung Heroes: The World War II Chaplain Who Survived The Bataan Death March http://taskandpurpose.com/unsung-heroes-the-world-war-ii-chaplain-who-survived-the-bataan-death-march/.

332 Ibid.

333 Edward Pentin. 03/27/2014 http://www.ncregister.com/daily-news/pope-francis-president-obama-discuss-religious-freedom-life-issues-and-immi/#ixzz3kz0Vyoep.

334 Vivian Yee, Andy Newman. "US Church, in Pope Francis' Afterglow, Sees Chance to Win Back Faithful." Oct. 2, 2015 http://www.nytimes.com/2015/10/03/nyregion/us-church-in-pope-francis-afterglow-sees-chance-to-win-back-faithful.html?_r=0.

335 http://www.elizabethfiles.com/act-of-uniformity-1559/3833/.

336 Ibid.

337 Lambert, Franklin T. (2003). *The Founding Fathers and the Place of Religion in America*. Princeton, NJ: Princeton University Press (published 2006). Retrieved 2015-03-07.

338 Ibid.

339 Quoted in *The New England Currant* (July 23, 1722), "Silence Dogood, No. 9; Corruptio optimi est pessima."

340 Religioustolerance.org/Deism, Jim Peterson (2007) "The Revolution of Belief: Founding Fathers, Deists, Orthodox Christians, and the Spiritual Context of 18th Century America." Robert L. Johnson, "The Deist Roots of the United States of America."

341 http://www.christianpost.com/news/georgia-mall-bans-christian-womens-group-from-praying-says-it-violates-code-of-conduct-policy-124424/.

342 http://www.pewresearch.org/2007/05/09/religion-in-the-public-schools/.

343 Ibid.

344 Ibid.

345 Ibid.

346 Ibid.

347 Ibid.

348 http://www.theblaze.com/stories/2012/06/25/today-marks-the-50th-anniversary-of-the-prayer-ban-in-public-schools-heres-the-history/.

349 Ibid.

350 Ibid.

351 https://www.au.org/resources/publications/prayer-and-the-public-schools.

352 Ibid.

353 Ibid.

354 http://wreg.com/2015/11/02/high-school-football-coach-suspended-for-praying-alone-after-games/.

355 http://www.christianpost.com/news/10-year-old-banned-from-writing-about-god-by-memphis-teacher-told-to-remove-paper-from-school-property-104426/.

356 Ibid.

357 https://swordattheready.wordpress.com/answering-the-charge-that-george-washington-was-a-deist/.

358 http://www.pattonhq.com/prayer.html.

359 http://www.schoolprayerinamerica.info/1separationchurchstate.html.

360 Ibid.

361 "National Defense Authorization Act for Fiscal Year 2014."

362 "Muslim Americans: Middle Class and Mostly Mainstream," Pew Research Center, 2007.

363 Ibid.

364 http://www.pewforum.org/2015/02/26/religious-hostilities/.

365 Ibid.

366 "Executive Order—Further Amendments to Executive Order 11478, Equal Employment Opportunity in the Federal Government, and Executive Order 11246, Equal Employment Opportunity." The White House. Office of the Press Secretary. July 21, 2014. Retrieved July 21, 2014.

367 http://www.supremecourt.gov/opinions/13pdf/13-354_olp1.pdf.

368 http://www.hrc.org/blog/entry/new-arkansas-rfra-still-empowers-discrimination.

369 http://www.nbcconnecticut.com/news/local/Malloy-to-Bar-State-Travel-to-Indiana-Amid-Religious-Freedom-Law-Backlash-298010911.html.

370 http://www.cnn.com/2015/04/02/living/indiana-religious-freedom-pizza-feat/.

371 Ibid.

372 Ibid.

373 http://abcnews.go.com/US/kentucky-clerk-kim-davis-licenses-issued-authority/story?id=33737136.

374 http://abcnews.go.com/US/kentucky-clerk-kim-davis-set-released-jail/story?id=33601309.

375 http://www.washingtonpost.com/wp-dyn/articles/A62581-2004Sep4.html.

376 Ibid.

377 Ibid.

378 https://swordattheready.wordpress.com/answering-the-charge-that-george-washington-was-a-deist/.

379 http://refspace.com/quotes/Nelson_Mandela/ Q1554

380 https://www.nps.gov/mamc/learn/historyculture/people_marymcleodbethune.htmhttp://www.tuskegee.edu/about_us/

legacy_of_leadership/booker_t_washington.aspx ; http://www.npr.org/news/specials/olemiss/.

381 http://www.chasingthefrog.com/reelfaces/rememberthetitans.php.

382 https://rankingamerica.wordpress.com/category/rankings/ranking-of-11-to-20-rankings/ 6 Jan 15.

383 http://www.governing.com/gov-data/education-data/state-high-school-graduation-rates-by-race-ethnicity.html.

384 Ibid.

385 http://nces.ed.gov/programs/coe/indicator_cce.asp.

386 Ibid.

387 Carolyn Williams. Demand Media. "The Average Salary Without a College Degree." http://work.chron.com/average-salary-college-degree-1861.html.

388 Ibid.

389 Ibid.

390 http://www.pewhispanic.org/2013/05/09/hispanic-high-school-graduates-pass-whites-in-rate-of-college-enrollment/.

391 http://www.ed.gov/news/press-releases/more-40-low-income-schools-dont-get-fair-share-state-and-local-funds-department-education-research-finds.

392 Ibid.

393 https://www.census.gov/newsroom/releases/archives/income_wealth/cb12-172.html.

394 Ibid.

395 Ibid.

396 http://data.bls.gov/timeseries/LNS14000000.

397 Ibid.

398 Ibid.

399 Calmes, Jackie (July 28, 2014). "Advocates Shun 'Pro-Choice' to Expand Message." *New York Times*. Retrieved August 4, 2014.

400 Peter Engelman, *A History of Birth Control in America*, Prager, New York, 2010.

401 Beaucar Vlahos, Kelley (April 24, 2008). "Pastors Accuse Planned Parenthood for 'Genocide' on Blacks." Fox News. Retrieved July 30, 2015.

402 Arina Grossu, "Margaret Sanger, Racist Eugenicist Extraordinaire: The founder of Planned Parenthood would have considered many Americans unworthy of life." *Washington Times*, May 5, 2014.[1] Retrieved July 27, 2015.

403 Ibid.

404 Somashekhar, Sandhya; Ohlheiser, Abby (July 21, 2015). "Antiabortion group releases second Planned Parenthood video." *The Washington Post*. Retrieved July 27, 2015.

405 Roberts, Dan (August 3, 2015), "Republicans' Planned Parenthood defunding push fails in the Senate." *The Guardian*, retrieved August 3, 2015.

406 Howard N. Snyder, Ph.D., Joseph Mulako-Wangota, PhD, FBI, Uniform Crime Reporting Program.

407 Ibid.

408 Ibid.

409 Ibid.

410 Bureau of Justice Statistics, National Prisoner Statistics Program, 2012–13.

411 Ibid.

412 Ibid.

413 Jared Taylor, American Renaissance, July 1, 2015, New DOJ Statistics on Race and Violent Crime http://www.amren.com/news/2015/07/new-doj-statistics-on-race-and-violent-crime/.

414 Ibid.

415 Ibid.

416 Miller, J.G. (1996). *Search and Destroy*. New York: Cambridge University Press.

417 Ibid.

418 Ibid.

419 Alexander, M. (2010). *The New Jim Crow*. New York: The New Press.

420 Glover, K. (2009). *Racial Profiling*. Lanham: Rowman and Littlefield.

421 Alexander, M. (2010). *The New Jim Crow*. New York: The New Press.

422 Mohamed and Fritsvold. (2010). *Dorm Room Dealers*. Boulder, Co.: Lynne Rienner.

423 Miller, J.G. (1996). *Search and Destroy*. New York: Cambridge University Press.

424 Shelden, R. (2008). *Constructing the Dangerous Classes*. Boston: Allyn and Bacon.

425 Miller, J.G. (1996). *Search and Destroy*. New York: Cambridge University Press.

426 Ibid.

427 Bickel, C. (2012). "The Drug War and Plantations to Prisons." Cal Poly, Lecture. San Luis Obispo, CA.

428 Jared Taylor, American Renaissance, July 1, 2015, New DOJ Statistics on Race and Violent Crime http://www.amren.com/news/2015/07/new-doj-statistics-on-race-and-violent-crime/.

429 Ibid.

430 Ibid.

431 Ibid.

432 Miller, J.G. (1996). *Search and Destroy*. New York: Cambridge University Press.

433 Bickel, C. (2012). "The Drug War and Plantations to Prisons." Cal Poly, Lecture. San Luis Obispo, CA.

434 http://www.brainyquote.com/quotes/quotes/m/mothertere130839.html.

435 Centers for Disease Control and Prevention, National Center for Injury Prevention and Control. Web based Injury Statistics Query and Reporting System (WISQARS) [online]. (2012) [cited 2014 Dec 17]. Available from www.cdc.gov/injury/wisqars.

436 Ibid.

437 Centers for Disease Control and Prevention. Youth risk behavior surveillance—United States, 2013. MMWR, Surveillance Summaries 2014; 61 (no. SS-4).

438 www.cdc.gov/violenceprevention.

439 http://video.foxnews.com/v/4131470919001/brutal-beating-of-teen-on-philadelphia-subway-platform-/?#sp=show-clips.

440 American culture in decline? November 11, 2013 / Fox News, http://www.foxnews.com/on-air/the-five/article/2013/11/11/american-culture-decline.

441 http://www.cbssports.com/collegefootball/eye-on-college-football/25100482/mississippi-state-qb-dak-prescott-attacked-while-on-spring-break.

442 "Record Share of Americans Have Never Married." 24 Sep 2014 http://www.pewresearch.org/.

443 http://www.pewresearch.org/fact-tank/2014/12/22/less-than-half-of-u-s-kids-today-live-in-a-traditional-family/.

444 "Record Share of Americans Have Never Married." 24 Sep 2014 http://www.pewresearch.org/.

445 Ibid.

446 Ibid.

447 Neyland, Shon. *Loving When You Don't Feel Like It*. Tate Publishing, 2014.

448 https://www.census.gov/newsroom/releases/archives/income_wealth/cb12-172.html.

449 Ibid.

450 Ibid.

451 Paul R. Amato. "The Impact of Family Formation Change on the Cognitive, Social, and Emotional Well-Being of the Next Generation." http://www.princeton.edu/futureofchildren/publications/journals/article/index.xml?journalid=37&articleid=107&sectionid=69.

452 Ibid.

453 Ibid.

454 http://datacenter.kidscount.org/data/tables/107-children-in-single-parent-families-by#detailed/1/any/false/36,868,867,133,38/10,168,9,12,1,13,185/432,431.

455 Ibid.

456 http://www.heritage.org/research/reports/1999/06/ broken-families-rob-children-of-their-chances-for-future-prosperity

457 *"Roe v. Wade* and Beyond." *Frontline*, PBS (2006-01-19): "While reaffirming the central holding of *Roe v. Wade*, the court rejected 'Roe's rigid trimester framework.'"

458 Cole, George; Frankowski, Stanislaw. "Abortion and protection of the human fetus: legal problems in a cross-cultural perspective," p. 20 (1987): "By 1900 every state in the Union had an anti-abortion prohibition." Via Google Books. Retrieved (2008-04-08).

459 McCorvey, Norma and Meisler, Andy. *I Am Roe: My Life, Roe V. Wade, and Freedom of Choice.* (Harper Collins 1994).

460 http://law.justia.com/cases/federal/district-courts/FSupp/ 314/1217/1472349/.

461 Greenhouse, Linda (2005). *Becoming Justice Blackmun: Harry Blackmun's Supreme Court Journey.* New York: Times Books.

462 McCorvey, Norma. Testimony to the Senate Subcommittee on the Constitution, Federalism and Property Rights (1998-01- 21), also quoted in the parliament of Western Australia (PDF) (1998-05-20): "The affidavit submitted to the Supreme Court didn't happen the way I said it did, pure and simple." Retrieved 2007-01-27.

463 Partial-Birth Abortion Ban Act of 2003, Enrolled as Agreed to or Passed by Both House and Senate (HTML); * same, from the US Government Printing Office.

464 http://www.cdc.gov/reproductivehealth/data_stats/.

465 Ibid.

466 Ibid.

467 Ibid.

468 http://www.cdc.gov/mmwr/preview/mmwrhtml/ss6015a1.htm#Tab12.

469 Ibid.

470 Tyson JE, Parikh NA, Langer J, Green C, Higgins RD (April 2008). "Intensive care for extreme prematurity—moving beyond gestational age." N. Engl. J. Med. 358 (16): 1672–81. doi:10.1056/NEJMoa073059. PMC 2597069. PMID 18420500. Luke B, Brown MB (December 2006). "The changing risk of infant mortality by gestation, plurality, and race: 1989-1991 versus 1999-2001." *Pediatrics* 118 (6): 2488– 97. doi:10.1542/peds.2006-1824. PMID 17142535. The American College of Obstetricians and Gynecologists (September 2002). "ACO Practice Bulletin: Clinical Management Guidelines for Obstetrcian-Gynecologists: Number 38," September 2002. "Perinatal care at the threshold of viability." *Obstet Gynecol* 100 (3): 617–24. PMID 12220792.

471 http://www.pewforum.org/2013/08/15/abortion-viewed-in-moral-terms/.

472 Ibid.

473 Ibid.

474 2011 The Economic Impact of Illicit Drug Use on American Society. Washington, DC: United States Department of Justice.

475 Ibid.

476 http://www.drugabuse.gov/related-topics/trends-statistics.

477 Ibid.

478 http://www.drugabuse.gov/national-survey-drug-use-health.

479 http://www.justice.gov/archive/ndic/pubs38/38661/drugImpact.htm.

480 Ibid.

481 Ibid.

482 https://www.samhsa.gov/data/sites/default/files/NSDUHresults PDFWHTML2013/Web/NSDUHresults2013.htm#2.7.

483 Ibid.

484 Ibid.

485 Ibid.

486 Ibid.

487 https://www.nytimes.com/2017/02/13/us/overdose-cases-kentucky.html?_r=0, "A Spike in Overdose Emergency Calls Is Seen in Kentucky" By Christine Hauser, Feb. 13, 2017.

488 Ibid.

489 Ibid.

490 Ibid.

491 Centers for Disease Control and Prevention. *Estimated HIV incidence among adults and adolescents in the United States, 2007–2010*. HIV Surveillance Supplemental Report 2012;17. 4). http://www.cdc.gov/hiv/topics/surveillance/resources/reports/#supplemental. Published December 2012.

492 Ibid.

493 Ibid.

494 Ibid.

495 Ibid.

496 Ibid.

497 Ibid.

498 Ibid.

499 Ibid.

500 Ibid.

501 http://store.jfklibrary.org/one-person-can-make-a-difference-framed-jfk-quote/padcibjcicdlmjle/product.

502 http://www.mentoring.org/about_mentor/value_of_mentoring.

503 Ibid.

504 Ibid.

505 http://hirr.hartsem.edu/research/fastfacts/fast_factshtml#numcong.

506 http://www.cogic.org/urbaninitiatives/vision-mission/.

507 April 2014 Violence Policy Center, Hispanic Victims of Lethal Firearms Violence in the United States.

508 http://www.brainyquote.com/quotes/quotes/m/martinluth101472.html.

509 http://wgntv.com/2015/03/23/police-officer-helps-woman-who-lost-over-200-pounds-cross-10k-finish-line/.

510 Ibid.

511 Dan Good and Ariella Weintraub, "Off Duty Army Captain Pulls Man from Fiery North Carolina Car Crash." http://abcnews.go.com/US/off-duty-army-captain-pulls-man-fiery-north/story?id=31142141.

512 http://abcnews.go.com/US/off-dutyarmy-captain-pulls-man-fiery-north/story?id=31142141.

513 http://wate.com/2015/04/18/grandfather-with-cancer-takes-up-uber-driving-to-pay-off-home-for-family/ April 18, 2015, 10:01 a.m.

514 Ibid.

515 Martin Luther King Jr., "Strength to Love." Stanford. Retrieved 2011-08-23.

516 http://www.history.com/topics/black-history/selma-montgomery-march.

517 Ibid.

518 Ibid.

519 Ibid.

520 Ibid.

521 http://millercenter.org/president/speeches/speech-3386.

522 http://www.sweetspeeches.com/s/602-martin-luther-king-jr-address-concluding-the-selma-to-montgomery-march#ixzz3qOYmI6jz.

523 cbrainyquote.com/quotes/quotes/g/georgewash146823.html.

CPSIA information can be obtained
at www.ICGtesting.com
Printed in the USA
LVOW03*0556211117
557062LV00003B/8/P